AI-Driven Innovations in Last-Mile Delivery

Omar Ali
Abdullah Al Salem University, Kuwait

IGI Global
Scientific Publishing
Publishing Tomorrow's Research Today

Vice President of Editorial	Melissa Wagner
Director of Acquisitions	Mikaela Felty
Director of Book Development	Jocelynn Hessler
Production Manager	Mike Brehm
Cover Design	Jose Rosado

Published in the United States of America by
IGI Global Scientific Publishing
701 East Chocolate Avenue
Hershey, PA, 17033, USA
Tel: 717-533-8845 | Fax: 717-533-7115
Website: https://www.igi-global.com E-mail: cust@igi-global.com

Library of Congress Cataloging-in-Publication Data

LCCN: 2025026730 (CIP Data Pending)
ISBN13: 9798337328331
Isbn13Softcover: 9798337328348
EISBN13: 9798337328355
British Cataloguing in Publication Data
A Cataloguing in Publication record for this book is available from the British Library.

Table of Contents

Detailed Table of Contents

The world of supply chain management is changing faster than ever, bringing new challenges, such as unexpected disruptions, inefficiencies, and a lack of real-time transparency. In this chapter, we explore how cutting-edge technologies, specifically the Internet of Things (IoT) and Artificial Intelligence (AI), are transforming supply chains by providing real-time visibility. These innovations empower businesses to boost efficiency, proactively manage risks, and make smarter decisions. By leveraging IoT-powered sensors, RFID, GPS, and AI-driven analytics, companies can achieve end-to-end tracking, predictive insights, and automated decision making, ultimately creating a more resilient and adaptive supply chain. This chapter also discusses emerging technologies, real-world case studies, key enablers of real-time visibility, and future research opportunities, providing a comprehensive look at how AI and IoT are shaping the future of supply chain management.

This chapter explores the transformative role of Federated Learning (FL) in enabling secure, privacy-preserving, and collaborative intelligence across modern supply chain ecosystems. Unlike traditional centralized AI approaches, FL facilitates model training across distributed enterprises without the need to share sensitive operational data, thereby maintaining data sovereignty and compliance with regulations like GDPR. The chapter discusses various FL architectures and types (HFL, VFL, FTL), their advantages, and real-world supply chain applications in demand forecasting, inventory optimization, logistics, and risk mitigation. It further elaborates on FL's integration with emerging technologies such as blockchain, IoT, and digital twins to enhance visibility, traceability, and sustainability. Through case studies and industry practices, the chapter emphasizes FL's potential in aligning AI-driven

last-mile delivery. Leveraging predictive analytics offers a transformative solution by harnessing AI-driven algorithms to forecast consumer demand with high accuracy. These tools analyze historical sales data, consumer behaviors, and external factors, such as weather or regional events, to anticipate future demand patterns. Predictive analytics allows businesses to optimize inventory levels, ensuring that products are available without overstocking or waste, which is particularly crucial for perishable goods like fresh produce. Additionally, predictive analytics plays a key role in optimizing last-mile delivery by enabling real-time route planning and minimizing delivery costs. As the industry continues to expand, integrating predictive analytics will be crucial for maintaining competitiveness, sustainability, and customer satisfaction, marking a step toward supply chain optimization in e-grocery services.

On-time delivery in India's heavy commercial vehicle logistics sector is critical for operational efficiency and customer satisfaction. However, issues like poor infrastructure, traffic congestion, regulatory delays, driver shortages, and end-of-month invoicing disruptions contribute to frequent delivery delays. This book examines strategies to address these challenges using emerging technologies, data-driven decision-making, optimized route planning, predictive analytics, and end-to-end delivery management. Telematics tracking & digital documentation enhance transparency and responsiveness across the logistics value chain. Effective collaboration among logistics providers, government agencies, and tech firms can streamline operations. Faster payment processing cycles for service providers are crucial for timely deliveries. HCV logistics firms can improve delivery timelines, reduce costs, and increase customer satisfaction. This research offers practical insights to enhance reliability and competitiveness in India's evolving logistics sector.

The maintenance of electric motors is being transformed by the implementation of machine learning algorithms and RPM data analysis, with the objective of enhancing operational efficiency and minimizing unforeseen failures. These advanced models examine current performance indicators and past records to detect patterns and

Preface

It is with great pleasure that I present *AI-Driven Innovations in Last-Mile Delivery*. The rapid growth of e-commerce has transformed consumer expectations and placed unprecedented demands on logistics and supply chain networks. Nowhere are these pressures more acute than in last-mile delivery, the critical final step in ensuring goods reach customers. Long recognized as the most expensive and complex part of the supply chain, last-mile delivery faces challenges ranging from traffic congestion and escalating operational costs to environmental concerns and customer service demands.

In this context, artificial intelligence (AI) emerges not merely as a tool but as a transformative enabler. Intelligent algorithms, predictive models, and autonomous technologies are redefining how goods are moved from distribution centers to doorsteps. From AI-powered route optimization and dynamic delivery scheduling to autonomous delivery vehicles and drones, the logistics industry is witnessing a revolution that promises to make last-mile delivery faster, more efficient, and more sustainable. Just as importantly, AI is shaping a more customer-centric delivery ecosystem, one that offers personalization, real-time visibility, and flexible fulfillment options.

This book brings together leading research, case studies, and critical perspectives to explore how AI is reshaping the last-mile delivery landscape. It examines not only the operational benefits, such as reduced costs, improved scalability, and environmental sustainability, but also the ethical, social, and regulatory challenges that accompany AI adoption. Issues of data privacy, cybersecurity, workforce transformation, and equitable access are all central to understanding the true impact of these technologies.

The chapters collected here are designed to serve a wide audience: industry professionals seeking actionable strategies, academics and researchers exploring new horizons in AI and logistics, policymakers shaping urban infrastructure and regulations, and innovators and investors driving technological advancements in the delivery ecosystem. By bringing these voices together, the book aims to bridge theory and practice, offering both conceptual frameworks and real-world insights.

CHAPTER OVERVIEWS

Chapter 1: Real-Time Supply Chain Visibility Using IoT and AI: Enhancing Efficiency, Resilience, and Decision-Making

This chapter examines how IoT and AI technologies enable real-time visibility in supply chains, critical for optimizing last-mile delivery. Through IoT-powered sensors, RFID, GPS, and AI-driven analytics, businesses achieve end-to-end tracking, predictive insights, and automated decision-making to mitigate disruptions and enhance efficiency. Featuring case studies and emerging technologies, the chapter offers practical strategies for logistics professionals, theoretical insights for researchers, and a roadmap for leveraging IoT and AI to build adaptive, resilient supply chains.

Chapter 2: Federated Learning for Cross-Enterprise Supply Chain Collaboration

Focusing on federated learning (FL), this chapter explores its role in fostering secure, privacy-preserving collaboration across supply chain enterprises. By enabling distributed AI model training without sharing sensitive data, FL supports applications in demand forecasting, inventory optimization, logistics, and risk mitigation while ensuring compliance with regulations like GDPR. The chapter integrates FL with blockchain, IoT, and digital twins, offering case studies and insights into aligning AI-driven decisions with ESG goals. It serves as a guide for industry leaders, researchers, and policymakers seeking ethical and intelligent supply chain solutions.

Chapter 3: Supply Chain 4.0: The Digital Twin Revolution

This chapter investigates the transformative potential of digital twin technology in modern supply chain management, with a focus on last-mile delivery. By creating real-time, data-driven simulations, digital twins enhance logistics, inventory management, demand forecasting, and sustainability tracking. The chapter explores how enabling technologies like IoT, AI, and cloud computing drive agility and resilience, while addressing ethical, legal, and regulatory challenges. It provides actionable guidelines for industry adoption, policy recommendations for regulators, and identifies research gaps for academics, positioning digital twins as a cornerstone of sustainable and efficient supply chains.

Chapter 4: Optimizing Last-Mile Delivery Using AI-Powered Route Optimization and Personalization

This chapter reviews the literature on AI-powered route optimization and personalization in last-mile delivery. It synthesizes advancements in reducing delivery times and enhancing customer experiences through tailored solutions, while identifying gaps for future research. The chapter offers a foundation for industry practitioners to implement AI-driven strategies, policymakers to promote equitable technology adoption, and researchers to explore real-world applications across diverse industrial and geographical contexts.

Chapter 5: Demand Forecasting and Optimized Inventory Management in E-Grocery Last-Mile Delivery: Leveraging Predictive Analytics

This chapter addresses the unique challenges of e-grocery last-mile delivery, where predictive analytics transforms demand forecasting and inventory management. By analyzing historical sales, consumer behavior, and external factors like weather, AI-driven algorithms optimize stock levels for perishable goods and streamline delivery routes. The chapter provides practical insights for e-grocery businesses aiming to reduce waste and costs, theoretical frameworks for researchers, and strategies for enhancing customer satisfaction and sustainability in a competitive market.

Chapter 6: Reducing Delivery Delays and Improving Customer Satisfaction in Indian Heavy Commercial Vehicle Logistics

Focusing on India's heavy commercial vehicle logistics, this chapter tackles delays caused by infrastructure challenges, regulatory hurdles, and driver shortages. It explores how telematics, predictive analytics, and optimized route planning enhance transparency and efficiency. The chapter provides practical solutions for logistics firms, collaboration strategies for policymakers and tech providers, and insights for improving customer satisfaction and competitiveness in India's evolving logistics sector.

Chapter 7: Proactive Life Cycle Management: Developing a Machine Learning Model for Predictive Maintenance of Electric Motors Using RPM Data

This chapter delves into the application of machine learning for predictive maintenance of electric motors in last-mile delivery vehicles. By analyzing RPM data to detect performance anomalies, these models extend equipment life, reduce downtime, and lower maintenance costs. The chapter offers practical guidance for fleet operators, theoretical insights for researchers, and a framework for adopting data-driven maintenance practices to ensure reliable and efficient delivery operations.

Ultimately, *AI-Driven Innovations in Last-Mile Delivery* underscores the dual role of AI as both a driver of efficiency and a catalyst for systemic change. As cities become smarter, consumers more demanding, and environmental sustainability more urgent, AI will remain at the heart of solutions that enable the logistics sector to thrive in a rapidly evolving world.

I am grateful to the contributors whose expertise and vision have shaped this volume, and I trust that the knowledge contained herein will inspire continued innovation and responsible application of AI in last-mile delivery.

Omar Ali

Abdullah Al Salem University, Kuwait

Chapter 1
Real-Time Supply Chain Visibility Using IoT and AI:
Enhancing Efficiency, Resilience, and Decision-Making

Muhammad Nadeem
American University of the Middle East, Kuwait

Wael A. Farag
https://orcid.org/0000-0002-9191-1824
Cairo University, Egypt

ABSTRACT

The world of supply chain management is changing faster than ever, bringing new challenges, such as unexpected disruptions, inefficiencies, and a lack of real-time transparency. In this chapter, we explore how cutting-edge technologies, specifically the Internet of Things (IoT) and Artificial Intelligence (AI), are transforming supply chains by providing real-time visibility. These innovations empower businesses to boost efficiency, proactively manage risks, and make smarter decisions. By leveraging IoT-powered sensors, RFID, GPS, and AI-driven analytics, companies can

DOI: 10.4018/979-8-3373-2833-1.ch001

achieve end-to-end tracking, predictive insights, and automated decision making, ultimately creating a more resilient and adaptive supply chain. This chapter also discusses emerging technologies, real-world case studies, key enablers of real-time visibility, and future research opportunities, providing a comprehensive look at how AI and IoT are shaping the future of supply chain management.

1. INTRODUCTION

A supply chain is a system of organizations, people, activities, technology, information, and resources involved in moving a product or service from suppliers to customers (Mentzer et al., 2001). It is typically composed of several key components that work in unison to ensure an efficient flow of goods, services, and information from the point of origin to the final consumer. These components include suppliers, who provide the raw materials or components; manufacturers, who convert these inputs into finished goods; distributors and wholesalers, who handle the storage and bulk transportation of products; retailers, who make the goods available to end customers; and finally, the consumers themselves. In addition, essential support functions, such as procurement, production planning, inventory management, warehousing, transportation, and order fulfillment enable coordination across the chain. Seamless integration of these elements, often supported by digital technologies, is critical for maintaining supply chain efficiency, agility, and resilience.

The key functions involved in managing a supply chain are given below, which encompass a wide range of interrelated activities that ensure a smooth flow of goods and information:

1. *Procurement* involves sourcing and acquiring raw materials or components from the suppliers.
2. *Production planning* ensures that manufacturing processes align with demand forecasts and resource availabilities.
3. *Inventory management* focuses on maintaining optimal stock levels to balance availability and cost efficiency.

4. *Warehousing* involves storing goods in strategic locations in order to support timely distribution.
5. *Transportation and logistics* coordinate the physical movement of goods across a supply chain network. Order fulfillment ensures accurate and timely delivery of products to customers.

Additionally, supply chain coordination and integration synchronize the activities of all stakeholders, facilitated by information systems and analytics that support real-time decision making. These functions collectively contribute to the responsiveness, resilience, and competitiveness of modern supply chains.

Supply Chain Visibility (SCV) has become a cornerstone of modern logistics and operational management. It refers to the ability to track and monitor products, components, and information as they move through the supply chain in real-time (Kumar, Viehmann, Sunmola). SCV can be categorized into four primary constructs (Wei & Wang, 2007, 2010):

- o Visibility of sensing directly influences strategic performance by allowing firms to detect changes and disruptions early.
- o The visibility of learning aids in adapting and improving processes based on new information.
- o Visibility for coordinating enhances collaboration and synchronization among supply chain partners; and
- o The visibility for integration ensures seamless information integration across the supply chain, thereby boosting overall performance.

SCV offers several benefits, including risk mitigation by minimizing waste, environmental footprints, and disruptions, thereby enhancing the social, ethical, and performance aspects of the supply chain (Apeji & Sunmola, 2022). Operational efficiency is improved through technologies such as IoT, RFID, and blockchain, which provide real-time data for smarter decision making, accurate demand forecasting, and optimized inventory management (Michaelides & Forster, 2013). SCV also contributes to resilience by enabling proactive management and improved risk assessment (Mirzaei et al., 2025). Additionally, high levels of visibility are essential for achieving sustainability objectives through quality information-sharing and automation (Kalaiarasan et al., 2022).

Figure 1 illustrates the projected expansion of a specific market over a seven-year period, measured in billion U.S. dollars. The data reveal a consistent year-on-year increase in market size, indicating a strong growth momentum. The chart demonstrates a compound annual growth trend, with an approximate increase of $2.5–$3.3 billion per year. In 2023, technology accounted for 30% of businesses, with equipment manufacturing second at 25%. The remaining businesses are equally distributed among various industries such as packaged products, utilities, and consultancy. As seen in Figure 1, experts estimate that worldwide supply chain management will surpass $30 billion by 2026 (Department, 2023)

Figure 1. Supply chain visibility market size

(Department, 2023)

Figure 1 illustrates how the priority of supply chain visibility shifted between 2022 and 2023 across manufacturing enterprises of different sizes (fictive enterprises). Overall, 55% of manufacturing-related businesses identified improving supply chain visibility as their top strategic priority in 2023, reflecting a growing emphasis on transparency, agility, and responsiveness. However, a closer look reveals distinct patterns based on the company size. Among small enterprises (with fewer than 2,500 employees), the focus on visibility declined sharply from 77% in 2022 to just 38% in 2023, suggesting a shift in priorities, possibly driven by resource limitations or a renewed focus on cost efficiency. Medium-sized companies (2,500–5,000 employees) also showed a reduction from 55% in 2022 to 30% in 2023, potentially redirecting their efforts toward enhancing supply chain resilience and agility, rather than visibility alone. In contrast, large enterprises (more than 5,000 employees) maintained a steady commitment to visibility, with 57% in 2022 and 56% in 2023, likely because of their greater capacity to invest in long-term digital infrastructure and advanced analytics. These trends suggest that, while supply chain visibility remains a critical industry objective, its prioritization varies significantly based on organizational size, operational complexity, and strategic focus.

Figure 2. prioritizing supply chain visibility by companies of different sizes

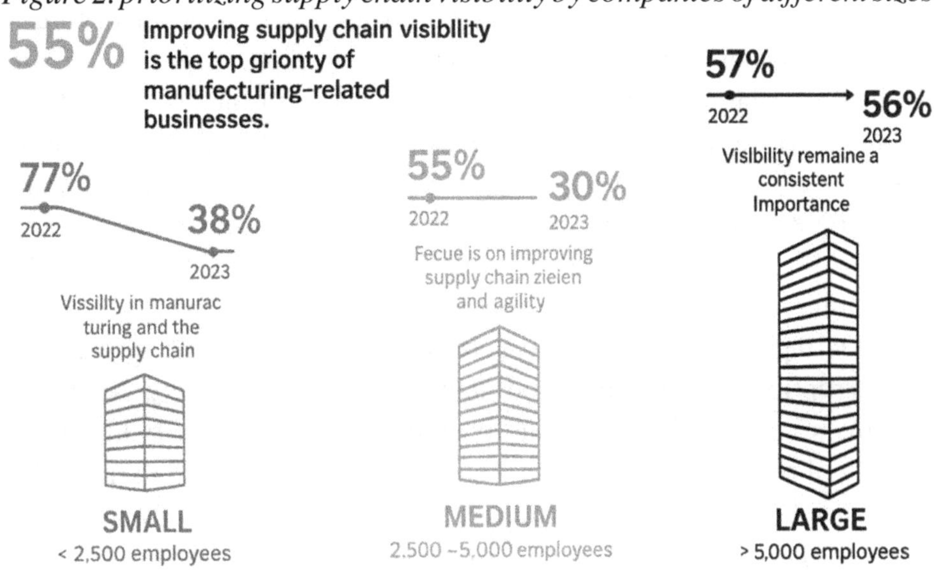

(Fictiv, 2023)

Traditional supply chain monitoring faces several significant challenges that hinder its efficiency, responsiveness, and reliability. One of the most critical issues is the lack of real-time data, often stemming from centralized data management systems that delay data retrieval and processing (Muthu & Kartheeban, 2023; Vora et al., 2022). This centralized approach not only creates bottlenecks but also poses risks of system failure and cybersecurity threats. Additionally, fragmented information flows across supply chain entities result in isolated 'information islands' that obstruct seamless communication and coordination (Rashed et al., 2025). Another major limitation is the manual tracking processes, which involve time-consuming counting and locating activities that are prone to human errors and inconsistencies (Anandhi et al., 2019). These systems also struggle with data validation, making it difficult to ensure information accuracy and trustworthiness (Pise et al., 2024). Furthermore, the lack of full upstream and downstream visibility in traditional supply chains impairs their ability to holistically monitor processes and make informed decisions (Boudouaia et al., 2024). This absence of transparency can lead to mistrust among stakeholders and delays in their execution (Kim & Davis, 2019; Muthu & Kartheeban, 2023). Quality control is another concern, as traditional monitoring systems are often insufficient to detect deviations or counterfeit goods, which is an especially critical issue in sensitive sectors, such as pharmaceuticals and cosmetics (Pise et al., 2024; Sreerakhi et al., 2022). Operationally, these traditional systems lack the scalability and interoperability needed to integrate with emerging technologies and face increasing pressure to address environmental and sustainability challenges in a globally dispersed infrastructure (Rashed). These limitations became more apparent during global crises such as the COVID-19 pandemic, geopolitical conflicts, and harsh weather, resulting in interruption in production and delays in delivery. Getting goods for customers and satisfying demand becomes increasingly difficult in the absence of efficient logistics and distribution. These issues highlight the urgent need for digital transformation in supply chain monitoring.

The integration of IoT and AI has significantly transformed supply chain management by enhancing visibility and transparency. IoT devices such as sensors, GPS trackers, and RFID tags provide real-time data on the location, condition, and status of goods throughout the supply chain, ensuring correct handling and timely arrival. AI processes these data, enabling predictive analytics and real-time decision-making to anticipate disruptions, optimize routes, and effectively manage inventory (Stephen

& Archana, 2025). It uses historical data and market trends for predictive analytics, improving inventory management and reducing stockouts or overstocking. By analyzing traffic patterns and external factors, AI suggests efficient routes, reduces transportation costs, and improves delivery times. IoT-driven solutions enable anticipatory maintenance through constant surveillance and identify potential issues before they become significant problems. The combination of IoT and AI enhances supply chain resilience and agility, allowing quick adaptation to change and disruptions, such as those experienced during the COVID-19 pandemic. Integrating blockchain with IoT and AI further enhances transparency and trust by providing a secure, immutable record of transactions and product movements, ensuring that all stakeholders have access to accurate, real-time information about a product's journey, which is crucial for compliance and quality assurance (Mustapha et al., 2024).

2. IOT TECHNOLOGIES FOR REAL-TIME SUPPLY CHAIN MONITORING

IoT technologies play a transformative role in real-time supply chain monitoring by enabling enhanced visibility, operational efficiency, and data-driven decision making. The deployment of interconnected sensors, devices, and communication systems allows supply chain stakeholders to continuously collect, transmit, and analyze real-time data across various stages, from production and warehousing to transportation and delivery. This level of continuous monitoring helps organizations identify bottlenecks, track inventory movements, monitor environmental conditions, and predict potential disruptions. Consequently, companies are better equipped to respond proactively to dynamic supply and demand conditions, reduce operational risks, and optimize resource utilization, ultimately leading to more agile, resilient, and transparent supply chain systems.

2.1. RFID & Barcode Systems – Automated tracking of inventory and shipments

These technologies play a vital role in enhancing supply chain efficiency by enabling automated identification, data capture, and tracking of inventories and shipments. Radio Frequency Identification (RFID) tags allow for wireless scanning of items, even without line-of-sight, significantly reducing manual labor and improving the speed and accuracy of logistics operations. This enhances tracking and identification by automatically identifying and tracking items throughout the supply chain, providing real-time information, and improving the inventory accuracy. This reduces labor costs by automating the identification process, thus lowering the need for manual labor and simplifying business processes. It significantly improves efficiency by cutting ordering lead times, reducing inventory control costs, and increasing the number of inventories turns (Zhu2012). Their ability to register multiple items simultaneously is particularly useful for large-scale operations without human intervention, which enhances the accuracy and speed of data collection. However, the implementation of RFID systems can be expensive, which may prohibit some businesses. There are also ongoing concerns regarding the lack of standardization and potential security vulnerabilities of RFID technology (Michael & McCathie, 2005).

Barcode technology involves printing a unique code on a label that can be scanned using optical devices, such as laser- or camera-based barcode scanners. Each barcode represents specific data, such as product ID, batch number, or location, and is linked to a database that stores relevant product or shipment details (Alsubaiei, n.d.). As with RFID, Barcode technology plays a significant role in supply chain management by enhancing the efficiency and accuracy of tracking and managing goods throughout the supply chain. Over 90% of the retail industry uses barcodes, and their demand continues to grow owing to their reliability and cost-effectiveness (Kafi et al., 2022). However, barcodes have limited data storage capacity compared to RFID tags, which can store more detailed information and require line-of-sight. While RFID technology offers advanced capabilities, such as non-line-of-sight scanning and greater data storage, barcodes remain a popular choice owing to their low cost and simplicity. Barcodes are often used in conjunction with RFID to provide comprehensive solutions for supply chain management (Quinn, 2004).

2.2. GPS and Geolocation Tracking – Live monitoring of goods in transit.

Global Positioning System (GPS) technology is a satellite-based navigation system that enables the precise determination of the location, movement, and timing of objects anywhere on Earth. It uses signals from a network of satellites to triangulate the exact position of a GPS-enabled device or asset. The integration of GPS and geolocation tracking in supply chain management has significantly enhanced the efficiency, visibility, and reliability of logistics. The GPS technology provides precise real-time tracking of goods, vehicles, and shipments, ensuring continuous visibility throughout the supply chain. This real-time data helps monitor the location and status of shipments, thereby reducing the risk of delays and losses. By combining GPS with data analytics, supply chains can optimize routing decisions, reduce travel times, and fuel consumption, which is a key advantage for last-mile delivery and overall logistics performance (Lam). Furthermore, enhanced visibility through the GPS enables better control over inventory and production processes, allowing companies to make informed emergency ordering decisions. This contributed to reduced operational costs, improved inventory management, and increased responsiveness to disruptions. While GPS technology offers numerous benefits, the initial cost of implementation and maintenance can be high, especially for small and medium-sized enterprises

2.3. IoT Sensors & Smart Devices – Temperature, humidity, and condition monitoring of perishable goods.

The integration of IoT sensors and smart devices in supply chain management has transformed traditional logistics and inventory processes, enhancing efficiency, visibility, and decision making (Y. Khan et al., 2023). These sensors monitor key environmental parameters, such as temperature, humidity, pressure, vibration, and light exposure, which are particularly important for sensitive or perishable goods, such as food, chemicals, and pharmaceuticals. For example, temperature sensors embedded in cold chain logistics help maintain and document compliance with safety standards during transportation and storage. Vibration and shock sensors can detect handling issues in fragile items, thereby enabling real-time alerts and corrective actions. Smart devices also allow remote condition monitoring of assets and warehouse environments, reducing the need for manual inspections and minimizing response time to issues. The data collected by IoT devices enable better decision making through predictive analytics and real-time insights (Lushi et al., 2022). Predictive maintenance, for example, helps identify potential issues before they occur, reducing downtime and maintenance costs. The IoT helps maintain food safety standards, reduce waste, and manage variations in the food supply chain (Bigliardi et al., 2022). The IoT ensures the integrity of pharmaceutical products by monitoring storage conditions and preventing counterfeit drugs (Aslam, 2025).

Despite its benefits, the adoption of IoT in logistics faces challenges such as the need for policy support, standardization, and technological innovation (Jiang & Hao, 2011). Many companies face challenges in integrating IoT technologies with existing legacy systems, which can be complex and expensive (Aslam, 2025). The integration of IoT devices raises concerns about data security and privacy as sensitive information is transmitted and stored. Ensuring robust security measures and compliance with regulations are crucial for mitigating these risks. By delivering continuous, accurate, and location-specific data, IoT sensors and devices can empower companies to reduce spoilage, ensure product integrity, comply with regulatory requirements, and improve customer satisfaction.

2.4. Digital Twin Technology: Virtual representations of supply chain networks.

Digital twin (DT) technology involves creating a virtual replica of a physical object, system, or process. This digital counterpart is designed to accurately reflect a real-world entity and is updated in real time using data from sensors and other sources. DT technology is increasingly recognized as a transformative tool in supply chain management, offering virtual representations of supply chain networks that mirror physical assets and processes. This technology enables real-time monitoring, predictive analytics, and adaptive decision-making, which significantly enhances the efficiency and resilience of supply chains. DT provides real-time insights into supply chain operations, allowing immediate adjustments and optimizations (Alguirat et al., 2024). This capability is crucial for maintaining operational efficiency and swiftly responding to disruptions. By simulating various scenarios, digital twins can help forecast supply chain dynamics and potential issues, enabling proactive management. Predictive models can address challenges, such as demand forecasting, inventory planning, and risk management. Digital twins improve supply chain visibility, facilitating better communication and collaboration between stakeholders (Abbas et al., 2024). Visibility is essential for managing complex supply chains and ensuring that all parts of the network are aligned. Technology supports sustainable practices by optimizing resource use and reducing environmental impacts. It also helps to minimize waste and improve the overall efficiency of supply chain processes (Wang et al., 2022). Digital twins are widely used to optimize manufacturing processes, improve quality control, and enhance production planning. In the logistics sector, digital twins help optimize transport routes, improve delivery times, and reduce costs. They ensure food safety, reduce waste, and maintain traceability, which are critical for the food industry (Rashed et al., 2025). Integrating digital twins into existing supply chains can be complex and require significant investment in technology and training

2.5. Edge Devices and Gateways

Edge devices and gateways are essential components of edge computing and the Internet of Things (IoT). Edge devices, such as sensors, actuators, and smart devices, collect, process, and transmit data at the edge of the network closer to the data source. Gateways serve as intermediaries between these edge devices and the cloud or central datacenters, performing crucial functions such as data processing, protocol translation, and security. By filtering and preprocessing data, gateways ensure efficient communication and compatibility between different devices, while providing encryption and authentication to protect data during transmission. Edge devices and gateways enhance data processing efficiency, reduce latency and bandwidth usage, and improve security and reliability in various applications and industries.

Edge computing has emerged as a transformative technology in supply chain management (SCM) that offers numerous benefits and addresses various challenges. Edge computing enables real-time data processing, which is crucial for making timely decisions in supply chain management (SCM), thereby enhancing operational efficiency and responsiveness. By processing data locally, edge computing facilitates faster decision making, leading to more agile and efficient supply chains (Akbari, 2024). Integrating edge computing with blockchain technology can improve data security and transparency in SCM, thereby ensuring secure and efficient mutual authentication and data transmission. In addition, edge computing supports the seamless coordination of various supply chain elements, thereby improving production efficiency and resource allocation. By reducing the need for centralized data processing, edge computing can lower infrastructure costs and improve overall cost efficiency (Zhang et al., 2024). Edge computing is emerging as a transformative innovation in supply chain operations. In flexible assembly and disassembly lines, edge computing has been validated in laboratory models, demonstrating its effectiveness in real-time process control and decision making. In the maritime sector, it has been applied to marine IoT systems to support efficient data processing and task management, demonstrating its versatility in handling decentralized environments (Hu & Wang, 2024). In the automotive industry, especially within electric vehicle supply chains, edge computing improves traceability, enhances operational monitoring, and supports overall efficiency by enabling the localized processing of large volumes of sensor data (Kapsalis et al., 2024). These applications highlight the growing role of edge computing in building intelligent, responsive, and scalable supply chain systems.

Several challenges accompany the adoption of advanced technologies such as edge computing in supply chains. One major issue is workload balancing, because an increasing number of edge devices can result in an uneven distribution of processing tasks. Addressing this issue requires effective intra-gateway and inter-gateway methodologies to ensure efficient application execution and resource utilization. Another challenge is data integration and management, where the complexity of handling data from diverse sources can hinder real-time operation. Advanced approaches, such as collaborative large-scale information fusion and decentralized architectures, can help unify and manage such data efficiently. Security concerns also emerge owing to the heightened connectivity of SCM networks (Liu et al., 2020). These risks can be mitigated through robust mechanisms such as enhanced RFID authentication protocols and blockchain integration, which offer data integrity and secure access control. Finally, scalability is critical, ensuring that the system can grow without degrading performance. Techniques, such as lightweight deep neural network models and decentralized processing architectures, provide the necessary support to maintain performance at scale (Tošić et al., 2023). Together, these solutions lay the foundation for robust, scalable, and secure supply chain systems powered by edge and AI technologies.

2.6. Connected Vehicles and Assets

Connected vehicles and assets refer to systems in which vehicles and various physical assets are equipped with sensors, software, and connectivity to interact with each other and central systems. This connectivity enables real-time data collection, monitoring, and management and enhances efficiency and safety. Connected vehicles and assets play a transformative role in modern supply chain management by enabling real-time monitoring, automation, and data-driven decision making. These assets, ranging from smart trucks and delivery vans to forklifts, pallets, and containers, are equipped with IoT sensors, telematics, and communication modules that continuously transmit data on location, speed, fuel consumption, load status, and mechanical health (sharif). In logistics, connected vehicles allow for real-time fleet tracking, route optimization, and proactive maintenance scheduling, which minimizes downtime and reduces operational costs. Similarly, connected warehouse assets such as autonomous forklifts or smart shelves provide continuous status updates, improve inventory visibility, and enhance warehouse efficiency. These technologies also support predictive maintenance by identifying potential equipment failures before they occur, thus avoiding unexpected disruptions (Druehl). Furthermore, integrating connected assets into centralized platforms enables end-to-end visibility across the supply chain, enhances coordination between stakeholders, and supports compliance with safety and environmental standards. Overall, connected vehicles and assets help to create a more intelligent, responsive, and resilient supply chain ecosystem.

The integration of connected vehicles and assets into supply chain management offers numerous benefits, including enhanced efficiency, cost reduction, and improved sustainability. However, it also requires careful consideration of data security and collaborative efforts among stakeholders to fully realize its potential.

3. AI-DRIVEN ANALYTICS FOR SUPPLY CHAIN OPTIMIZATION

In today's highly dynamic and globally interconnected business environment, the supply chain has evolved into a complex web of operations that require sophisticated tools for effective management. Traditional supply chain models, which rely heavily on manual processes and historical data, are no longer sufficient to handle real-time challenges, such as fluctuating demand, geopolitical disruptions, pandemics, and rising consumer expectations. AI combined with advanced data analytics offers a powerful solution to these problems. AI-driven analytics plays a crucial role in optimizing supply chain operations across various industries. AI-driven analytics involves the use of machine learning algorithms, natural language processing, computer vision, and predictive modeling to process large volumes of structured and unstructured data (Samuels, 2025). These technologies enable supply chain managers to gain insight, forecast future scenarios, and automate decision-making processes. Consequently, companies can achieve greater efficiency, reduce costs, improve customer satisfaction, and increase overall agility.

3.1. Predictive Analytics: forecasting demand, supply fluctuations, and risk factors.

Accurate demand forecasting is one of the critical components of supply chain efficiency. AI enhances forecasting by analyzing vast datasets, including historical sales records, seasonal trends, weather patterns, social media sentiments, and macroeconomic indicators. Machine learning models, such as Long Short-Term Memory (LSTM) networks or ARIMA models, can detect complex patterns and make more accurate predictions than traditional statistical models. By improving demand forecasts, organizations can align production schedules, optimize inventory levels, and reduce both shortages and excess stock (Terrada et al., 2022). Hybrid models combining AI with traditional optimization techniques can improve demand forecasting accuracy by integrating vast amounts of data and providing real-time visibility into supply chain operations (Rui & Li, 2024). The use of predictive analytics and real-time data processing enables organizations to anticipate and respond to market changes swiftly. This reduces the risk of stockouts and surplus inventory, ensuring a balanced supply chain (riad). In addition, AI-driven predictive analytics models analyze large datasets to identify trends and patterns, which helps in making informed decisions regarding future demand (Hasan et al., 2024). AI-based automation of the demand-forecasting process minimizes human errors and streamlines operations, leading to increased efficiency and reduced operational costs.

Supply fluctuations caused by factors such as demand variability, supplier instability, transportation delays, and geopolitical or environmental disruptions can severely affect the operational continuity. AI plays a crucial role in predicting supply fluctuations by enabling data-driven proactive decision-making that enhances the agility and resilience of supply chains. It uses machine learning (ML) algorithms to analyze historical sales data, seasonal trends, consumer behavior, and external variables such as economic indicators, social media sentiment, and weather patterns. Models, such as time-series forecasting or neural networks (e.g., LSTM), can detect complex patterns and anomalies, improve the accuracy of demand forecasts, and anticipate fluctuations that traditional statistical models might miss. Through integration with IoT devices and enterprise systems (such as ERP and WMS), AI continuously monitors inventory levels, supplier lead-times, and order statuses. It can identify early warning signs of potential supply disruptions such as delayed shipments or production slowdowns, enabling companies to respond before the issue escalates.

Evaluating supply chain risks is a critical strategic function that enables organizations to ensure operational continuity, protect financial performance, and build long-term resilience. Without proper risk evaluation, these disruptions can cause delays, increased costs, lost revenue, reputational damage, and even complete operational breakdowns. AI evaluates supply chain risks by processing structured data (e.g., supplier performance records) and unstructured data (e.g., news articles, financial reports, and social media). Natural language processing (NLP) can extract sentiments and identify red flags, such as political unrest, strikes, or financial instability of vendors that may trigger supply fluctuations. AI enables the early identification of potential risks by analyzing large datasets from various sources, including historical transaction data and external market data (Kahya et al., 2025). This predictive capability helps foresee disruptions and take proactive measures to mitigate them.

In short, the evaluation of supply chain risks is not merely a defensive measure, but a strategic enabler of agility, resilience, and sustained growth in an increasingly volatile and complex global environment. AI significantly enhances supply chain risk management by providing predictive insights, improving decision making, and optimizing processes. However, successful implementation requires addressing the challenges related to data quality, organizational readiness, and ethical considerations. By leveraging AI, companies can build resilient, efficient, and transparent supply chains capable of navigating modern complexities and uncertainties.

3.2. Anomaly Detection – AI algorithms identifying fraud, delays, or unexpected disruptions.

In modern supply chains, disruptions can stem from various sources, including fraud, equipment failures, demand surges, transportation delays, and cyber threats. Traditional systems often struggle to detect anomalies over time, leading to losses in efficiency, customer trust, and revenue. AI has emerged as a transformative tool for addressing this challenge through automated anomaly detection.

Anomaly detection is critical in supply chains that identify fraudulent transactions, inventory errors, shipment delays, and unexpected demand shifts. AI can learn complex patterns and identify outliers more effectively than traditional rule-based systems by leveraging machine learning algorithms to monitor vast amounts of structured and unstructured supply chain data, such as sensor logs, shipment records, inventory levels, and vendor transactions, in real time. These algorithms learn normal operation patterns and are trained to identify deviations or outliers that could indicate potential issues. For example, a sudden spike in demand that does not align with seasonal trends, a missing shipment scan, or an unusual supplier transaction may be flagged as suspicious.

Among the most widely used AI methods for identifying fraud, autoencoders, which are a type of unsupervised neural network, stand out for their ability to learn complex patterns and detect anomalies based on reconstruction errors (parsnna). These are particularly effective in processing high-dimensional sensor data, such as temperature logs or real-time shipment monitoring. Isolation Forests, another popular choice, operate by isolating outliers using random partitioning, offering high scalability and speed, which is ideal for real-time anomaly detection in large-scale supply chains. One-Class Support Vector Machines (SVMs) are effective when anomalous examples are rare or unavailable because they train solely on normal data to flag deviations (Ali & Ali Hagag, 2024). Clustering algorithms such as K-means can also be employed to detect outliers based on the distance from cluster centers, providing a simple and interpretable approach. For time-series data, Recurrent Neural Networks (RNNs) and Long Short-Term Memory (LSTM) networks are used to capture sequential dependencies and temporal flag anomalies such as unexpected delivery delays (Kumari & Mittal, 2024). Bayesian Networks, which model probabilistic relationships among variables, are useful for incorporating domain knowledge and offering interpretable results. Additionally, ensemble methods, such as hybrid voting classifiers, enhance detection accuracy by combining multiple models. Together, these AI algorithms enable supply chain systems to monitor operations proactively, detect irregularities early, and support timely decision making to mitigate risks and optimize performance.

Similarly, to detect and manage unexpected delays in supply chain operations, various AI algorithms have been employed based on their ability to analyze time-dependent patterns, handle uncertainty, and learn from complex datasets. Recurrent Neural Networks (RNNs), particularly Long Short-Term Memory (LSTM) networks, are highly effective in capturing sequential dependencies in delivery timelines, enabling the prediction of expected arrival times and the detection of anomalies when delays occur (Ashraf et al., 2024; Viellechner & Spinler, 2020).

Time-series forecasting models such as ARIMA, Facebook Prophet, or DeepAR are also widely used to forecast delivery or production durations based on historical trends, helping organizations anticipate disruptions before they escalate. Autoencoders, when applied to sequential data, can learn normal operation patterns and identify delays by measuring the reconstruction errors. In scenarios with multiple influencing variables, such as weather, traffic, or supplier reliability, Bayesian Networks offer a probabilistic framework to model and infer the likelihood of delays, providing both prediction and interpretability. Additionally, Gradient Boosting algorithms, such as XGBoost and LightGBM, can predict delays by learning from structured data inputs and can effectively handle nonlinear relationships among features, such as order size, logistics constraints, and resource availability (Rezki & Mansouri, 2024). These AI algorithms are chosen not only for their predictive power, but also for their adaptability to real-time data, scalability, and suitability for dynamic and uncertain environments, making them valuable tools for minimizing supply chain delays and enhancing operational responsiveness.

3.3. Automated Decision-Making – AI-based recommendations for route optimization, inventory restocking, and supplier selection.

Artificial Intelligence (AI) plays a pivotal role in optimizing transportation routes within supply chain networks. Route optimization refers to the process of determining the most efficient path for delivering goods, with the aim of minimizing delivery time, fuel consumption, and operational costs (Lushi et al., 2022). AI algorithms, particularly machine learning models, analyze vast datasets, including historical traffic patterns, weather conditions, vehicle telematics, and GPS inputs (Ashkanani et al., 2025). These models can predict delays and recommend alternative routes in real-time. Reinforcement learning (RL) techniques are increasingly being used to simulate and adapt to complex logistics environments by learning from past delivery outcomes. Graph-based algorithms, such as Dijkstra's or A*, when enhanced with AI, can dynamically adjust routes based on live updates. The use of AI in route optimization leads to more timely deliveries, lower fuel costs, and improved customer satisfaction. For example, a logistics company may deploy an AI-driven system that learns to avoid congested urban areas during peak hours, thereby improving the delivery efficiency by 20%.

Inventory restocking is a core function in supply chain management that involves the replenishment of goods to ensure availability while minimizing holding costs. AI-based systems significantly enhance this process by using predictive analytics to forecast future demands. Algorithms such as ARIMA, Facebook Prophet, and LSTM neural networks analyze historical sales, seasonal trends, market shifts, and promotional campaigns to accurately predict when and how much inventory is required. Classification techniques can categorize products based on their sales volatility, allowing supply chain managers to apply restocking strategies accordingly. Moreover, reinforcement learning can automate replenishment decisions by continuously optimizing reorder quantities and intervals based on real-time sales and cost metrics. These approaches prevent overstocking and stockouts, reduce inventory-carrying costs, and improve customer service levels. For instance, a retail chain may use AI to anticipate a surge in demand for certain products during festive seasons, allowing timely restocking and minimizing lost sales.

Supplier selection is a strategic component of procurement and risk management in supply chains. AI enhances this process by enabling data-driven multidimensional evaluations of suppliers. ML algorithms integrated with multi-criteria decision-making models, such as the Analytic Hierarchy Process (AHP) or TOPSIS, assess suppliers based on key performance indicators, including cost, reliability, quality, and compliance. Furthermore, Natural Language Processing (NLP) techniques can scan and analyze supplier contracts, reviews, and regulatory filings to uncover hidden risks such as litigation history or inconsistent service. Clustering algorithms and anomaly detection models can identify underperforming suppliers by flagging unusual trends such as increased defect rates or delivery delays. The integration of AI in supplier selection not only improves sourcing decisions but also strengthens risk mitigation strategies and procurement transparency. For example, an electronics manufacturer may use an AI system to flag a supplier with a recent drop in on-time delivery performance, prompting a re-evaluation of vendor contracts.

4. INTEGRATION OF IOT AND AI

The integration of the Internet of Things (IoT) and Artificial Intelligence (AI) has significantly enhanced data security, traceability, and trust across modern supply chains. IoT devices, such as RFID tags, GPS trackers, and environmental sensors, collect real-time data on the movement, condition, and location of goods throughout the supply chain. This continuous data stream provides the foundation for end-to-end visibility and traceability.

4.1. Ensuring data security, traceability, and trust in the supply chain.

Securing a vast amount of data generated from logistics, procurement, inventory, and distribution activities is critical in today's highly connected and globalized supply chains. The integration of IoT and AI technologies plays a transformative role in strengthening data security by enabling real-time monitoring, automated threat detection, and predictive response capabilities across supply chain ecosystems. IoT devices, such as RFID tags, GPS trackers, temperature sensors, and smart meters, generate continuous streams of data regarding the condition, location, and status of products and assets. These devices automatically collect and transmit data without human intervention, thereby significantly reducing the risk of manual errors or data tampering.

To ensure data authenticity, IoT systems are configured with cryptographic signatures, secure communication protocols (e.g., TLS and MQTT with encryption), and device authentication layers to prevent unauthorized access or spoofing of devices. AI algorithms, particularly machine learning and deep learning models, are used to analyze IoT-generated data in real time. These algorithms can detect anomalies or suspicious patterns that may indicate security threats, such as data breaches, sensor manipulation, unauthorized device access, or fake delivery confirmations. For instance, if a shipment is logged as delivered, but the GPS data do not reach its destination, the AI system can flag the event for investigation. Techniques such as autoencoders, isolation forests, and neural network classifiers help identify both known and novel cyber threats in real time. In addition, if a supplier's IoT infrastructure begins to exhibit unusual data traffic or erratic sensor readings, AI can preemptively isolate the system or alert administrators. This predictive capability enhances cyber resilience and reduces the time interval between threat detection and response. Furthermore, IoT devices feed data into decentralized blockchain systems in which each event or transaction (such as product handovers, temperature checks, or delivery confirmations) is securely recorded in a tamper-proof ledger.

AI validates the integrity of data before it is added to the blockchain and can trigger smart contracts based on verified inputs (M. M. Khan et al., 2025). Consider a pharmaceutical supply chain that uses IoT sensors to monitor temperature during drug transportation. If a hacker attempts to spoof sensor data to hide a temperature breach, AI algorithms trained on normal shipment patterns will detect inconsistencies between real-time GPS and environmental data. The system can flag the anomaly, prevent tampered data from being entered into inventory systems, and even activate a smart contract to halt payments to the transporter until verification is complete. This triple-layered security—IoT for sensing, AI for validating, and blockchain for storing—creates a highly secure and traceable supply chain infrastructure.

4.2. Smart Contracts for the automated execution of supply chain agreements

Smart contracts are self-executing digital agreements written in code, where the terms of the contract are directly embedded into a blockchain (M. M. Khan et al., 2025). These contracts automatically perform predefined actions when specific conditions are met without requiring intermediaries. Once deployed, smart contracts are immutable, transparent, and trustless, meaning that all parties can verify outcomes without relying on central authority. In supply chain management, smart contracts are used to automate and enforce agreements between parties such as manufacturers, suppliers, logistics providers, retailers, and customers. They operate on blockchain platforms (e.g., Ethereum and Hyperledger Fabric) and are triggered by inputs such as timestamps, delivery confirmations, sensor data (IoT), or payment receipts. For example, smart contracts ensure that payments are released automatically once agreed-upon conditions are fulfilled. For example, a contract might stipulate that a payment is issued to a supplier once goods are delivered and verified through GPS data or RFID scans. This reduces delays, manual invoicing, and disputes over payment terms.

Smart contracts can also be linked to IoT devices (e.g., temperature sensors and GPS trackers), which monitor the conditions and locations of goods. If a shipment arrives on time and meets all the required quality conditions (e.g., temperature within range), the contract automatically confirms receipt and process-related tasks, such as inventory updates or delivery confirmation to end users. Supply contracts often include performance clauses such as penalties for delays or quality issues. Smart contracts can automatically enforce these rules. For instance, if a supplier fails to meet delivery deadlines, the smart contract can deduct penalties or withhold payment based on verifiable event logs from the blockchain or external data oracles. Every transaction or status update governed by a smart contract is recorded on the blockchain to ensure full visibility and tamper-proof auditing. This is critical for industries, such as pharmaceuticals, food, and electronics, where product origin and handling must be verified across the entire supply chain for compliance or ethical sourcing. Smart contracts can automate reorder processes by monitoring stock levels through integrated systems. When inventory drops below a certain threshold, the smart contract can initiate a new purchase order with a pre-approved supplier, streamline procurement, and reduce stockouts. For instance, a coffee company can use smart contracts to automate the entire life cycle of coffee bean procurement. The contract ensures that farmers receive payment instantly upon confirmation of ethically sourced beans, while transporters are compensated only if the shipment arrives on time and in good condition, as verified via IoT sensors. All records from farm to shelf were stored immutably in the blockchain.

4.3. Data interoperability and standardization challenges

Organizations often face significant data interoperability and standardization challenges when integrating the IoT and AI into supply chain systems. These issues can hinder seamless data exchange, analysis, and decision making across diverse platforms, devices, and stakeholders. Below is a detailed explanation of these challenges in the context of supply chain integration.

4.3.1. Heterogeneous Data Sources and Formats

Supply chains involve multiple stakeholders, such as manufacturers, warehouses, transport providers, and retailers, each potentially using different IoT devices and platforms. These devices generate data in various formats, schemas, and protocols (e.g., JSON, XML, CSV, MQTT, and CoAP), leading to compatibility issues. AI models require structured and clean data, but inconsistent data formats complicate the preprocessing, integration, and analytics pipelines.

4.3.2. Lack of Universal Standards for IoT Devices

Currently, there is no universally accepted communication or data standard for the IoT devices used in supply chains. Manufacturers often use proprietary systems or protocols, resulting in vendor lock-ins and fragmented ecosystems. This lack of standardization creates difficulties in connecting new IoT devices to the existing infrastructure and limits scalability.

4.3.3. Siloed Data Across Organizations

Supply chains often span multiple companies with different IT infrastructures and data governance policies. Data can be stored in isolated silos to prevent real-time sharing and holistic visibility. Interoperability is difficult when there is no agreement on data-sharing protocols, formats, or access rights. This hampers the ability of AI to generate accurate end-to-end insight.

4.3.4. Inconsistent Data Quality and Semantics

IoT-generated data may vary in quality, accuracy, and labeling standards, particularly when collected from legacy systems or low-cost sensors. Additionally, semantic inconsistencies, such as different definitions of delivery time, inventory status, or order priority, can lead to misinterpretations by AI algorithms. This negatively impacts the model training, decision accuracy, and overall system reliability.

4.3.5. Integration Complexity with Legacy Systems

Many supply chain systems rely on ERP platforms, spreadsheets, or manual processes, which may not support modern APIs or IoT connectivity. Integrating AI and IoT technologies into such legacy environments requires custom interfaces, middleware, or data translators, increasing the implementation time, cost, and risk of failure.

4.3.6. Real-Time Data Synchronization Challenges

IoT devices continuously generate real-time data, whereas AI models require synchronized, timely, and coherent data streams for accurate predictions. Variations in data update rates, network latencies, and inconsistent timestamping make it difficult to synchronize data across sources, thereby affecting the effectiveness of AI-driven insights.

4.3.7. Regulatory and Compliance Issues

Differences in data regulations (e.g., GDPR, CCPA) and industry-specific standards (e.g., ISO, GS1) across regions and supply chain partners can create legal barriers to data-sharing and standardization. This limits the interoperability of AI and IoT systems, which rely on cross-border data flow for decision-making and transparency.

5. CASE STUDIES & INDUSTRY APPLICATIONS

As global supply chains become increasingly complex, accurate demand forecasting has become essential for efficient inventory management, cost control, and customer satisfaction. Artificial Intelligence (AI) plays a pivotal role in enabling data-driven real-time forecasting in modern supply chain systems.

5.1. Retail & E-Commerce – AI-powered demand forecasting in supply chain.

Accurate demand forecasting has become the cornerstone of efficient supply chain management in the era of globalized commerce and increasingly complex consumer behavior. Walmart Inc., the world's largest retailer, offers a prime example of how artificial intelligence (AI) can be harnessed to revolutionize this critical function. Operating more than 10,000 stores across the globe and serving millions of customers through its physical and digital platforms, Walmart faced a persistent challenge: accurately forecasting demand across diverse regions, product categories, and sales channels.

Walmart sees big swings in demand around holidays, such as Christmas and Black Friday. Historically, the organization has relied on traditional statistical models such as ARIMA and moving averages to predict product demand (Iseal & Michael, 2025). While these models provided basic forecasts, they were inadequate for capturing dynamic shifts in consumer behavior, local demand fluctuations, and external variables such as weather patterns or major public events. This has resulted in frequent stockouts during periods of high demand, overstocking of slower-moving goods, and increased operational costs due to markdowns and inefficiencies. To address these limitations, Walmart implemented an AI-powered demand-forecasting system designed to provide real-time, granular, and adaptive predictions. The new solution combines machine learning algorithms such as gradient boosting and random forests with deep learning models such as Long Short-Term Memory (LSTM) networks. These models were trained on a vast array of data sources, including historical sales, promotional campaigns, social media sentiments, weather forecasts, and local events. The integration of cloud computing through Microsoft Azure allows Walmart to scale the system across its vast global operations efficiently and securely. The AI system operates through a multi-step process. First, real-time data were collected from point-of-sale (POS) systems, e-commerce platforms, IoT sensors, and third-party sources. Next, they engineered predictive features that reflected seasonal trends, customer preferences, and regional characteristics. Forecasts were then generated at the SKU-store-day level, providing highly localized insights. Finally, these forecasts were integrated into Walmart's inventory management and replenishment systems, enabling automated data-driven decisions on restocking, distribution, and logistics.

The results of this initiative were significant. The forecasting accuracy improved by 30%, particularly in high-velocity and perishable product categories. Stockouts were reduced by 20%, while inventory-holding costs dropped substantially because of more precise inventory alignment. Additionally, the system reduces waste, especially in fresh food items, by avoiding overordering. Customer satisfaction also improved owing to better product availability, faster order fulfillment, and fewer delivery delays. Beyond these operational benefits, the AI system enhanced Walmart's agility and resilience, enabling faster responses to unforeseen events, such as supply chain disruptions or demand spikes during the COVID-19 pandemic. Walmart's success in AI-powered demand forecasting underscores several critical success factors. The use of granular localized predictions ensures that each store and region receives the right products at the right time. Real-time analytics and automated decision-making capabilities allow the company to adapt quickly to changing conditions. Cross-functional collaboration between data science, IT, supply chains, and business units is instrumental in the system's implementation and continuous improvement. Additionally, cloud infrastructure enables scalable deployment, model retraining, and data management at a global level.

In conclusion, Walmart's experience demonstrates the transformative potential of AI in supply chain management. By shifting from reactive to predictive forecasting, Walmart not only optimized its inventory and logistics but also enhanced its customer service and environmental sustainability. This case serves as a benchmark for other retailers and supply chain operators seeking to leverage AI for smarter, faster, and more resilient demand forecasts.

5.2. Pharmaceutical Industry – IoT-enabled temperature monitoring for vaccine distribution.

The pharmaceutical industry, particularly in the distribution of vaccines, demands stringent environmental controls to ensure the safety and efficacy of products. One critical challenge is maintaining the required temperature range, commonly between 2 and 8°C, for cold-chain-dependent vaccines during storage and transit. Any deviation from this range can lead to product degradation, rendering the vaccines ineffective or unsafe. To address this, global pharmaceutical companies have increasingly turned to Internet of Things (IoT) technologies for real-time temperature monitoring throughout the supply chain. A notable real-world example is Pfizer's distribution of the COVID-19 mRNA vaccine, which requires ultra-cold storage conditions at approximately -70°C. To ensure temperature compliance at every stage of transport, Pfizer and its logistics partners deployed IoT-enabled temperature-tracking systems embedded in each thermal shipping container. These systems include GPS-enabled data loggers and IoT sensors capable of continuously measuring the temperature, location, humidity, and exposure to light. The collected data were transmitted in real time to cloud-based monitoring platforms, allowing stakeholders to track every shipment from production facilities to distribution centers and vaccination sites. The data flow enabled immediate alerts to be sent to operations teams if any container experienced a temperature excursion or route deviation, triggering corrective actions, such as route adjustments or replacement of compromised batches.

The benefits of this IoT-enabled system are therefore significant. It provides end-to-end visibility into the vaccine supply chain, increases data transparency, and ensures regulatory compliance with agencies such as the FDA and WHO. Moreover, it significantly reduces the wastage of temperature-sensitive vaccines, improves inventory management, and enhances public trust in the vaccine distribution process. The use of such technology was especially vital in delivering vaccines to remote or underserved regions, where infrastructure was limited and monitoring was previously a major challenge. In addition to Pfizer, companies such as Moderna and logistics firms such as DHL and FedEx have implemented similar IoT-based cold chain solutions for their vaccine supply operations. These systems not only track environmental conditions in transit, but also interface with blockchain platforms to ensure immutable recording of shipment data, further strengthening security and traceability.

This case exemplifies how the integration of the IoT into the pharmaceutical supply chain transforms traditional cold chain logistics into smart, responsive, and secure systems. By enabling real-time monitoring and proactive risk management, IoT technologies have proven to be essential components in the successful global distribution of life-saving vaccines, particularly during the COVID-19 pandemic. As pharmaceutical supply chains continue to expand globally, IoT-based solutions are expected to become standard practices to ensure product integrity, patient safety, and supply chain resilience.

5.3. Automotive & Manufacturing – AI-driven predictive maintenance and inventory tracking.

Siemens, a global leader in industrial automation and manufacturing, offers a compelling real-world example of how AI-driven predictive maintenance and inventory tracking can transform the operational efficiency. Siemens faced persistent challenges related to unplanned equipment downtime, excessive spare parts inventory, and inefficient maintenance scheduling within its large-scale manufacturing plants. These issues not only disrupted production lines but also increased operational costs and delayed order fulfillment.

To address these challenges, Siemens deployed an AI-powered predictive maintenance system integrated with its existing IoT infrastructure under its broader Industrial Internet of Things (IIoT) initiative, branded MindSphere. Sensors installed on critical assets, such as motors, turbines, and conveyors, collect real-time data on temperature, vibration, pressure, and usage hours. These data were transmitted to a centralized AI platform that used machine-learning algorithms to identify degradation patterns and predict equipment failures before they occurred. For example, anomalies in vibration data could indicate impending bearing failure, prompting maintenance crews to intervene before breakdown. Simultaneously, Siemens integrated AI-enabled inventory tracking with its enterprise resource planning (ERP) system. The platform uses historical usage data, predicted maintenance needs, and machine learning-based demand forecasts to optimize the inventory levels of spare parts.

Instead of maintaining a large buffer stock, Siemens implemented a just-in-time (JIT) replenishment strategy, reducing excess inventory and capital lock-in. The system can automatically generate procurement requests or transfer orders when the forecasted demand approaches a critical threshold. The impact of these AI-driven solutions is substantial. Siemens reported a 30% reduction in unplanned downtime, 20% lower maintenance costs, and up to a 25% reduction in inventory holding costs for spare parts. The improved visibility of asset health and part availability enabled more proactive planning, enhanced equipment reliability, and minimized disruptions to manufacturing schedules. Additionally, the predictive maintenance system helped extend the lifespan of machinery and reduce energy consumption by maintaining the equipment under optimal operating conditions.

This case study illustrates how the convergence of AI and IoT technologies can create self-learning, automated maintenance, and inventory ecosystems. By moving away from reactive maintenance and manual inventory tracking, Siemens achieved significant operational gains, demonstrating the value of AI in driving predictive intelligence, cost efficiency, and supply chain agility in the manufacturing sector.

5.4. IoT and GPS enabled fleet management

The United Parcel Service (UPS), one of the world's largest package delivery and supply chain management companies, has been at the forefront of using IoT and GPS technologies to optimize its fleet management. With over 125,000 vehicles operating daily across global routes, the UPS faced the challenge of maximizing delivery efficiency, reducing fuel consumption, and ensuring real-time visibility of vehicle status and driver behavior. Traditional fleet management systems lack the granularity and responsiveness needed to effectively manage such massive and dynamic operations.

To address these challenges, UPS implemented a comprehensive IoT and GPS-enabled fleet management system, known as On-Road Integrated Optimization and Navigation (ORION). Each delivery vehicle was equipped with GPS trackers, IoT sensors, and telematics devices to monitor location, speed, idling time, engine health, and environmental conditions. These real-time data were continuously transmitted to a central AI-powered analytics platform that dynamically optimized delivery routes, monitored fleet health, and provided live updates to fleet managers. One of the most significant features of this system is its ability to generate dynamic and optimized delivery routes each day.

ORION uses GPS data and predictive algorithms to reduce left-hand turns, avoid traffic congestion, and prioritize urgent deliveries while minimizing fuel consumption. Simultaneously, IoT sensors collect data on vehicle performance and usage patterns, enabling predictive maintenance alerts to prevent breakdowns and costly repairs. The impact of the IoT and GPS-enabled fleet management systems was substantial. The UPS reported savings of more than 10 million gallons of fuel annually, eliminating 100 million miles driven, and reducing carbon emissions by over 100,000 metric tons. The improved routing efficiency translates into shorter delivery times, fewer vehicle breakdowns, and lower operating costs. In addition, the system provides enhanced safety monitoring by tracking driver behavior, such as harsh braking or rapid acceleration, enabling targeted training and accident reduction.

This case study demonstrates how the integration of IoT and GPS in fleet management can revolutionize logistics operations by providing real-time intelligence, proactive maintenance, and data-driven route optimization. UPS's success of UPSs highlights the potential of these technologies to not only drive operational efficiency but also support sustainability goals in large-scale transportation networks.

6. CHALLENGES, ETHICAL CONSIDERATIONS, AND FUTURE DIRECTIONS

The integration of IoT and AI technologies into supply chain visibility brings transformative potential, but also introduces a complex set of technical, ethical, and strategic challenges. Among the primary obstacles are issues related to data interoperability, infrastructure scalability, and system integration, particularly because supply chains span multiple regions, platforms, and legacy systems.

6.1. Challenges

6.1.1. Data privacy & security risks in IoT-powered supply chains.

The integration of IoT and AI technologies into supply chain systems introduces significant cybersecurity and privacy challenges that must be carefully managed (Karai). The vast volume of real-time data generated by IoT devices, ranging from shipment locations and environmental conditions to machine performance and inventory levels, is continuously collected, transmitted, and analyzed by AI systems. This interconnected ecosystem significantly expands the potential attack surface, making it more vulnerable to cyber threats, such as data breaches, device spoofing, denial-of-service (DoS) attacks, and unauthorized access. Malicious actors may exploit vulnerabilities in the sensor firmware, unsecured communication channels, or cloud storage to intercept or manipulate critical operational data. As a result, ensuring robust cybersecurity measures, such as encryption, secure authentication protocols, anomaly detection, and regular security updates, is essential to maintaining the integrity and confidentiality of supply chain information (Nazari).

In parallel, the widespread deployment of IoT devices raises privacy concerns, particularly when data involves sensitive business operations, customer information, or employee tracking. While visibility and traceability are vital for efficiency and compliance, excessively or improperly governed data collection can infringe on privacy rights and lead to regulatory violations. Striking the right balance between operational transparency and individual or organizational privacy is a complex challenge. It requires the implementation of data minimization practices, role-based access controls, anonymization techniques, and strict adherence to privacy regulations, such as the GDPR or CCPA (Chandankhede & Gourshettiwar, 2025). Ultimately, managing cybersecurity and privacy risks is not merely a technical issue, but also a strategic imperative that requires continuous risk assessment, cross-functional collaboration, and policy-driven governance across the supply chain ecosystem (Ajibesin et al., 2025).

6.1.2. Infrastructure and Integration

Implementing IoT and AI technologies in the supply chain requires a robust and often costly infrastructure, which poses a significant barrier to widespread adoption, particularly among small to medium enterprises (SMEs) and organizations operating in developing markets (Chandankhede & Gourshettiwar, 2025). The high installation costs associated with deploying IoT sensors, communication networks, edge-computing devices, AI platforms, and secure data storage systems can be prohibitive. These expenses include not only hardware and software investments but also the costs of skilled labor, training, system maintenance, and ongoing upgrades. For many companies, especially those with limited capital or operating in resource-constrained environments, return on investment may not be immediately evident, further discouraging adoption.

In addition to the financial challenges, system integration is a major technical hurdle. Many organizations operate legacy enterprise resource planning (ERP) systems, warehouse management systems (WMS), or transportation management systems (TMS) that are not designed to interact with IoT devices or advanced AI platforms (Nazari). Integrating these heterogeneous technologies, along with other digital innovations, such as blockchain or cloud-based analytics, requires the development of custom APIs, middleware solutions, and interoperability frameworks. This process is not only time-consuming and costly but also introduces risks related to system compatibility, data consistency, and cybersecurity. Without standardized protocols and cohesive architectures, achieving seamless communication and real-time data exchange across platforms has become a complex endeavor (Ghosh et al., 2024). Consequently, both infrastructure investment and technological integration remain critical challenges that must be addressed to unlock the full potential of IoT and AI in modern supply chains.

6.1.3. Data Quality and Management

Data quality and management are fundamental to the successful integration of IoT and AI technologies in the supply chain because the reliability and accuracy of AI-driven decisions are directly tied to the integrity of the data being analyzed. One of the most critical challenges is the data quality. IoT devices often operate in diverse and dynamic environments, where they are susceptible to errors, such as sensor drift, data loss, environmental interference, and hardware malfunctions. If the data collected are inaccurate, incomplete, or inconsistent, AI algorithms may produce flawed insights, resulting in poor decision making, operational inefficiencies, and even financial losses. For instance, erroneous temperature readings in a cold chain supply system could mislead AI models in allowing the delivery of compromised goods, thereby undermining product quality and safety (Gosh).

Compounding this issue is the problem of data overload. The sheer volume of data generated by IoT devices can be staggered, ranging from real-time location tracking and environmental monitoring to asset performance metrics. Without robust data architecture and advanced management tools, organizations can quickly become overwhelmed, leading to delays in data processing, bottlenecks in analytics pipelines, and difficulties in extracting actionable insights. Effective data governance strategies, including data filtering, edge computing, storage optimization, and automated cleansing protocols, are essential for efficiently managing this influx. Additionally, adopting scalable cloud infrastructure and AI-enhanced data management platforms can help organizations maintain high data quality standards while ensuring timely, accurate, and context-aware decision making across the supply chain (Drake, 2022).

6.1.4. Scalability and Operability

Scalability and operability are critical considerations when deploying IoT and AI solutions in supply chain environments, particularly as businesses expand, and supply networks become increasingly complex. One of the primary challenges lies in scalability; as the number of connected devices, data points, and operational nodes increases, maintaining the performance, connectivity, and responsiveness of IoT-AI systems becomes increasingly difficult. Many solutions that function well in pilot programs or small-scale deployments struggle to perform efficiently. Constraints, such as limited bandwidth, network latency, increased data storage demands, and processing power requirements, can inhibit broader implementation. Without scalable infrastructure and cloud-native architectures, organizations may be unable to adapt these technologies to larger, multi-regional operations, ultimately stalling digital transformation efforts (Chandankhede & Gourshettiwar, 2025).

Equally important are the operability complications arising from deploying IoT devices and AI systems in various environments. Supply chain operations span diverse conditions, from climate-controlled warehouses and manufacturing plants to outdoor logistics routes and cross-border facilities, each of which presents unique technical challenges. Ensuring that IoT sensors, gateways, and AI analytics platforms function reliably across these different settings requires robust hardware, adaptive software, and consistent system calibrations. Environmental factors such as temperature extremes, humidity, signal interference, or power fluctuations can compromise device performance and data accuracy. Moreover, maintaining consistent operability often demands significant IT support, standardized protocols, and real-time monitoring systems. Addressing these challenges is essential to ensure that IoT and AI technologies not only scale with business growth, but also deliver consistent, reliable performance across the supply chain ecosystem.

6.1.5. Resistance to Adoption

Resistance to adoption remains a notable barrier to the successful integration of IoT and AI technologies into supply chain management. One of the primary sources of this resistance stems from reliance on legacy systems, which are often deeply embedded within an organization's operational workflows, infrastructure, and enterprise software. Although outdated, these systems are perceived as stable and familiar, and their replacement can pose significant technical and financial risks. Transitioning from legacy platforms to modern IoT-enabled and AI-driven solutions often requires extensive re-engineering, data migration, and compatibility adjustments. For many organizations, especially those with limited IT resources or highly customized systems, this transformation is viewed as disruptive and cost-intensive, discouraging innovation (Ajibesin et al., 2025).

In addition to technological barriers, change management challenges significantly impact adoption. Implementing IoT and AI technologies involves more than deploying hardware and software; they require fundamental shifts in organizational culture, decision-making processes, and employee responsibilities. Employees may be reluctant to embrace new tools because of fear of job displacement, lack of digital skills, or discomfort with automated decision systems. Similarly, middle and senior management may resist altering established operational models and fear a loss of control or accountability. Overcoming this resistance requires strong leadership, clear communication, employee training, and a phased implementation strategy that demonstrates early win. Without proactive change management, even the most advanced technologies may fail to gain traction, limiting the potential benefits of digital transformation in the supply chain (Gosh).

6.2. Ethical and Regulatory Challenges

Ethical and regulatory challenges represent significant obstacles to the widespread adoption of AI and IoT technologies in supply chains. As AI systems increasingly influence decision making, such as in demand forecasting, supplier selection, route planning, and workforce management, they raise important ethical considerations. A key concern is the transparency and accountability of AI-driven decisions. When AI models make complex recommendations or automated choices, it is often difficult to trace the rationale behind these outcomes, particularly in black-box systems. This lack of explainability can lead to mistrust among stakeholders and raise questions about who is responsible for decisions that may negatively impact workers, partners, or customers. Additionally, the use of vast datasets collected from IoT devices, including personal or behavioral data, can create privacy risks and ethical dilemmas regarding consent, surveillance, and data ownership (Ugrinov et al., 2024).

Simultaneously, organizations must navigate a rapidly evolving landscape of regulatory compliance across different countries and industries. Supply chains often span multiple jurisdictions, each with their own data protection laws, cybersecurity mandates, and AI governance frameworks. Regulations such as the General Data Protection Regulation (GDPR) in Europe, the California Consumer Privacy Act (CCPA) in the U.S., and industry-specific guidelines for pharmaceuticals, food safety, and critical infrastructure impose strict rules on how data must be collected, stored, and processed. Ensuring compliance with these diverse regulations requires significant investments in legal expertise, compliance monitoring systems, and adaptive data governance practices. Noncompliance can result in reputational damage, financial penalties, and disruption of operations. Therefore, addressing both the ethical and regulatory dimensions of AI and IoT integration is essential for building trust, ensuring lawful operations, and achieving long-term sustainability in digital supply chain transformation (Nabli).

6.3. Future Directions

6.3.1. Interoperable Standards

The future of AI and the IoT in supply chain visibility hinges on the development of interoperable standards that allow devices, platforms, and systems from different vendors to communicate and share data seamlessly. Currently, the lack of standardized communication protocols and data formats creates integration bottlenecks, particularly when connecting legacy systems with modern IoT sensors and AI platforms. Interoperability ensures that information flows smoothly across the entire supply chain, enabling real-time decision making and eliminating data silos. Industry-wide adoption of standards such as the OPC UA, MQTT, GS1, and ISO/

IEC frameworks will be crucial for fostering open ecosystems and scalable implementations.

6.3.2. Edge Computing for Real-Time Analytics

As supply chains become more distributed and data-intensive, edge computing will play a vital role in processing data closer to its source, such as at warehouses, trucks, or factory floors, rather than relying solely on centralized cloud systems. By enabling local data processing and AI inference at the edge, organizations can achieve real-time analytics with reduced latency, improved bandwidth efficiency, and enhanced responsiveness. This is especially critical for time-sensitive operations such as cold chain monitoring, predictive maintenance, and dynamic route optimization. Edge computing also strengthens data security by limiting the amount of sensitive information transmitted over the networks.

6.3.3. Explainable AI Models

As AI becomes more integral to decision making in supply chains, the need for explainable AI (XAI) will increase. Explainable AI refers to systems that not only make accurate predictions, but also provide transparent, understandable justifications for those decisions. In supply chain contexts, such as supplier risk scoring, demand forecasting, or fraud detection, stakeholders must understand why certain recommendations are made to ensure trust, regulatory compliance, and ethical accountability. Future AI models will increasingly need to balance predictive accuracy with interpretability to enable users to audit algorithms, identify biases, and make informed adjustments.

6.3.4. Blockchain Integration for Secure, Tamper-Proof Data Sharing

Blockchain technology complements AI and the IoT by providing a secure, decentralized, and tamper-proof ledger for recording supply chain transactions and events. When integrated with IoT devices, blockchain can record immutable data points, such as temperature logs, shipping milestones, or delivery confirmations. This enhances traceability and accountability across the supply chain, making it easier to verify product authenticity, ensure regulatory compliance and resolve disputes. Combined with AI, blockchain can enable smart contracts that automatically execute actions, such as payments or alerts based on validated conditions, further automating and securing the supply chain ecosystem.

6.3.5. Cultivating Trust

Technological advancement alone is not sufficient; the future of digital supply chains also depends on cultivating trust among all stakeholders, including suppliers, logistics providers, customers, and regulators. Trust is built through transparency, data integrity, and ethical handling of information. Ensuring that AI systems are fair, unbiased, and auditable, as well as safeguarding privacy and cybersecurity, is fundamental to driving adoption and collaboration.

6.3.6. Cross-Functional Collaboration

The effective integration of AI and IoT into supply chains requires cross-functional collaboration among IT, operations, procurement, logistics, compliance, and executive leadership. These technologies impact multiple areas of business, and siloed implementation efforts can lead to misalignment, inefficiencies, or resistance. Future-ready organizations need to foster interdisciplinary teams and establish unified strategies that align technological initiatives with their business goals.

6.3.7. Ethical Governance

Finally, ethical governance is essential to guide the responsible development and deployment of AI and IoT technologies. This includes policies that address data privacy, algorithmic bias, employee surveillance concerns, and the social impact of automation. Establishing ethical oversight committees, implementing transparent decision frameworks, and engaging with external regulatory bodies will help organizations ensure that innovation in supply chain visibility supports long-term sustainability and social responsibility.

7. CONCLUSION

This chapter explores how the convergence of IoT and AI technologies has revolutionized supply chain visibility. Real-time monitoring, predictive analytics, and autonomous decision-making are no longer futuristic concepts but present-day realities. Organizations that embrace these tools can build more responsive, resilient, and intelligent supply chains. Going forward, collaborative efforts between industry, academia, and policymakers are essential to unlock the full potential of digital transformation in supply chain management.

REFERENCES

Abbas, H. M., Kumar, V. N., Ashlin Deepa, R. N., Bansal, S., Senthil Kumar, R. S., & Krishnakumar, K. (2024). Digital Twins for Real-Time Supply Chain Visibility and Optimization. *2nd IEEE International Conference on IoT, Communication and Automation Technology, ICICAT 2024*, 1132–1137. DOI: 10.1109/ICICAT62666.2024.10923493

Ajibesin, A. A., Çela, E., Vedishchev, A., & Vajjhala, N. R. (2025). Future Horizons in Explainable AI and Blockchain for Supply Chain Management. In *Explainable AI and Blockchain for Secure and Agile Supply Chains* (pp. 197–213). Enhancing Transparency, Traceability, and Accountability., DOI: 10.1201/9781003497363-14

Akbari, M. (2024). Revolutionizing supply chain and circular economy with edge computing: Systematic review, research themes and future directions. *Management Decision*, *62*(9), 2875–2899. DOI: 10.1108/MD-03-2023-0412

Alguirat, I., Zouari, A., & Lehyani, F. (2024). Exploring the Role of Digital Twins in Future Supply Chain Industry: Characteristics, Technologies, and Applications. *2024 IEEE 15th International Colloquium of Logistics and Supply Chain Management, LOGISTIQUA 2024*. DOI: 10.1109/LOGISTIQUA61063.2024.10571453

Ali, A. H., & Ali Hagag, A. (2024). An enhanced AI-based model for financial fraud detection. *International Journal of Advanced and Applied Sciences*, *11*(10), 114–121. DOI: 10.21833/ijaas.2024.10.013

Alsubaiei, F. (n.d.). *OGAR: Augmented Reality Application for Assisting Workers in the Oil and Gas Industry*.

Anandhi, S., Anitha, R., & Sureshkumar, V. (2019). IoT Enabled RFID Authentication and Secure Object Tracking System for Smart Logistics. *Wireless Personal Communications*, *104*(2), 543–560. DOI: 10.1007/s11277-018-6033-6

Apeji, U. D., & Sunmola, F. T. (2022). Principles and Factors Influencing Visibility in Sustainable Supply Chains. *Procedia Computer Science, 200*, 1516–1527. DOI: 10.1016/j.procs.2022.01.353

Ashkanani, M., AlAjmi, A., Alhayyan, A., Esmael, Z., AlBedaiwi, M., & Nadeem, M. (2025). A Self-Adaptive Traffic Signal System Integrating Real-Time Vehicle Detection and License Plate Recognition for Enhanced Traffic Management. *Inventions (Basel, Switzerland), 10*(1), 14. DOI: 10.3390/inventions10010014

Ashraf, M., Eltawil, A., & Ali, I. (2024). Disruption detection for a cognitive digital supply chain twin using hybrid deep learning. *Operations Research, 24*(2), 23. Advance online publication. DOI: 10.1007/s12351-024-00831-y

Aslam, M. S. (2025). IoT and Its Role in Sustainable Pharmaceutical Supply Chains. In *Sustainable Pharmaceutical Product Development and Optimization Processes* (pp. 141–161). From Eco-Design to Supply Chain Integrity., DOI: 10.1007/978-981-97-9707-3_6

Bigliardi, B., Bottani, E., & Filippelli, S. (2022). A study on IoT application in the Food Industry using Keywords Analysis. *Procedia Computer Science, 200*, 1826–1835. DOI: 10.1016/j.procs.2022.01.383

Boudouaia, M. A., Ouchani, S., Qaisar, S. M., & Almaktoom, A. T. (2024). Supply Chain 5.0: Vision, Challenges, and Perspectives. *21st International Learning and Technology Conference: Reality and Science Fiction in Education, L and T 2024*, 203–208. DOI: 10.1109/LT60077.2024.10469476

Chandankhede, A., & Gourshettiwar, P. (2025). A Review of IoT-Driven Innovations in Supply Chain Management. *3rd International Conference on Electronics and Renewable Systems, ICEARS 2025 - Proceedings*, 781–787. DOI: 10.1109/ICEARS64219.2025.10940471

Department, S. R. (2023). Supply chain management (SCM) market size worldwide from 2020 to 2026. In *Statista*. https://www.statista.com/statistics/1181996/supply-chain-management-market-size-worldwide/

Drake, M. J. (2022). The Application of the Internet of Things in Managing Supply Chains. In *Encyclopedia of Data Science and Machine Learning* (pp. 2298–2312). DOI: 10.4018/978-1-7998-9220-5.ch138

Fictiv. (2023). 2023 State of Manufacturing Report. In *Fictiv*. https://www.fictiv.com/ebooks/2023-state-of-manufacturing-report

Ghosh, D., Dutta, P. K., & Abotaleb, M. (2024). Harnessing the power of hybrid models for supply chain management and optimization. In *Hybrid Information Systems* (pp. 407–426). Non-Linear Optimization Strategies with Artificial Intelligence., DOI: 10.1515/9783111331133-019

Hasan, M. Z., Hussain, M. Z., Umair, S., & Waqas, U. (2024). Understanding Artificial Intelligence in Supply Chain and Innovation Performance. In *Human Perspectives of Industry 4.0 Organizations* (pp. 131–154). Reviewing Sustainable Performance., DOI: 10.1201/9781032616810-7

Hu, Y., & Wang, F. (2024). The Task Collaborative Migration Method for Marine IoT Based on Edge Computing-RESTful Architecture. *6th International Conference on Artificial Intelligence in Information and Communication, ICAIIC 2024*, 446–451. DOI: 10.1109/ICAIIC60209.2024.10463387

Iseal, S., & Michael, H. (2025). *Demand Forecasting in E-Commerce Using AI & ML.*

Jiang, Y., & Hao, S. (2011). Research on the development of intelligent logistics based on internet of things. *2011 International Conference on Remote Sensing, Environment and Transportation Engineering, RSETE 2011 - Proceedings*, 5254–5257. DOI: 10.1109/RSETE.2011.5965498

Kafi, M. A., Saifudin, A. B. M., Zainuddin, N. B., Shahron, S. A., Abualrejal, H., & Mohamad, M. (2022). Essential of RFID Technology in Supply Chain Management: A review on Digital Perspective. *International Conference on Intelligent Technology, System and Service for Internet of Everything, ITSS-IoE 2022*. DOI: 10.1109/ITSS-IoE56359.2022.9990933

Kahya, I., Huschbeck, T., & Markovič, P. (2025). Predictive Risk Management in the Supply Chain. In *Studies in Systems* (Vol. 578, pp. 41–57). Decision and Control., DOI: 10.1007/978-3-031-80935-4_3

Kalaiarasan, R., Olhager, J., Agrawal, T. K., & Wiktorsson, M. (2022). The ABCDE of supply chain visibility: A systematic literature review and framework. *International Journal of Production Economics, 248*, 108464. Advance online publication. DOI: 10.1016/j.ijpe.2022.108464

Kapsalis, P., Rimassa, G., Zeydan, E., Via, S., Risso, F. G., Chiasserini, C. F., & Vivo, G. (2024). A Next Generation Architecture for Internet of Things in the Automotive Supply Chain for Electric Vehicles. *Proceedings of the International Symposium on Mobile Ad Hoc Networking and Computing (MobiHoc)*, 428–433. DOI: 10.1145/3641512.3690035

Khan, M. M., Khan, F. S., Nadeem, M., Khan, T. H., Haider, S., & Daas, D. (2025). Scalability and Efficiency Analysis of Hyperledger Fabric and Private Ethereum in Smart Contract Execution. *Computers, 14*(4), 132. DOI: 10.3390/computers14040132

Khan, Y., Su'ud, M. B. M., Alam, M. M., Ahmad, S. F., Ahmad, A. Y. A. B., & Khan, N. (2023). Application of Internet of Things (IoT) in Sustainable Supply Chain Management. *Sustainability (Switzerland), 15*(1). Advance online publication. DOI: 10.3390/su15010694

Kim, Y. H., & Davis, G. F. (2019). Challenges for global supply chains and opportunities for social innovation. In *Handbook of Inclusive Innovation: The Role of Organizations* (pp. 305–320). Markets and Communities in Social Innovation., DOI: 10.4337/9781786436016.00027

Kumari, P., & Mittal, S. (2024). Fraud Detection System for Financial System Using Machine Learning Techniques: A Review. *2024 11th International Conference on Reliability, Infocom Technologies and Optimization (Trends and Future Directions), ICRITO 2024*. DOI: 10.1109/ICRITO61523.2024.10522197

Liu, Z., Hu, B., Zhao, Y., Lang, L., Guo, H., Florence, K., & Zhang, S. (2020). Research on Intelligent Decision of Low Carbon Supply Chain Based on Carbon Tax Constraints in Human-Driven Edge Computing. *IEEE Access : Practical Innovations, Open Solutions, 8*, 48264–48273. DOI: 10.1109/ACCESS.2020.2978911

Lushi, A., Daas, D., & Nadeem, M. (2022). IoT-Based Public Transport Management System. *2022 IEEE Global Conference on Artificial Intelligence and Internet of Things (GCAIoT)*, 69–75.

Mentzer, J. T., DeWitt, W., Keebler, J. S., Min, S., Nix, N. W., Smith, C. D., & Zacharia, Z. G. (2001). Defining supply chain management. *Journal of Business Logistics*, *22*(2), 1–25. DOI: 10.1002/j.2158-1592.2001.tb00001.x

Michael, K., & McCathie, L. (2005). The pros and cons of RFID in supply chain management. *4th Annual International Conference on Mobile Business, ICMB 2005*, 623–629. DOI: 10.1109/ICMB.2005.103

Michaelides, Z., & Forster, R. (2013). The Use of RFID Technologies for E-Enabling Logistics Supply Chains. In *E-Logistics and E-Supply Chain Management* (pp. 198–217). Applications for Evolving Business., DOI: 10.4018/978-1-4666-3914-0.ch011

Mirzaei, M., Dehe, B., Weerasinghe, K., & Srivastava, H. (2025). Enhancing Supply Chain Visibility in the Fishing Industry: The Role of Emerging Technologies and Their Affordances. *Operations and Supply Chain Management*, *18*(2), 146–160. DOI: 10.31387/oscm0610462

Mustapha, I., Khan, N., Qureshi, M. I., Sikandar, H., Hassan, M., & Simarmata, J. (2024). Revolutionizing Supply Chain Processes: Harnessing the Power of IoT and Blockchain Technology to Enhance Opportunities. In *SpringerBriefs in Applied Sciences and Technology: Vol. Part F2588* (pp. 87–94). DOI: 10.1007/978-3-031-55558-9_10

Muthu, S. E., & Kartheeban, K. (2023). Blockchain Enabled Secure Agri-Goods Traceability using RFID in Supply Chain Management. *Proceedings - 2023 3rd International Conference on Ubiquitous Computing and Intelligent Information Systems, ICUIS 2023*, 301–310. DOI: 10.1109/ICUIS60567.2023.00057

Pise, R., Patil, S., Patil, S., Shinde, S., & Gavkare, S. (2024). Decentralizing the Cosmetic Supply Chain with Hyperledger Fabric. *2024 IEEE International Conference on Blockchain and Distributed Systems Security, ICBDS 2024*. DOI: 10.1109/ICBDS61829.2024.10837300

Quinn, P. (2004). Bar code: Stronger than ever. *Supply Chain Systems Magazine, 24*(10), 16–20. https://www.scopus.com/inward/record.uri?eid=2-s2.0-10444290713&partnerID=40&md5=6ee80358db84297bf590eab9ef5fb3a8

Rashed, M. S., Fakhry, S., Satour, R., Abdelkarim, E. A., Sobhy, M., & Pathania, S. (2025). IoT and Digital Twins for Ssmart Food Supply Chains. In *Sustainable Development Goals Series: Vol. Part F102* (pp. 249–273). DOI: 10.1007/978-3-031-76758-6_16

Rezki, N., & Mansouri, M. (2024). MACHINE LEARNING FOR PROACTIVE SUPPLY CHAIN RISK MANAGEMENT: PREDICTING DELAYS AND ENHANCING OPERATIONAL EFFICIENCY. *Management Systems in Production Engineering*, *32*(3), 345–356. DOI: 10.2478/mspe-2024-0033

Rui, G., & Li, M. (2024). Utilizing Internet Big Data and Machine Learning for Product Demand Forecasting and Analysis of Its Economic Benefits. *Tehnicki Vjesnik (Strojarski Fakultet)*, *31*(4), 1385–1394. DOI: 10.17559/TV-20240318001408

Samuels, A. (2025). Examining the integration of artificial intelligence in supply chain management from Industry 4.0 to 6.0: A systematic literature review. *Frontiers in Artificial Intelligence*, *7*, 1477044. DOI: 10.3389/frai.2024.1477044 PMID: 39902380

Sreerakhi, V., Balagopal, N., & Mohan, A. (2022). Transforming supply chain network and logistics using blockchain – a survey. *International Journal of Business Information Systems*, *39*(2), 193–218. DOI: 10.1504/IJBIS.2022.121430

Stephen, R. K., & Archana, T. (2025). IoT and AI integration for real-time supply chain monitoring. In *Ecological and Human Dimensions of AI-Based Supply Chain* (pp. 339–372). DOI: 10.4018/979-8-3693-7478-8.ch015

Terrada, L., El Khaili, M., & Ouajji, H. (2022). Demand Forecasting Model using Deep Learning Methods for Supply Chain Management 4.0. *International Journal of Advanced Computer Science and Applications*, *13*(5), 704–711. DOI: 10.14569/IJACSA.2022.0130581

Tošić, A., Vičič, J., Burnard, M., & Mrissa, M. (2023). A Blockchain Protocol for Real-Time Application Migration on the Edge. *Sensors (Basel), 23*(9), 4448. Advance online publication. DOI: 10.3390/s23094448 PMID: 37177653

Ugrinov, S., Ćoćkalo, D., Terek Stojanović, E., Stanisavljev, S., Bakator, M., & Gluvakov, V. (2024). Enhancing Efficiency in Food and Beverage Supply Chains †. *Engineering Proceedings*, *79*(1), 2. Advance online publication. DOI: 10.3390/engproc2024079002

Viellechner, A., & Spinler, S. (2020). Novel data analytics meets conventional container shipping: Predicting delays by comparing various machine learning algorithms. *Proceedings of the Annual Hawaii International Conference on System Sciences, 2020-Janua*, 1278–1287. DOI: 10.24251/HICSS.2020.158

Vora, D. K., Patel, J. H., Shah, D., & Mehta, P. (2022). Application of Blockchain in Different Segments of Supply Chain Management. *Lecture Notes in Electrical Engineering*, *840*, 537–548. DOI: 10.1007/978-981-16-9012-9_43

Wang, L., Deng, T., Shen, Z.-J. M., Hu, H., & Qi, Y. (2022). Digital twin-driven smart supply chain. *Frontiers of Engineering Management*, *9*(1), 56–70. DOI: 10.1007/s42524-021-0186-9

Wei, H.-L., & Wang, E. T. G. (2007). Creating strategic value from supply chain visibility- The dynamic capabilities view. *Proceedings of the Annual Hawaii International Conference on System Sciences*. DOI: 10.1109/HICSS.2007.157

Wei, H.-L., & Wang, E. T. G. (2010). The strategic value of supply chain visibility: Increasing the ability to reconfigure. *European Journal of Information Systems*, *19*(2), 238–249. DOI: 10.1057/ejis.2010.10

Zhang, C., Zhang, J., Sangaiah, A. K., Li, D., & Li, W. (2024). Evaluating edge artificial intelligence-driven supply chain management platforms using collaborative large-scale fuzzy information fusion. *Applied Soft Computing*, *159*, 111686. Advance online publication. DOI: 10.1016/j.asoc.2024.111686

Chapter 2

Federated Learning for Cross-Enterprise Supply Chain Collaboration

R. N. Ravikumar
https://orcid.org/0009-0009-3705-1681
Marwadi University, Rajkot, India

S. Aarthi
https://orcid.org/0009-0006-9064-2091
Marwadi University, Rajkot, India

ABSTRACT

This chapter explores the transformative role of Federated Learning (FL) in enabling secure, privacy-preserving, and collaborative intelligence across modern supply chain ecosystems. Unlike traditional centralized AI approaches, FL facilitates model training across distributed enterprises without the need to share sensitive operational data, thereby maintaining data sovereignty and compliance with regulations like GDPR. The chapter discusses various FL architectures and types (HFL, VFL, FTL), their advantages, and real-world supply chain applications in demand forecasting, inventory optimization, logistics, and risk mitigation. It further elaborates on FL's integration with emerging technologies such as blockchain, IoT, and digital twins to enhance visibility, traceability, and sustainability. Through case studies and industry practices, the chapter

DOI: 10.4018/979-8-3373-2833-1.ch002

emphasizes FL's potential in aligning AI-driven decision-making with ESG goals, highlighting its promise in building intelligent, ethical, and resilient supply chains.

1. INTRODUCTION

In the age of globalized markets and multi- enterprises logistics networks, cooperation on supply chain level is required to increase efficiency, agility, and resilience. Nevertheless, the exchange of sensitive operation data between any organizations, even organization boundaries, brings about a lot of concern over privacy, security, and ownership of data. Conventional centralized machine learning that needs centralization of data on a central server are not practical or do not comply with regulatory policy like General Data Protection Regulation (GDPR). Federated Learning (FL) appears as a potential way to address them, as it allows several stakeholders to be able to jointly train machine learning models without sharing raw data.

Through this chapter, the authors investigate the use of the concept of federated learning to optimize cross-enterprise collaboration in supply chain under the view of how decentralized intelligence can improve demand prediction, inventory optimization, and logistics coordination without jeopardizing data confidentiality (Atadoga et al., 2024). FL enables people to be involved in a global model but deliver their input independently and maintain complete control over information, which leads to trust and collaboration in the supply chain ecosystems. The chapter also looks into the role of FL in combination with technologies such as blockchain, IoT, digital twins, to establish transparent, responsive and sustainable supply chains. This introductory section forms the foundation on which to elaborate more on how FL could transform the future environment of intelligent and privacy-supportive supply chain management.

1.1 Background of AI in Supply Chain Management

Artificial Intelligence (AI) has become an innovative development in Supply Chain Management (SCM), which has impacted the process of planning, forecasting, executing, and reacting to market changes in business operations. With AI, real-time insights are now possible using predictive analytics, demand sensing, route optimization and risk mitigation, what this means is that supply chains can be made more agile, more resilient and cost-effective. The ML models are more and more used to forecast the demand, plan the inventories, and detect the anomalies, and Natural Language Processing (NLP) is used to facilitate communication with the suppliers and manage the contracts (Chen et al., 2024). The automation and quality inspection of warehouse is facilitated by robotics and computer vision. As AI is incorporated, supply chains are being made smarter as self-correcting and adaptive ecosystems that are no longer reactive. Nevertheless, such developments are most dependent on the availability of vast amount of quality data. This data is commonly isolated and distributed across several enterprises and systems in more classical SCM arrangements which restricts efficiency of centralized AI applications (P. Zhang et al., 2024). Due to the increased complexity of supply chains and links among various organizations worldwide, it is essential to develop collaborative AI systems allowing to leverage distributed data without affecting the security and competitive confidentiality of each company at the macro level, thus, turning AI adoption in the supply chain into an adaptable and safe practice.

1.2 Need for Cross-Enterprise Collaboration

Contemporary supply chains cannot be locked in one company only but spread out in a cluster of suppliers, manufacturers, logistics, distributors, and retailers. The synergy of these parties is important in promoting the visibility, limited disruptions, and improvement of the overall supply chain performance. Conventional enterprise-contracted solutions can no longer keep up with the need to make real time decisions, coordinate logistical operations, and synchronised planning (Dayan et al., 2021). The complexity of the global trade, the just-in-time system of manufacturing, and customer demands that the ordered goods arrive quickly increase the requirement of smooth cross-enterprise integration.

Moreover, any troubling situation like geopolitical tensions, pandemics, climatic events, etc., demonstrates the instability of a disintegrated supply chain and the need to share information and collective intelligence.

Cross-enterprise integration gives the stakeholders a chance to not only share their resources, also align services and make combined decisions that ensure resiliency, cost decrease and a boost of service levels (Chukwu et al., 2024). Nevertheless, the achievement of such a high level of integration requires complex technologies that cannot work in a distributed heterogeneous environment but keep the data sovereignty protocol intact. Never has the demand of collaborative but secure AI models been more important: i.e. which can learn on decentralized data across companies. This paves the way towards using the Federated Learning in the supply chain ecosystems.

1.3 Challenges of Data Sharing and Privacy

Even though cross-enterprise cooperation in supply chains is the key to its efficiency and innovative power, it is discouraged by data security, privacy, and competitive disadvantage issues being too severe. Exchange of operational data such as inventory status, sales projections, supplier efficiency or client behavior among various companies frequently attracts legal, as well as strategic issues. Other companies are frightened by the possibility of sharing sensitive data with their partners or enemies, and this creates the fear of sharing even anonymized data. More so, there are no unification of data formats and interoperability among enterprise systems which warrant the ease of data exchange (Dong et al., 2022). Other standard forms of data governance, including policies imposed by sector regulators and sovereign data protection legislation, including the General Data Protection Regulation (GDPR) provide further limitations on storage, transfer and processing of data. Data pooling necessities of centralized models increase the risk of data hacks and unauthorized access to data. Supply chains face challenges that do not allow getting full use of AI-driven insights. Thus, the models that comply with data sovereignty, limit the data swapping of the raw data, and secure strong privacy guarantees are of the essence, which requires deploying privacy-preserving technologies, such as Federated Learning.

1.4 Federated Learning: A Privacy-Preserving Solution

Federated Learning (FL) is a new paradigm providing collaborative machine learning in a group of organizations without the actual sharing of raw data. Rather than centralizing data, in FL each participant (or node) can train a local model on its own data and only share parameters with a central aggregator (or coordination server) learned (e.g., weights, gradients). This will remarkably minimize the risk of exposing data and help to comply with data protection regulations. When applied to supply chain collaboration, FL enables stakeholders, including supply chain partners, suppliers, manufacturers, and logistic partners to collaboratively design predictive models to make demand predictions, optimize the shipment, or risk assessment without having to share their proprietary data (Dora et al., 2022). A decentralized training process will lead to trust, prevent the leakage of intellectual property, and generalize the model using scattered data distributions across the enterprise. Also, along with FL, other security-enhancing technology previously described, including differential privacy, homomorphic encryption, and blockchain, can be used to achieve transparency, accountability, and auditability. Consequently, the Federated Learning can be seen as a potential privacy-preserving method to allow the use of AI across enterprise boundaries, which will give a possibility to establish a smart, collaborative, and safe supply chain environment.

1.5 Objectives

In this chapter, the authors will seek to discuss the transformational nature of Federated Learning (FL) on facilitating secure, collaborative intelligence across enterprise boundaries in contemporary supply chains. The most important thing is to show how FL could help with the urgent problem of data privacy, inter-organizational trust, and optimized operations and enable real-time AI-enabled decision-making throughout a decentralized environment.

The specific objectives of this chapter are as follows:

- To introduce the foundational concepts and architecture of federated learning in the context of supply chain management.

- To analyze the key applications of FL in demand forecasting, inventory optimization, transportation planning, and logistics visibility.
- To explore the integration of FL with enabling technologies such as blockchain, IoT, and digital twins to enhance transparency, traceability, and decision support.
- To evaluate the implications of FL in advancing sustainability goals and Environmental, Social, and Governance (ESG) compliance through collaborative optimization.
- To highlight real-world use cases, success stories, and implementation challenges faced by industry leaders and startups.
- To identify current limitations, research gaps, and future directions for federated learning in supply chain collaboration.

2. FUNDAMENTALS OF FEDERATED LEARNING

Federated Learning (FL) stands in the form of a decentralized machine learning algorithm which allows a set of participants to train a common model without communication of their (local) data to a central server (Eyo-Udo, 2024). As an alternative, each of the participants trains a model using their local dataset and only distributes the model parameters or gradients to a central aggregator. This approach guarantees privacy of data, decreases the cost of communication and keeps the regulations in check like the GDPR. FL accommodates many topologies such as centralized, peer-to-peer as well as hierarchical with a combination of security methods such as differential privacy and secure aggregation that makes it feasible with sensitive and distributed settings such as supply chain.

2.1 Concept and Architecture of Federated Learning

Federated Learning (FL) is a distributed machine learning method, where different clients, be they organizations, devices, or nodes, jointly train a global model without their raw data being shared or communicated to any other agent. The main idea behind FL is that the data stays on-site whereas only the learned parameters (e.g. model weights or gradients) are shared with a coordination server or peer nodes (Falcone et al., 2019).

This enables all participants to enjoy shared intelligence without privacy or ownership of data. An FL system in the classic architecture consists of three main parts: local clients (e.g., enterprises in a supply chain), the central aggregator (or the coordination server), and a secure means of transmitting the model update. This is done by an iterative process in which the clients calculate updates on their local data and transmit them to the server who combines the updates (powerfully achieved by methods such as Federated Averaging) until the global model is refined. This model is, in its turn, redistributed among clients, the next round of training (Kaya, 2024). Higher-level FL structures are Hierarchical FL (multi-tier), and between large organizations (cross-silo FL). Edge computing and blockchain can be additionally integrated to boost its functionality and auditory. As an application to supply chains, FL allows a decentralized set of stakeholders to have a privacy-preserving and scalable methodology of together making a decision. The figure,1 illustrates the basic architecture of Federated Learning, where multiple client devices train models locally on their private data (Mo, 2024). Only model updates are shared with a central server, preserving data privacy while enabling collaborative learning.

Figure 1. Concept and Architecture of Federated Learning

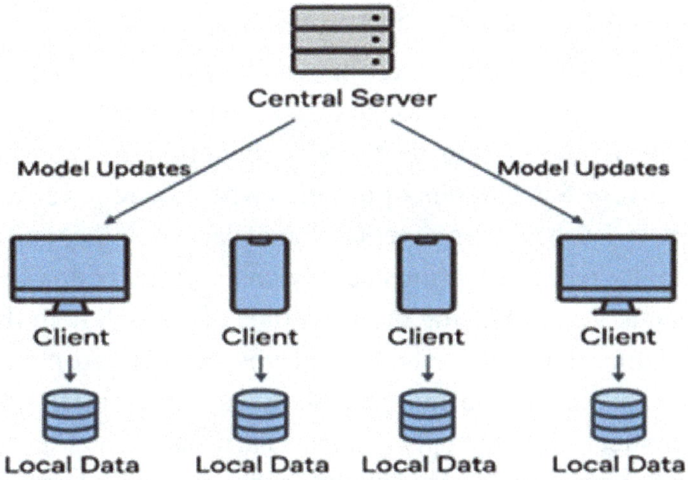

2.2 Types of Federated Learning (Horizontal, Vertical, Federated Transfer)

Federated Learning is broadly classified into three main varieties that depend on the type of data spread among the participants: Horizontal FL, Vertical FL and Federated Transfer Learning (FTL).

Horizontal Federated Learning (HFL) is used in the situation that distinct organizations or clients have datasets that share a common feature space but do not share user samples. To use one illustration, several logistics firms with similarities in logistics attributes (e.g., the time of delivery, cost in different regional markets) may use HFL to work together (Narmadha & Varalakshmi, 2022). Concerted sharing occurs on a larger presentation suits each client but the shared model is trained on each of these mutual representative users in itself.

Vertical Federated Learning (VFL): the datasets may have different feature spaces but contain common user identifiers. As an example, the same customers may be measured differently by a manufacturer and a retailer (e.g. the manufacturer is interested in production data, whereas the retailer is interested in sales data) (Narmadha & Varalakshmi, 2022). VFL enables such organizations to jointly train models in an end-to-end free manner without exposing their proprietary attributes.

The Federated Transfer Learning (FTL) can be applied in the case where the sample space as well as the feature space varies across organizations yet there is a need to transfer knowledge. This kind is very applicable in the case of very few datasets or in fields where there is variance in the line of business. Each of them covers different data situations and enhances the applicability of FL to various supply chain partnerships (Narmadha & Varalakshmi, 2022). Having the right type of FL will help them learn without violating data silos. The table 1 contrasts Horizontal, Vertical, and Federated Transfer Learning based on data distribution, participant roles, and applicability in supply chain scenarios and The Figure.2classifies Federated Learning into Horizontal, Vertical, and Federated Transfer Learning based on feature and sample alignment. It includes real-world examples to illustrate the relevance of each type in diverse collaborative environments.

Figure 2. Types of Federated Learning: HFL, VFL, and FTL

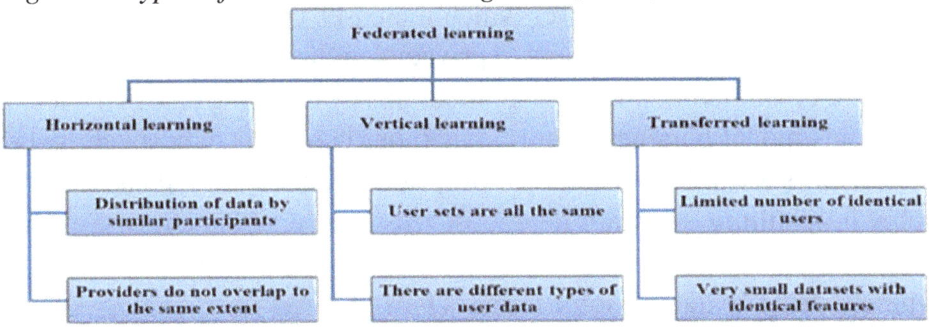

Table 1. Comparison of Federated Learning Types in Supply Chains

Aspect	Horizontal FL (HFL)	Vertical FL (VFL)	Federated Transfer Learning (FTL)
Data Distribution	Same feature space, different sample space	Different feature space, same sample space	Different feature and sample spaces
Typical Participants	Similar companies with different customers (e.g., regional logistics firms)	Different departments handling same customers (e.g., manufacturer + retailer)	Unrelated entities with minimal overlap (e.g., new entrant collaborating with leader)
Use Case in Supply Chain	Demand forecasting across multiple regional distributors	Joint customer profiling by manufacturers and retailers	Cold-start problem resolution or low-data collaboration
Data Privacy	High no raw data shared; model weights aggregated	Moderate only shared entities enable joining models	High leverages transfer learning with privacy-preserving techniques
Challenges	Model heterogeneity, convergence on non-IID data	Alignment of different feature spaces, encryption overhead	Limited shared context, higher complexity in transfer setup

2.3 Key Advantages Over Centralized AI Approaches

In comparison with the classical centralized AI, the Federated Learning approach has a number of relevant benefits when applied in multi-organization ecosystems, such as supply chains. The first advantage is privacy and security of data. Raw data in the centralized models have to be relayed to a central server which increases chances of data breach, leakage and also does not adhere to privacy regulations such as the GDPR or HIPAA (Muthaluri, 2024). FL reduces this by retaining data in the local and sends model parameters only. The other benefit is data sovereignty. Organizations can keep their own proprietary or sensitive data and this helps in instilling a certain degree of trust and enablement of a wider sharing of data. This plays a major role in competitive supply chain setup where sharing of data in some cases is barred.

Scalability and robustness are also possible in FL. Since the processing of data is localized, it does not require large bandwidth and storage infrastructure in central location. In addition, the decentralized training process becomes more tolerant to single points of failure or server outages (Nisha, 2025). FL enhances model generalization because of the presence of a wide range of data distributions of different stakeholders. This causes stronger models that work well under many circumstances. Last, FL is a good fit when real-time, distributed intelligence needs to be deployed, which allows scaling AI to edge devices, remote operations, and disconnected systems, thus, highly flexible to support the modern supply chains as they change.

2.4 Security, Privacy, and Data Governance Features

One of the big strengths of Federated Learning is its security and privacy, and thus it is a very good fit in highly sensitive and multi stakeholder environments such as supply chains. Also, FL does not have the same data exposure risk that the traditional AI approach presents since it only distributes a model update to the nodes and the aggregator, not the raw data. This automatically contributes to data privacy and fewer attacker areas (Wang, 2024). In further efforts to increase privacy, FL can be integrated with other methods including Differential Privacy (DP) which involves adding noisy mathematical values into model updates so as to obscure individual contribution to data and Secure Multi-Party Computation (SMPC) which lets more parties collaboratively compute a given functionality without compromising their respective input. An additional layer of protection is brought by Homomorphic Encryption (HE) that allows calculation to be directly performed on encrypted information (He et al., 2023).

FL offers sound data governance, too, no matter regarding laws of data residency and policy requirements of enterprises. The data requires no transfer of its locality, and hence it becomes simpler to comply with the demands of other international regulations like GDPR, CCPA, and HIPAA (Biswal et al., 2021). Furthermore, the FL framework can implement access control, audit logging and blockchain to be able to trace and track the accountabilities. Such functionalities are used to develop trust between the entities that are working together and have a secure, transparent, and compliant AI forum within the supply chain network.

3. SUPPLY CHAIN APPLICATIONS OF FEDERATED LEARNING

The idea behind Federated Learning (FL) is to allow supply chain partners namely manufacturers, suppliers, distributors and retailers to learn an AI model collectively without transferring sensitive information. This enables a broad set of applications, such as demand forecasting, in which aggregated data increases regional forecasting accuracy; inventory optimization, in which inventory levels are optimized based on real-time and decentralized data; transportation planning, such as the path planning of delivery, which can be enhanced based on collaborative traffic and logistics information (Briggs et al., 2020). FL also facilitates risk identification and resilience of supply chain, whereby, the organizations can predict interruption. Through these applications, it is possible to see that FL supports intelligent, privacy-preserving collaboration among different stakeholders within contemporary supply chains and improves agility, visibility, and decision-making. The table 2 Summarizes major FL applications such as demand forecasting, inventory optimization, logistics planning, and risk prediction, along with expected benefits.

Table 2. Key Applications of Federated Learning in Supply Chain Management

Application Area	Description	Expected Benefits
Demand Forecasting	Collaborative forecasting models trained across manufacturers, wholesalers, and retailers	Improved accuracy, seasonal/ regional trend capture, privacy-preserving intelligence
Inventory Optimization	Real-time inventory management using distributed data from suppliers and retailers	Balanced stock levels, reduced holding costs, minimized stockouts and overstocking
Logistics & Transportation	Decentralized models using vehicle, route, and traffic data from logistics partners	Optimized routing, cost reduction, real-time responsiveness to disruptions
Risk Prediction & Disruption	Joint models trained on local incident and environmental data from different partners	Early warnings, adaptive response strategies, enhanced supply chain resilience

3.1 Demand Forecasting with Collaborative Intelligence

The demand forecasting is an important step in realizing efficient and affordable supply chain activities. Nevertheless, fragmentation of supply chain information usually does not allow individual organizations to see the whole picture. Federated Learning (FL) supports collaborative intelligence by means of allowing several enterprises (manufacturers, wholesalers, and retailers) to jointly constructed unified demand forecasting model without disclosing own sales, customer and inventory information (Dayan et al., 2021). Under FL, every participant trains his/her own model against their local data, and the newly trained parameters are shared with a central server or other peer nodes. This puts the global model on steroids and the varied demand signals including the seasonal and regional trends, including the behavioural patterns of customers, do not compromise the privacy of information. The end outcome is a generalized and precise forecasting model that is representative of market dynamics.

Through this collaborative forecasting, the production, procurement and distribution planning come into coordinate with each other, reducing the instances of stock out, overproduction and wastage. It is also useful in demand sensing in the context of disruption such as during a pandemic or geopolitical crisis where signals are merged among partner groups under disruption (Fantacci & Picano, 2020). On the supply chain side, decentralized predictive demand gives a stakeholder the benefits of supply chain in the form of agility, lowered operations costs, and improved timeliness in adapting to the change in consumer demand without losing management of sensitive information.

3.2 Inventory Optimization Across Partner Networks

Inventory control is the art of trying to keep up with customer demand and at the same time keep holding costs to a minimum. With isolated data silos, volatile demand and a lack of cross-partner visibility, in cross-enterprise supply chains it is tricky to ensure optimal levels of inventory. Federated Learning (FL) proposes the privacy preserving method because it allows cooperating optimization models of inventory to take into account distributed inventory data, lead times, and demand predictions of all network nodes. In FL, every organization, suppliers, distributers, retails, can train the local models with stock levels, orders history and replenishments. Learnings on these insights are pooled together into a common global model that learns interdependencies and demand patterns throughout the ecosystem (Chen et al., 2024). Through this collective intelligence, there is the possibility of superior reorder point calculations, dynamic setting of safety stock and dynamic replenishment policies.

Besides, FL enables co-ordination of partners so as to avoid cases of overstocking and stockouts. To illustrate, upstream suppliers are able to plan demand peaks depending on trends in the retailer that they will not even get actual figures of the sales made. This results in more aligned processes, less bullwhip, and effective supply chains, in general (Husnoo et al., 2022). Businesses that employ FL in inventory optimization can balance their services provision at high levels, eliminate undue inventory as well as use their working capital better- without privatizing and facing competition.

3.3 Real-Time Logistics and Transportation Planning

Transportation and logistics are so crucial parts of the supplies chain which define the levels of services, the schedule of the delivery, and the satisfaction of the customers in general. Optimization of a traditional logistics is usually characterized by the inability to become a carrier, warehouses, and last-mile providers. Federated Learning (FL) arose as an alternative to this collaboration-an independent model can be created, since the stakeholders can interact to create a mutually beneficial model that will minimize the costs of routes, predict the delayed deliveries, and monetize the fleet, without exchanging secret or company data (Jacobs et al., 2023). Using FL, the logistics companies, manufacturers, and distributors can train local models on the live data of vehicles status, fuel consumption, and traffic, as well as the volume of shipments. The combination of these insights can help the global model to make knowledgeable routing choices, forecast possible bottlenecks, and streamline resource use throughout the transportation framework.

The federated process helps the process of a dynamic and flexible logistics planning, in multi modal and complex supply chains (where road, rail, sea and air transport are utilized). It also improves res responsiveness times in situations of disruptions like port congestions, strikes or events of extreme weather conditions by incorporating decentralized intelligence in near real time. FL helps to create the cost savings, increase on-time performances, drive of end-to-end visibility through enabling time-sensitive cooperation in logistics on a privacy-preserving basis (Kaissis et al., 2021).

3.4 Risk Prediction and Disruption Response

There has been a rise in the vulnerabilities of supply chain networks to disruptions like the failures of suppliers, geopolitical tensions, natural disasters, cyber threats and world pandemics. An early supply chain risk detection and reaction are critical to the continuity of supply chains. Federated Learning (FL) is the technique of unified danger forecast that permits decentralized organizations (manufacturers, logistics providers, and procurement units) to cooperate in machine learning model training without data exchange. Individual parties bring their local disruptions, delays, or even environmental events, and accumulate, to provide early warning signs and suggest proactive measures, such as changing suppliers or rerouting logistics (Loftus et al., 2022). FL also promotes adaptive learning based on the past events coming up with risk model refinements to fit the changing events. When combined with real-time IoT sensor data and external feeds (e.g. a news or a weather update), FL enhances real-time situational awareness and response. Enhanced visibility and the ability to plan resilience in unison, and the ability to maintain business continuity in dynamic conditions, give stakeholders in the supply chain the power to better manage the uncertainty and in a more sustainable way.

4. INTEGRATION WITH EMERGING TECHNOLOGIES

Federated Learning (FL) can still be even stronger when combined with other emerging technologies (IoT, blockchain, digital twins, and edge computing). IoT lets us access real-time information on different entries of the supply chain, and edge computing makes it possible to process on-site with the shortest lags. Blockchain provides tamper-proof, transparent and secure model transaction and data logs. Real life supply chain operation can be simulated with digital twins enabling FL models to be trained and tested in dynamic virtual environments (Moshawrab et al., 2023). This merging makes a very strong, smart, privacy preserving supply segment chain environment that can optimize in real-time, spot anomalies and make predictive choice past the territories of organizations. The table 3 Outlines how FL combines with IoT, Blockchain, Digital Twins, and Big Data to enable secure, real-time, and scalable supply chain intelligence.

Table 3. Integration of Federated Learning with Emerging Technologies

Technology	Integration with FL	Impact on Supply Chain
IoT	Provides real-time data from sensors and devices for local model training	Enables real-time decision-making, enhances operational visibility across distributed environments
Blockchain	Maintains secure, tamper-proof logs of model updates and contributions	Ensures transparency, trust, and auditability in collaborative training across enterprise boundaries
Digital Twins	Simulates real-world operations with FL-trained models on virtual replicas	Supports scenario testing, anomaly detection, and predictive maintenance in a privacy-preserving manner
Big Data Analytics	Combines FL with multimodal, high-volume datasets from diverse sources	Enhances the depth and scope of decision support while maintaining data sovereignty and privacy

4.1 Federated Learning and Digital Twins for Real-Time Visibility

Digital twins are computer models of a real system, which allow simulating operations in real-time, using actual data collected by sensors, and IoT devices as well as enterprise systems. By being combined with Federated Learning (FL), digital twins facilitate the real-time and highly accurate visibility and predictive modelling throughout the supply chain (Narmadha & Varalakshmi, 2022). A digital twin of the operations may be developed by each stakeholder, including a manufacturer, a warehouse, or a logistics provider, supplying it with local data to train FL models without data sharing. This will enable testing of scenario in real-time, detection of anomalies, and forecast of performance in a secure and privacy-preserving way.

As an example, a digital twin of a production line can identify any inefficiencies or anticipate a failure of an equipment based on locally trained FL-models but remain a part of a global model that can be accessed by other members of the supply chain. This shared wisdom enables practical reaction to perturbation, facilitates ongoing advancement and increases the appeal of the supply chain (Park & Son, 2023). The expertise of digital twins in providing simulations along with the collaborative nature of FL enables supply chains to run as synergetic adaptive ecosystems. Through this integration, not only are decisions made better, but there is an increase in service levels and the establishment of operational resilience- at the same time that data confidentiality has been secured enabling data governance rules to be met.

4.2 Blockchain for Secure, Auditable Model Updates

Blockchain, in its turn, is complementary to Federated Learning (FL) as it offers a secure, decentralized record (ledger) to keep track of and certify the model updates among the members of the supply chain. Maintaining the integrity, transparency and trustworthiness of contributions of each party can be cited as one of the major challenges in collaborative AI (Fantacci & Picano, 2020). Blockchain resolves this by storing the record of every model update or every contribution to the gradient in a non-writable and auditable log that cannot be tampered and accessed by unauthorized users. In incidents of the combination of FL and blockchain, the model parameters of each participant are hashed cryptographically and documented as transactions. This will make the aggregation process traceable and every time a model is updated there will be verification. The validation and rewarding mechanism may also be automatized through smart contracts, which will promote honest work during the collaborative training process.

Blockchain is also beneficial in supply chain settings, where relationships among stakeholders depend on trust. Blockchain increases the level of accountability in the system and reduces the possibility of model poisoning or data alteration attempts or malicious actions. This is more crucial in the cross-border, multi-vendor ecosystem where conventional trust systems are inefficient (Wang, 2024). Dually, FL and blockchain comprise a sound base of privacy-secure and trust-based AI collaboration and build up smart supply chain intelligence with data-driven and safe decision-making without compromising privacy or compliance. The Figure. 3 depicts how client model updates are sent to a central server, then securely hashed and recorded on a blockchain ledger. It ensures trust, transparency, and auditability in collaborative learning environments.

Figure 3. Integration of Blockchain with Federated Learning for Secure Model Tracking

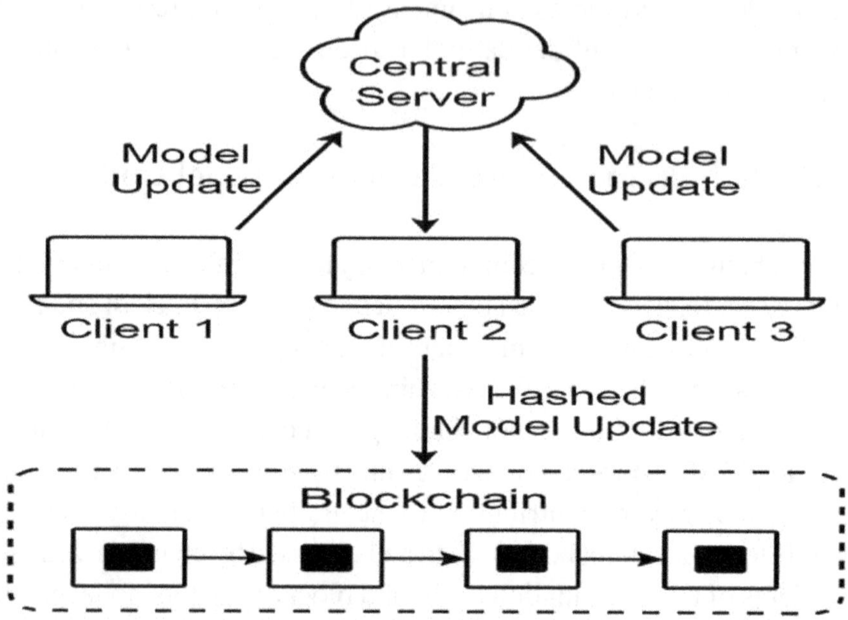

4.3 Big Data Analytics for Multimodal Decision Support

Modern supply chains produce a vast amount of heterogeneous information supplied by various sources, sensors, ERPs, GPS, and customer equipment. This big data is structured as well as semi-structured and unstructured and includes anything as transactional data to real-time shipments data. Multimodality was a new opportunity in the supply chain when big data analytics was combined with Federated Learning (FL) types of decision support. The FL allows the stakeholders to analyze such a large amount of data together without necessarily concentrating sensitive data. Training distributed models using local databases enables organizations to derive value out of the inventory levels, weathers, sales patterns, and machine telematics, without sharing the data (He et al., 2023). Multimodal FL models have the capability of working with various types of data e.g., images collected by warehouse cameras, conversations with customers in customer service, or data collected by other sensors to draw more comprehensive information.

It could mean that a retailer can leverage its POS data and weather patterns to optimize stock, and a logistics partner will leverage fleet sensor information to ensure its delivery routes optimally utilize the resources available. When all these insights are fed into a federated model, the system that will come out will be more intelligent, more adaptive, and more predictive than the others. Such combination of big data analytics and FL will enhance real-time decision making in a context-aware manner throughout the entire supply chain enhancing responsiveness and customer satisfaction as well as overall operational efficiency.

4.4 Interoperability Challenges and Solutions

The problem of interoperability creates a critical issue in the implementation of Federated Learning (FL) in multi-enterprise supply chains since implementing AI frameworks, data format, hardware, and compliance policies differ. The heterogeneity of data to train the model and coordinate is a challenge since they can be different relational databases to time-series logs (F. Zhang & Hu, 2024). Also, lack of unified protocols in communications, aggregation and security verification may impede model performance and convergence. Some solutions to this may be the usage of interoperable data schemes, containerization (ex. Docker) and inter-platform frameworks such as TensorFlow Federated. The synchronization and reliability is provided by federated orchestration layers. The FL collaboration defines the supply chain across multiple stakeholders; the use of international standards (e.g., IEEE, ISO) will be necessary to create scalable, secure, privacy-preserving FL collaboration.

5. ENABLING SUSTAINABILITY AND ESG GOALS

Federated Learning (FL) helps to achieve sustainability and ESG (Environmental, Social, and Governance) objectives by allowing multiple organizations to optimize their respective activities with a shared goal of having privacy of data. FL enables smart logistics, emission-conscious routing, and waste management to benefit through learning with decentralized information over partners in supply chains (P. Zhang et al., 2024). It encourages transparency and traceability of where the materials were sourced, optimized resource allocation, and predictable maintenance, cutting carbon footprints at no cost of data sovereignty. In addition, FL can also be used to improve ESG reporting by providing effective and reliable data-driven conclusions through various stakeholders. This coordination of ESG compliance with AI-powered optimization by FL can be the key to developing transparent, accountable, and green supply chains, thereby ensuring a direct relationship between eco-friendly supply chains and global sustainability as well as committing to net-zero contributions. The table 4 Highlights how FL contributes to emissions reduction, waste minimization, ethical AI practices, and ESG metric tracking across the supply chain.

Table 4. ESG Objectives Supported by Federated Learning

ESG Focus Area	FL Contribution	Impact on Supply Chain
Emission Reduction	Enables emission-aware routing by training decentralized models on local traffic and fuel data	Optimizes transport efficiency, reduces carbon footprint, aligns with environmental goals
Waste Minimization	Facilitates dynamic packaging and production planning across partners using localized data	Reduces excess inventory, packaging waste, and promotes circular economy practices
Ethical AI Implementation	Preserves data sovereignty, prevents surveillance, and supports fairness through decentralized learning	Builds trust, ensures compliance with AI ethics, and encourages responsible innovation
ESG Metric Tracking	Allows real-time monitoring and decentralized audit trails using FL + blockchain integration	Improves transparency, traceability, and accountability across diverse stakeholder networks

5.1 Emission-Aware Routing and Transport Optimization

Transportation is one of the most high-potential greenhouse gas sources in supply chains and still, traditional optimization ignores the impact on the environment. Emission-aware routing may be achieved with Federated Learning (FL), which means that AI models can be trained by different stakeholders in the logistics sector without sharing sensitive data. These models determine the less emission path, balance loads and mix loads to shipments to achieve maximum efficiency. FL can enable live route optimization with respect to weather or traffic jam while protecting data privacy (Chilimattur, 2025). This shared practice will diminish ESG effect on the environment, promote ESG objectives, and guarantee regulatory conformity, thereby making supply chains greener without flattening service levels or manufacturing privacy.

5.2 Waste Reduction and Dynamic Packaging

The current supply chains face problems such as packed wastes and surplus inventory as a major sustainability challenge. FL tackles all these issues by allowing the enterprise partners (suppliers, manufacturers, and retailers) to collaboratively train models for dynamic packaging and inventory policies without exchanging sensitive data. FL-Based Models can be used to predict order quantities, minimize utilization of packaging materials, and suggest sustainable packages in terms of constraints that are localized such as legislations, product fragility, and transportation modes. This promotes less but safe packaging designs. FL also provides better demand forecasting and production coordination thereby preventing wastage due to off-track production (Ikpe & Shamsuddoha, 2024). FL promotes recycling, therefore, supporting the circular economy and sustainability through the optimization of materials and packaging in an individual way. The figure.4 illustrates how suppliers, manufacturers, and retailers collaboratively train FL-based models to reduce packaging waste and excess inventory. The flow highlights sustainability benefits in decentralized supply chain optimization.

Figure 4. Federated Learning for Waste Reduction and Dynamic Packaging

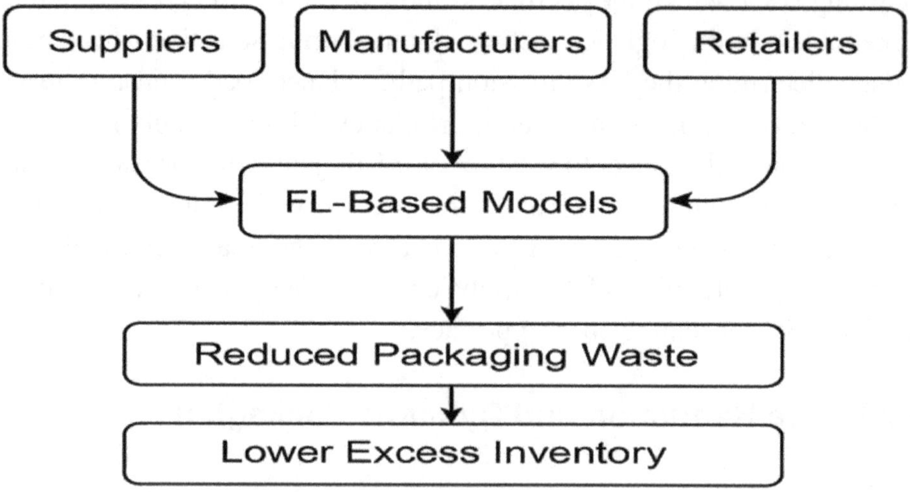

5.3 Ethical AI and Responsible Supply Chain Innovation

The issues of transparency, fairness and accountability are on the rise as AI can penetrate in the workings of the supply chain more than ever. By itself, Federated Learning (FL) enables the design of ethical artificial intelligence (AI) including the concepts of data sovereignty and responsible innovation. The FL reduces the chances of surveillance, misuse of data, and invasion of privacy since data is not centralized (Ivanov & Dolgui, 2021). It makes it possible to train models on a local level, decreasing the impact of biased or non-representative uncapped datasets and facilitating local understanding of fairness.

Since FL can also be combined with privacy-enhancing methods like differential privacy and secure multiparty computation, it also defends individual and organizational data against inference attack. Based on governance perspective, FL promotes shared ownership where you can have various stakeholders participate in jointly developing AI policies based on ethical principles such as those developed by OECD, UNESCO, and EU AI principles. In practice, ethical AI enabled by FL has the potential to enable responsible sourcing, monitor labour rights, and methods of supplier selection, enhancing ESG promises. With the increasing AI-fiction of supply chains, FL takes a central stage in the streamlining the innovation process with ethics in mind, guaranteeing transparency, trust, and inclusivity, ethics, and social responsibility in the adoption of AI on a global level and throughout the global supply chain ecosystem (Khan & Tabasum, 2025).

5.4 Metrics and Benchmarks for ESG in FL Systems

Organizations should implement explicit metrics and thresholds to consider Federated Learning (FL) a proper strategy to facilitate ESG objectives. Environmental indicators are measured in terms of emission and energy reduction and reduction of waste on packaging and social indicators measured in terms of labour disclosure and fair sourcing. Metrics on governance are concerned with the auditing, control, and ensuring compliance with privacy regulations such as GDPR. Such measures as emissions saved per shipment, and rates of responsible AI adoption are examples of KPIs that allow consistent measurement (Kim et al., 2025). Such tools as ESG scorecard and the federated audit trails facilitate tracking in real time. The established/standard metrics will help optimize transparency, fuel constant improvements, and illustrate FLs worth throughout the development of sustainable, ethical, and compliant supply chain ecosystems.

6. CASE STUDIES AND INDUSTRY PRACTICES

The aspect of being able to share intelligence safely and at the same time maintaining data privacy in a business environment makes Federated Learning (FL) gain popularity in real-life supply chain contexts. With the help of FL, companies such as Siemens apply predictive maintenance, increasing the uptime of equipment in factories scattered around the world, without exchanging sensitive sensor information. Alibaba uses FL to make demand predictions within its network of vendors, upgrading its inventory capabilities without revealing its sales information. DHL uses FL by using it to improve the route planning process; reducing the emission factor of the vehicles in the process by sharing vehicle data (Melesse et al., 2023). Other startups include Consortium.ai which offers FL platforms with blockchain and digital twin integrations. These illustrations indicate the possible use of FL to support secure, efficient, and ESG-compatible innovations in the supply chain.

6.1 Case Study 1: Siemens – Predictive Maintenance in Smart Factories

Siemens, one of the world leaders in industrial automation, implemented Federated Learning (FL) on its network of smart factories so that to enhance predictive maintenance at the cost of very limited data privacy. Historically, predictive models have used centralized deployments, where raw data collected by the sensors (e.g., temperature, vibration, usage patterns) had to be sent to a central server, which was risky in terms of data privacy and non-compliance with regulatory framework such as GDPR. In order to resolve these issues, Siemens has integrated FL that enables each factory unit to train AI models within its proprietary data locally. Only encrypted model parameters were sent to a central aggregator, rather than raw data, and confidentiality as well as data sovereignty were maintained (Ikpe & Shamsuddoha, 2024). The Figure.5 illustrates the measurable benefits of applying Federated Learning in Siemens' smart factory operations. Key improvements include a 30% reduction in unplanned downtimes, 25% increase in equipment lifespan, 40% decrease in data transmission overhead, and 15% improvement in production uptime highlighting the role of decentralized AI in boosting efficiency and maintaining data privacy.

Figure 5. Impact of Federated Learning on Siemens' Predictive Maintenance

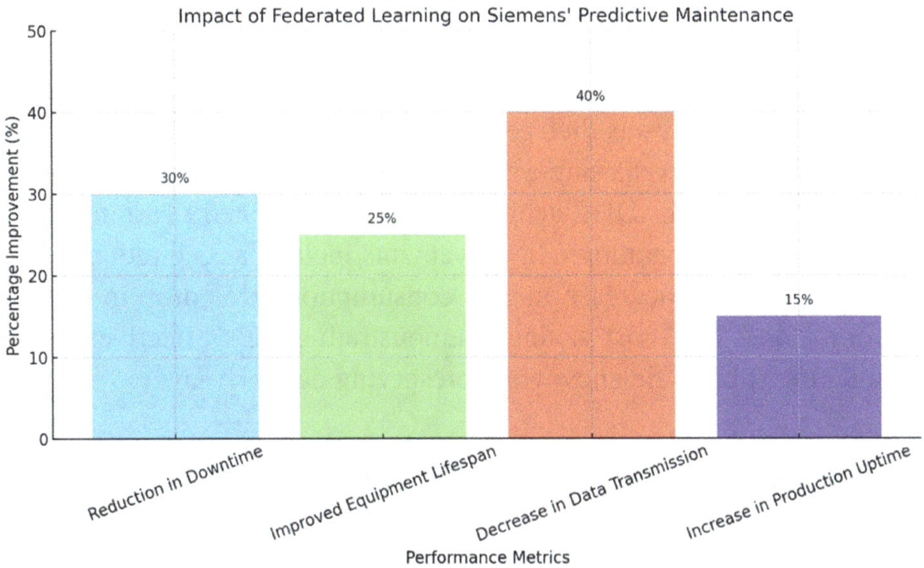

The consequences were tremendous. With better early fault detection and intelligent, decentralized maintenance time-table, Siemens managed to achieve 30% loss in uncoordinated downtimes of machines and 25% enhancement in the lifetime of equipment. Moreover, it was reported that the company experienced 40 percent reduction in the overhead data transmission, which improved the level of efficiency and security. The usage of production time also went up by 15% and this translated to more productivity and less operational risk. This deployment is an indication of how Siemens conforms to the concept of Industry 4.0- the use of distributed intelligence to see better performance, mitigate risk, and privacy. This success of this FL application is indicative of how secure, scalable decentralized AI can be highly useful.

6.2 Case Study 2: DHL – Route Optimization Using Federated Learning

DHL is one of the largest logistics providers in the world, and it deployed Federated Learning (FL) to improve the process of route optimization within its last-mile delivery operation and maintain data privacy. Rather than use a centralized AI system, and thus the need to have sensitive data about customers and routes being centralized, DHL enabled its distribution centers to train local models based on the vehicle load, fuel usage, delivery times and local traffic patterns data (Atadoga et al., 2024). This locally trained model was then centrally aggregated into a single optimization model- and never a single raw data moved. The Figure.6 highlights the performance gains DHL achieved through Federated Learning in its last-mile delivery operations. Improvements include a 35% reduction in delivery time, 20% decrease in fuel consumption, 28% drop in carbon emissions, and 18% cost savings demonstrating FL's effectiveness in boosting logistical efficiency while preserving data privacy.

Figure 6. Impact of Federated Learning on DHL's Route Optimization

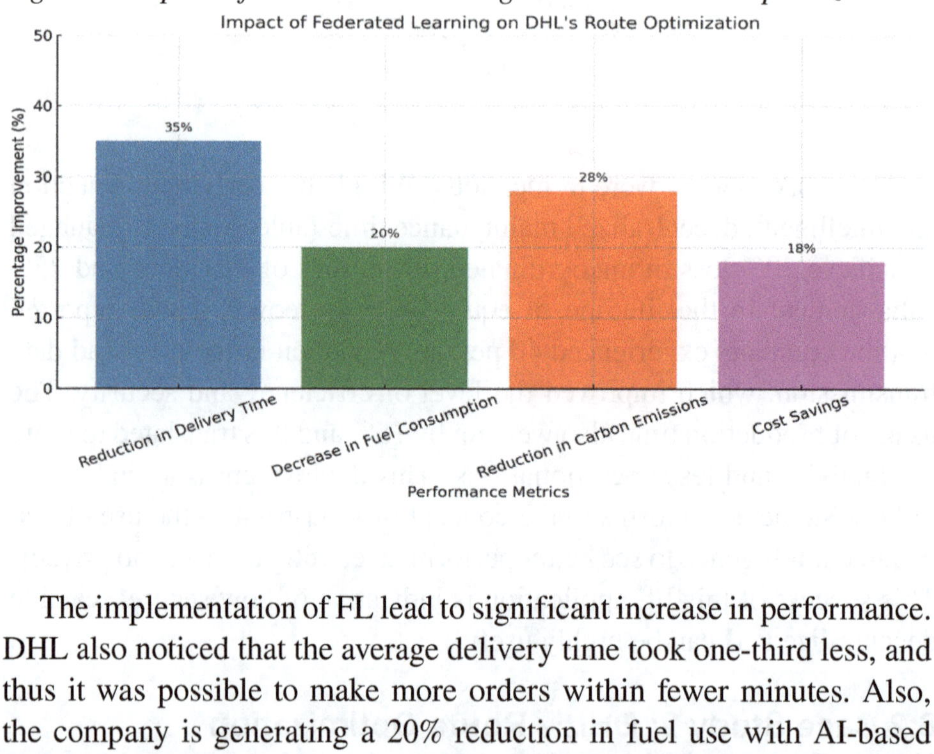

The implementation of FL lead to significant increase in performance. DHL also noticed that the average delivery time took one-third less, and thus it was possible to make more orders within fewer minutes. Also, the company is generating a 20% reduction in fuel use with AI-based dynamic route optimization powered by local real-time data as well as a 28% reduction in carbon emissions in pilot areas. More so, DHL has experienced 18% savings on the cost of last-mile logistics operations as a result of a higher level of fleet coordination and balance load. DHL has managed to protect both its operational and customer data and explain that decentralized privacy-aware AI model can assist in addressing environmental sustainability as well as serve logistical efficiency worldwide through the use of FL.

7. CHALLENGES AND RESEARCH OPPORTUNITIES

Nonetheless, one of the main problems that Federated Learning (FL) in supply chains has exposed is the issue of data heterogeneity, communication latency, and inter-operative model convergence issues operating in the event of varying surroundings. Interoperability, strong protection, and regulatory compliance are difficult to sustain, especially within a multi-national environment. Besides, there are risks, such as model poisoning, free-riding and inefficient aggregation, which may impede trust and scalability (Jacobs et al., 2023). Nevertheless, such difficulties open up fruitful avenues of research- How to design adaptive aggregation algorithms, incentives schemes and privacy preservation methods like homomorphic encryption and differential privacy. It is also recommended in the future to standardized frameworks, real-time FL on edge systems, and integration with ESG monitoring as such to increase resiliency and sustainability.

7.1 Model Convergence and Communication Overhead

One of the key issues of Federated Learning (FL) is how to bring convergence on the model on the heterogeneous supply chain set-up of non-identically distributed (non-IID) data. The differences in data quality, batch size, and participation causes biased local updates to impact the global model accuracy. There is also the fact that high frequency communications between clients and servers lead to high overhead particularly in low bandwidth requirements such as in warehouses or remote centers. The model compression, Sparsification, adaptive learning rates, and asynchronous FL of solutions are the ones that lower communication expense and enhance the scalability (Taik & Cherkaoui, 2020). Convergence also finds support in research on the personalized and federated averaging methods.

These are critical obstacles to the implementation of precise, effective FL models throughout the multi-tiered supply chains.

7.2 Security Risks: Poisoning Attacks and Trust Management

Although Federated Learning (FL) can be used to achieve privacy of data, it presents security risks in forms of model poisoning and unscrupulous participant behavior. When the participants in a supply chain are semi-trusted or even competitive, they can use local updates to skew the global model or otherwise affect its quality. The other issue is trusting management because FL offers no awareness of what each participant contributes, rendering systems susceptible to free-riding or Byzantine attacks. Mitigation solutions consist of sound aggregation techniques (e.g. Krum), outlier detection and reputation-based trust models (Chukwu et al., 2024). Security is boosted with the use of services such as blockchain, SMPC, and difference privacy. Multi-layered defense is designed to deliver FL resilience to critical supply chain systems.

7.3 Legal and Ethical Concerns in Collaborative AI

Federated Learning (FL) exists within a challenging legal and Ethical system thereby in the multinational supply chains. Whereas FL reserves the minimum data sharing, it does not exempt the institutions exacted by laws like GDPR, CCPA, or HIPAA in complete protection of data. Because of the potential inference attacks on the model parameters, even in the case of anonymization, there is the issue of data ownership, accountability, and privacy compliance. On an ethical level, FL brings queries concerning algorithm fairness, responsibility regarding model errors, and explanations of decisions produced by AI systems taught collectively (Patel, 2025). As an example, in case a model, which was trained jointly, does not perform well in a particular area because the data is not equally divided, it is hard to establish liability. On the same note, various organizations can have varying definitions of what impacts a good AI, thus making it difficult when organizations are supposed to govern together.

Intellectual property (IP)-related problems also exist such as who owns the federated model, how are the contributions quantified and rewarded? There are also no legal precedents with decentralized collaboration of AI which further creates doubt (Sani et al., 2022). To overcome these issues, explainability tools, well-defined governance policies, and contractual agreements having definitions of data rights, model usage, and dispute resolution mechanisms should be built into future FL implementations. Such an approach also requires the creation of cross-border standards of FL compliance and ethical certifications of AI in order to make that practical and widespread, and responsible.

7.4 Future Research Directions in FL for Supply Chains

Due to the increased use of Federated Learning (FL) in supply chain, new promising directions of research emerge that may help improve performance, security, and scalability. The building of FL architectures with the domain-specific models, geared towards the supply chain work like real-time routing, ESG tracking, and cold chain monitoring, is one of the promising vectors. These models must reckon with multimodal data, time-series modelling and region-bound conditions (Ruiz-Morales et al., 2021). The other important one is adaptive/personalised FL - where models are dynamically modified depending on the environment, infrastructure and data quality of a particular participant. This is so as to make FL inclusive and correct at varied levels of the supply chain and geographies.

Federated reinforcement learning across silos may also make autonomous decisions in dynamic settings such as logistics and inventory management. In the meantime, digital twins and edge AI together with blockchain-powered audit trails have the potential to build self-learning, self-optimizing and transparent supply chain ecosystems (Santhiyagu A et al., 2025). Lastly, the standardization frameworks, energy-efficient FL and incentive mechanisms to promote honest collaboration in collaborative AI require some study. The challenge of translating theoretical research to implementation in practice is one traditional priority. In the event of such directions being followed the prospects of FL will be fully realized resulting in sustainable, intelligent, and ethically managed supply chains of the coming generation of international trade.

8. CONCLUSION

The increasingly complex nature and interdependence of global supply chains requires novel developments that drive collaboration, data-based decision-making, and supply chain agility with an appreciation on privacy and security of data. Federated Learning (FL) is a revolutionary opportunity on that regard as it allows different supply chain members to train collective AI models without disclosing their sensitive data. The chapter has discussed how FL solves some of the major issues that face contemporary supply chain, such as the disjointedness of data, institutional lack of trust, and regulatory restrictions, in addition to improving the accuracy of forecasts, inventory optimization, and efficient movement of or goods and optimizing the effective management of risk. By case studies and practice, we showed that FL is not merely an abstract model but a growing practice to drive a cross-enterprise intelligence. Combined with other technologies like digital twins, blockchain and edge computing, FL can provide real-time view, trackable collaborations, and secure decentralization decision-making within networks that are highly complex.

Critically, FL is also linked to Environmental, Social and Governance (ESG) objectives, to help enable both emission-conscious routing, waste minimization, ethical sourcing and responsible use of AI. In spite of the promise, FL is subject to some of the drawbacks associated with model convergence, communication overhead, security vulnerabilities, and interoperability. The scale of the problems involved necessitates the cooperation of different fields, multidisciplinary research of AI and supply chain management, cybersecurity, and legal spheres. A significant improvement in the security against attacks, imposing just contribution principles, and meeting the global standards of data governance are necessary futuristic measures to introduce FL.

Furthermore, the set of ethical and legal aspects, including algorithm fairness and IP rights, should be found carefully as a way to establish trust between stakeholders and implement and deploy responsible AI.

The transparent governance structure, regulatory compliance plans, and uniform measures of technical performance and impact to ESG must be put in place to support Federated Learning systems. In future, domain-specific frames, personalized and adaptive FL models and incentivized collaborative networks are the key areas of FL in supply chains. Use of FL in the general context of digital transformation will help in developing intelligent, resilient, and sustainable supply chains, which will respond to dynamic global situations. To sum up, Federated Learning can be regarded as a key driver during the development of supply chain management. It fills the corridor between privacy and cooperation, between intelligence and decentralization, innovation and regulation. Since most companies pursue the vision of smarter, more sustainable, and ethically managed supply chain ecosystems, FL provides one of the most promising futures-based on new ways of utilizing, sharing, and securing data cross the enterprise boundary.

REFERENCES

Atadoga, A., Obi, O. C., Osasona, F., Onwusinkwue, S., Daraojimba, A. I., & Dawodu, S. O. (2024). AI in supply chain optimization: A comparative review of USA and African Trends. *Int. J. Sci. Res. Arch., 11*(1), 896–903. DOI: 10.30574/ijsra.2024.11.1.0156

Biswal, M., Tayeen, A. S., & Misra, S. (2021). AMI-FML: A privacy-preserving federated machine learning framework for AMI.

Briggs, C., Fan, Z., & Andras, P. (2020). Privacy preserving demand forecasting to encourage consumer acceptance of smart energy meters.

Chen, H., Wang, Z., & Zhang, M. (2024). Mechanism study on innovative influences of AI and blockchain on supply chain logistics: Case study of JD and Alibaba. Advances in Economics. *Management and Political Sciences, 109*(1), 94–100. DOI: 10.54254/2754-1169/109/2024BJ0116

Chilimattur, N. M.Nazia Mahammadrafiq Chilimattur. (2025). Intelligent food waste management in supply chains using deep Dense Networks and image processing. *Comm. Appl. Nonlinear Anal., 32*(10s), 117–134. DOI: 10.52783/cana.v32.4696

Chukwu, N., Yufenyuy, S., Ejiofor, E., Ekweli, D., Ogunleye, O., Clement, T., Obunadike, C., Adeniji, S., Elom, E., & Obunadike, C. (2024). Resilient chain: AI-enhanced supply chain security and efficiency integration. *International Journal of Scientific and Management Research, 07*(03), 46–65. DOI: 10.37502/IJSMR.2024.7306

Dayan, I., Roth, H. R., Zhong, A., Harouni, A., Gentili, A., Abidin, A. Z., Liu, A., Costa, A. B., Wood, B. J., Tsai, C.-S., Wang, C.-H., Hsu, C.-N., Lee, C. K., Ruan, P., Xu, D., Wu, D., Huang, E., Kitamura, F. C., Lacey, G., & Li, Q. (2021). Federated learning for predicting clinical outcomes in patients with COVID-19. *Nature Medicine, 27*(10), 1735–1743. DOI: 10.1038/s41591-021-01506-3 PMID: 34526699

Dong, Z., Liang, W., Liang, Y., Gao, W., & Lu, Y. (2022). Blockchained supply chain management based on IoT tracking and machine learning. *EURASIP Journal on Wireless Communications and Networking, 2022*(1), 127. DOI: 10.1186/s13638-022-02209-0 PMID: 36597502

Dora, M., Kumar, A., Mangla, S. K., Pant, A., & Kamal, M. M. (2022). Critical success factors influencing artificial intelligence adoption in food supply chains. *International Journal of Production Research, 60*(14), 4621–4640. DOI: 10.1080/00207543.2021.1959665

Eyo-Udo, N. L. (2024). Leveraging artificial intelligence for enhanced supply chain optimization. *Open Access Res. J. Multidiscip. Stud., 7*(2), 1–15. DOI: 10.53022/oarjms.2024.7.2.0044

Falcone, E., Kent, J., & Fugate, B. (2019). Supply chain technologies, interorganizational network and firm performance. *International Journal of Physical Distribution & Logistics Management, 50*(3), 333–354. DOI: 10.1108/IJPDLM-08-2018-0306

Fantacci, R., & Picano, B. (2020). Federated learning framework for mobile edge computing networks. *CAAI Transactions on Intelligence Technology, 5*(1), 15–21. DOI: 10.1049/trit.2019.0049

He, X., Hu, X., Wang, G., Yu, J., Zhao, Z., & Lu, X. (2023). Towards efficient federated learning using agile aggregation in Internet of vehicles. *Security and Communication Networks, 2023*, 1–20. DOI: 10.1155/2023/2265852

Husnoo, M. A., Anwar, A., Hosseinzadeh, N., Islam, S. N., Mahmood, A. N., & Doss, R. (2022). *FedREP: Towards horizontal federated load forecasting for Retail Energy Providers*. ArXiv. [Cs.DC]

Ikpe, V., & Shamsuddoha, M. (2024). Functional model of supply chain waste reduction and control strategies for retailers—The USA retail industry. *Logistics (Basel), 8*(1), 22. DOI: 10.3390/logistics8010022

Ivanov, D., & Dolgui, A. (2021). A digital supply chain twin for managing the disruption risks and resilience in the era of Industry 4.0. *Production Planning and Control, 32*(9), 775–788. DOI: 10.1080/09537287.2020.1768450

Jacobs, P.-P., Ehrengut, C., Bucher, A. M., Penzkofer, T., Lukas, M., Kleesiek, J., & Denecke, T. (2023). Challenges in implementing the local node infrastructure for a national federated machine learning network in radiology. *Healthcare (Basel)*, *11*(17), 2377. DOI: 10.3390/healthcare11172377 PMID: 37685411

Kaissis, G., Ziller, A., Passerat-Palmbach, J., Ryffel, T., Usynin, D., Trask, A., Lima, I.Jr, Mancuso, J., Jungmann, F., Steinborn, M.-M., Saleh, A., Makowski, M., Rueckert, D., & Braren, R. (2021). End-to-end privacy preserving deep learning on multi-institutional medical imaging. *Nature Machine Intelligence*, *3*(6), 473–484. DOI: 10.1038/s42256-021-00337-8

Kaya, A. (2024). Impact of artificial intelligence on supply chain efficiency in Turkey. *International Journal of Technology and Systems*, *9*(3), 25–37. DOI: 10.47604/ijts.2814

Khan, S., & Tabasum, S. (2025). Real-time health supply chain optimization using digital twin technology. *Int. J. Sci. Res. Arch.*, *15*(2), 1275–1289. DOI: 10.30574/ijsra.2025.15.2.1556

Kim, D.-H., Kim, G.-Y., & Do Noh, S. (2025). Digital twin-based prediction and optimization for dynamic supply chain management. *Machines (Basel)*, *13*(2), 109. DOI: 10.3390/machines13020109

Loftus, T. J., Ruppert, M. M., Shickel, B., Ozrazgat-Baslanti, T., Balch, J. A., Efron, P. A., Upchurch, G. R.Jr, Rashidi, P., Tignanelli, C., Bian, J., & Bihorac, A. (2022). Federated learning for preserving data privacy in collaborative healthcare research. *Digital Health*, *8*, 20552076221134456. DOI: 10.1177/20552076221134455 PMID: 36325438

Melesse, T. Y., Franciosi, C., Di Pasquale, V., & Riemma, S. (2023). Analyzing the implementation of digital twins in the agri-food supply chain. *Logistics (Basel)*, *7*(2), 33. DOI: 10.3390/logistics7020033

Mo, X. (2024). AI-based supply chain risk management. *Applied and Computational Engineering*, *106*(1), 125–130. DOI: 10.54254/2755-2721/106/20241297

Moshawrab, M., Adda, M., Bouzouane, A., Ibrahim, H., & Raad, A. (2023). Reviewing federated machine learning and its use in diseases prediction. *Sensors (Basel)*, *23*(4), 2112. DOI: 10.3390/s23042112 PMID: 36850717

Muthaluri, J. (2024). Optimizing supply chain management and marketing strategies: AI and ML integration for competitive advantage. Educational Administration: Theory and Practice, 8990–8997.

Narmadha, K., & Varalakshmi, P. (2022). Federated Learning in healthcare: A privacy preserving approach. *Studies in Health Technology and Informatics*, *294*, 194–198. DOI: 10.3233/SHTI220436 PMID: 35612055

Nisha. (2025). Federated AI approaches in pandemic outbreak forecasting. South Asian Journal of Engineering and Technology, 15(2), 46–56.

Park, K.-J., & Son, S.-Y. (2023). Residential load forecasting using modified federated learning algorithm. *IEEE Access : Practical Innovations, Open Solutions*, *11*, 40675–40691. DOI: 10.1109/ACCESS.2023.3268530

Patel, J. (2025). Leveraging digital twins for real-time supply chain visibility and decision-making. *International Journal on Science and Technology*, *16*(2).

Ruiz-Morales, B., Miranda-Ackerman, M. A., & Espitia-Moreno, I. C. (2021). Logistic strategies to minimize losses and waste in food supply chains. In *Research Anthology on Food Waste Reduction and Alternative Diets for Food and Nutrition Security* (pp. 302–314). IGI Global. DOI: 10.4018/978-1-7998-5354-1.ch015

Sani, S., Schaefer, D., & Milisavljevic-Syed, J. (2022). Utilising digital twins for increasing military supply chain visibility. In *Advances in Transdisciplinary Engineering*. IOS Press.

Santhiyagu, A. C., Vengadesh, S., & Chinna, P. R. (2025). The implications of digitalization in logistics after COVID-19. *International Research Journal of Multidisciplinary Scope*, *06*(01), 509–527. DOI: 10.47857/irjms.2025.v06i01.02336

Taik, A., & Cherkaoui, S. (2020, June). Electrical load forecasting using edge computing and federated learning. ICC 2020 - 2020 IEEE International Conference on Communications (ICC). DOI: 10.1109/ICC40277.2020.9148937

Wang, H. (2024). Linking AI supply chain strength to sustainable development and innovation: A country-level analysis. *Expert Systems: International Journal of Knowledge Engineering and Neural Networks*, *41*(5), e12973. DOI: 10.1111/exsy.12973

Zhang, F., & Hu, J. (2024). Research on logistics supply chain optimization strategy based on machine learning. In M. Mikusova (Ed.), International Conference on Smart Transportation and City Engineering (STCE 2023). SPIE. DOI: 10.1117/12.3024778

Zhang, P., Chen, G., Sun, L., & Wang, S. (2024). A framework for demand response load forecasting based on federated learning. *Journal of Physics: Conference Series*, *2914*(1), 12008. DOI: 10.1088/1742-6596/2914/1/012008

KEY TERMS AND DEFINITIONS

Blockchain: A decentralized ledger that records transactions securely and immutably, supporting auditability in FL.

Data Sovereignty: The principle that organizations retain ownership and control over their own data, central to FL.

Differential Privacy: A method that introduces noise into model updates to protect individual data contributions in FL.

Digital Twin: A virtual model of a physical system that simulates real-time performance using live sensor or system data.

Edge Computing: A method of processing data at or near the source (e.g., sensors), reducing latency in FL training.

ESG (Environmental, Social, Governance): A framework for measuring the sustainability and ethical impact of business practices.

Federated Learning (FL): A decentralized machine learning technique where multiple participants collaboratively train a model without sharing raw data.

Federated Transfer Learning (FTL): FL used when both features and samples differ, enabling collaboration in sparse data scenarios.

Horizontal FL (HFL): FL where data across participants has the same features but different samples (e.g., regional retailers).

Interoperability: The ability of diverse systems and organizations to work together effectively within a federated network.

IoT (Internet of Things): A network of connected devices that collect and exchange data in real-time across the supply chain.

Model Poisoning: A security threat where malicious participants intentionally manipulate model updates to degrade accuracy.

Secure Multi-Party Computation (SMPC): A cryptographic technique allowing parties to jointly compute a function without revealing their inputs.

Vertical FL (VFL): FL where participants share common users but with different features (e.g., manufacturer and retailer).

Chapter 3
Supply Chain 4.0:
The Digital Twin Revolution

Ananya Pandey
https://orcid.org/0000-0002-2419-6314
Christ University, India

ABSTRACT

The chapter explores the transformative role of digital twin technology in the evolution of modern supply chains. As businesses confront increasing complexity, volatility, and sustainability demands, digital twins offer real-time, data-driven solutions to simulate, monitor, and optimize supply chain processes. This chapter examines the integration of digital twins across logistics, inventory, demand forecasting, and sustainability tracking, highlighting their ability to enhance agility, resilience, and efficiency. It also addresses critical enablers such as IoT, AI, cloud computing, and discusses ethical, legal, and regulatory considerations in implementation. Through a strategic lens, it offers guidelines for adoption, policy recommendations, and identifies research gaps for future exploration. Positioned at the intersection of Industry 4.0 and sustainability, the digital twin revolution is redefining the future of supply chain management.

DOI: 10.4018/979-8-3373-2833-1.ch003

INTRODUCTION

Over the past few decades, supply chain management (SCM) has undergone a dramatic transformation, transitioning from linear, functionally siloed operations into interconnected, intelligent systems. This evolution is shaped by globalization, increasing customer expectations, volatile market dynamics, and, more recently, the profound influence of digital technologies. Traditional supply chains were primarily focused on cost-efficiency, inventory control, and logistics optimization. They relied heavily on manual processes, batch production, and reactive decision-making, which often led to inefficiencies, delayed responses to disruptions, and a lack of end-to-end visibility (Christopher, 2016). As markets globalized and consumer demands diversified, these traditional models began to falter in their ability to manage complexity and uncertainty.

The emergence of smart supply chains marks a significant departure from traditional models. Smart supply chains, often referred to as Supply Chain 4.0, are characterized by the integration of advanced technologies such as the Internet of Things (IoT), artificial intelligence (AI), machine learning (ML), blockchain, and digital twin systems to enable real-time data analytics, predictive decision-making, and autonomous operations (Ivanov et al., 2019). These systems facilitate dynamic responsiveness to supply and demand fluctuations, automate routine tasks, enhance visibility across the value chain, and improve resilience against disruptions. The smart supply chain is not merely an upgraded version of its predecessor but represents a paradigm shift in how organizations perceive, plan, and execute their logistics and production strategies.

Supply Chain 4.0 specifically refers to the digitization and integration of all elements of the supply chain ecosystem through Industry 4.0 technologies. It encapsulates a holistic approach where physical and digital components interact in real-time to optimize efficiency, agility, and sustainability. As a concept, Supply Chain 4.0 reflects the strategic evolution from reactive and siloed processes to a predictive and interconnected network where decisions are data-driven, collaborative, and customer-centric (Schrauf & Berttram, 2016). It is a response to the increasing need for supply chains to become not only faster and more cost-effective but also more adaptable, transparent, and environmentally responsible.

One of the most compelling aspects of Supply Chain 4.0 is the adoption of key enabling technologies that collectively reshape the supply chain landscape. IoT devices are instrumental in tracking goods, monitoring environmental conditions, and providing real-time location data. Artificial intelligence and machine learning enable advanced demand forecasting, anomaly detection, and automated decision-making. Blockchain technology enhances data security and traceability, particularly in sectors where provenance and compliance are critical, such as pharmaceuticals and food supply chains (Treiblmaier, 2018). Additionally, robotics and automation streamline warehousing and manufacturing processes, while cloud computing facilitates centralized data management and collaborative platforms.

Among these technologies, the concept of the Digital Twin has emerged as a revolutionary force in Supply Chain 4.0. A digital twin is a virtual representation of a physical object, system, or process that continuously updates in real time using sensor data and advanced analytics (Tao et al., 2019). In supply chain contexts, digital twins can model logistics networks, simulate warehouse operations, or predict the impact of disruptions in manufacturing lines. This capability allows for proactive risk management, dynamic scenario planning, and operational efficiency improvements across the value chain. Digital twins, when integrated with AI and big data analytics, provide a powerful tool for organizations seeking to achieve end-to-end supply chain visibility, agility, and sustainability.

The drivers behind the adoption of Supply Chain 4.0 are multifaceted. On the one hand, companies face increasing pressure to reduce operational costs, improve customer satisfaction, and deliver products faster and more reliably. On the other hand, global supply chains are more vulnerable than ever to geopolitical tensions, pandemics, climate change, and cyber threats. The COVID-19 pandemic underscored the fragility of traditional supply chains and acted as a catalyst for digital transformation across industries (Ivanov, 2020). Moreover, regulatory mandates and corporate sustainability commitments have prompted organizations to incorporate ESG (Environmental, Social, and Governance) considerations into their supply chain strategies, where digital technologies can play a pivotal role in enabling traceability, reporting, and compliance.

The objectives of this chapter are to establish a foundational understanding of Supply Chain 4.0, delineate its evolution from traditional supply chain models, and identify the key technologies that are shaping this new paradigm. It seeks to offer a conceptual framework for understanding how digitalization, connectivity, and real-time data analytics are converging to revolutionize supply chain operations. The chapter also aims to set the stage for subsequent discussions on digital twins and their role in enhancing supply chain resilience, agility, and sustainability. By exploring the technological enablers, strategic imperatives, and future directions of Supply Chain 4.0, this chapter provides the necessary context for comprehending the broader implications of the digital twin revolution in supply chain management.

Supply Chain 4.0 represents a significant leap forward in the digital transformation of global supply chains. It reflects a fundamental shift in how organizations design, operate, and optimize their value networks. By embracing advanced technologies such as IoT, AI, blockchain, and digital twins, organizations can not only enhance their competitive advantage but also contribute to a more sustainable, resilient, and customer-oriented supply chain ecosystem. As this book unfolds, the intricate interplay between these technologies and their practical applications in real-world supply chain scenarios will be explored in depth, with particular emphasis on the transformative potential of digital twins.

UNDERSTANDING DIGITAL TWINS

Digital Twin technology, a pivotal innovation within Industry 4.0 and Supply Chain 4.0 paradigms, refers to a virtual representation of a physical object, system, or process that enables real-time monitoring, simulation, and optimization. Originating from NASA's use of mirrored systems for spacecraft in the early 2000s (Glaessgen & Stargel, 2012), digital twins have evolved into sophisticated digital replicas that are dynamically updated with real-time data. The convergence of physical and digital worlds through digital twins allows for enhanced decision-making, operational efficiency, and predictive capabilities across diverse domains, especially within modern supply chains.

Digital twins are broadly categorized into three types: product twins, process twins, and system twins. Product twins represent individual physical assets such as machinery or components, enabling lifecycle tracking and performance optimization. Process twins model operational workflows—such as manufacturing lines or logistics processes—facilitating efficiency improvements and bottleneck identification. System twins encompass an interconnected network of processes and products, providing a holistic view of the supply chain or production environment (Tao et al., 2019). These categories are not mutually exclusive but often interact within comprehensive digital twin ecosystems that replicate entire supply networks or production facilities.

The core components that enable digital twin functionality include a mix of sensors, Internet of Things (IoT) devices, data analytics, and artificial intelligence (AI). Sensors embedded in physical systems collect data such as temperature, pressure, speed, and location, transmitting this data via IoT networks to digital platforms. This real-time data stream is essential for maintaining an accurate and current digital representation of the physical asset or system. Advanced data analytics, including machine learning algorithms and big data techniques, are then applied to interpret these data streams and predict outcomes (Kritzinger et al., 2018). AI further enhances these analytics by enabling cognitive functions such as anomaly detection, autonomous decision-making, and prescriptive maintenance, transforming digital twins from passive models into intelligent, interactive agents.

One of the most transformative aspects of digital twins lies in their capacity for real-time data integration and predictive modeling. Unlike traditional simulation models, which rely on historical or static data, digital twins ingest live data and continuously update their parameters. This dynamic nature allows for real-time status monitoring, performance forecasting, and rapid scenario testing. Predictive models powered by digital twins enable supply chain managers to anticipate equipment failures, forecast demand fluctuations, and simulate the impact of disruptions such as supply shortages or logistics delays (Negri et al., 2017). By running "what-if" scenarios within a risk-free virtual environment, organizations can explore contingency strategies and optimize resource allocation in advance.

The adoption of digital twins brings substantial benefits, but it also presents notable challenges. On the benefits side, digital twins offer enhanced visibility, traceability, and control across the supply chain. They can lead to increased operational efficiency, cost savings through predictive maintenance, reduced downtime, and more sustainable practices via energy monitoring and waste reduction (Jones et al., 2020). In industries like automotive, healthcare, and manufacturing, digital twins have proven instrumental in product development, quality control, and customer personalization. However, the challenges are non-trivial. Implementing digital twins requires significant investment in infrastructure, including high-quality sensors, connectivity networks, and computational power. Additionally, interoperability with legacy systems, data standardization, and integration complexities often hinder smooth deployment. Concerns about data privacy, cybersecurity, and intellectual property rights further complicate adoption, particularly in regulated industries or across international supply chains (Fuller et al., 2020). Moreover, organizations face a shortage of skilled professionals capable of developing, deploying, and managing digital twin systems, necessitating investment in workforce development and training.

In sum, digital twin technology represents a paradigm shift in how supply chains are managed and optimized in the digital era. Its ability to merge the physical and digital realms enables unprecedented levels of control, foresight, and adaptability. As technologies such as IoT, AI, and cloud computing continue to mature, digital twins are poised to become foundational components of Supply Chain 4.0 architectures. However, unlocking their full potential will require addressing technical, organizational, and regulatory barriers through strategic planning, cross-sector collaboration, and forward-looking policy frameworks.

THE INTEGRATION OF DIGITAL TWINS IN SUPPLY CHAINS

The integration of digital twins into modern supply chains marks a transformative shift in how organizations manage, optimize, and predict the behavior of interconnected logistical processes. Digital twins—virtual replicas of physical systems, processes, or products—enable supply chain professionals to simulate, analyze, and improve real-world operations in a data-driven and dynamic environment. One of the most impactful areas of application is demand forecasting. Traditional forecasting models, often reliant on historical data, fail to account for real-time market volatility and external disruptions. Digital twins, however, integrate live data streams from IoT devices, customer behavior analytics, and market trends, facilitating a dynamic, continuous forecasting process. This ensures that organizations can anticipate demand fluctuations and respond proactively. According to Ivanov et al. (2022), digital twins enhance forecast accuracy by enabling scenario planning and predictive modeling, thereby reducing stockouts and overstocking.

Equally critical is real-time inventory management, a long-standing challenge in supply chain logistics. With digital twins, companies can virtually monitor inventory movement across various nodes—warehouses, distribution centers, and retail points—ensuring precise inventory visibility and synchronization. This capability significantly enhances Just-in-Time (JIT) and lean inventory strategies, helping organizations reduce carrying costs and avoid obsolescence. For instance, a digital twin of a warehouse can simulate storage conditions, shelf life, and replenishment cycles to optimize inventory levels in real time (Negri et al., 2017). Additionally, when combined with automated guided vehicles (AGVs) and robotics, digital twins offer synchronized control, improving material handling and reducing human error. The result is a smarter, more responsive inventory system that can adapt to disruptions, such as supply chain delays caused by geopolitical issues or natural disasters.

In the realm of logistics and transportation optimization, digital twins revolutionize how goods are moved and delivered. Through integration with GPS data, traffic analytics, and vehicle telemetry, digital twins can simulate delivery routes, monitor vehicle performance, and optimize load planning. This real-time feedback loop allows logistics managers to identify bottlenecks, reroute vehicles dynamically, and reduce transportation costs and emissions. A study by Schluse et al. (2018) demonstrated how digital twins in logistics lead to increased asset utilization and energy efficiency, which is particularly vital in the context of carbon-neutral goals and sustainable logistics strategies. Furthermore, digital twins enhance collaboration between stakeholders—such as suppliers, third-party logistics providers, and retailers—by providing a unified view of shipment status and delivery timelines.

Another vital application is risk management and scenario simulation, where digital twins prove indispensable in preparing for uncertainties and complex interdependencies within the supply chain. By creating a virtual mirror of the end-to-end supply chain, organizations can simulate a wide range of "what-if" scenarios—from supplier failures and cyber-attacks to demand surges and climate-induced disruptions. These simulations enable preemptive risk mitigation strategies and resilience planning. For example, in the COVID-19 pandemic, organizations utilizing digital twin models were better equipped to pivot sourcing strategies, identify alternate suppliers, and maintain continuity (Wamba & Queiroz, 2022). The predictive capacity of digital twins enables real-time decision-making and stress-testing of the supply chain, making it possible to forecast the impact of disruption and optimize recovery paths.

Lastly, digital twins are pivotal in maintenance and asset monitoring, especially in capital-intensive industries such as manufacturing and energy. Through integration with IoT-enabled sensors and real-time analytics, digital twins provide a comprehensive health profile of critical equipment and infrastructure. This allows for predictive maintenance, where potential failures are detected and addressed before they escalate into costly breakdowns. For instance, a digital twin of a fleet of trucks or production line machinery can monitor parameters such as temperature, vibration, and wear levels to anticipate failures and schedule timely maintenance (Tao et al., 2019). This not only minimizes downtime but also extends asset lifespans and improves safety compliance. Furthermore, in industries where safety regulations are stringent, digital twins help simulate maintenance procedures and train personnel in a virtual environment, reducing operational risks.

In summary, digital twins are reshaping the future of supply chains by bringing intelligence, agility, and resilience to every stage of the value chain. From accurately forecasting demand and managing inventory in real time to optimizing logistics, simulating risk scenarios, and ensuring asset reliability, digital twins act as a digital backbone for Supply Chain 4.0. Their integration requires robust data governance, infrastructure, and a cultural shift toward digital maturity, but the benefits are evident across industries aiming for sustainability, efficiency, and adaptability in an increasingly uncertain world.

ARCHITECTURE AND INFRASTRUCTURE FOR DIGITAL TWIN IMPLEMENTATION

The successful implementation of digital twin technology in Supply Chain 4.0 hinges on a robust and adaptable architectural and infrastructural foundation. At the core of this foundation lies the data infrastructure, which enables the seamless flow of data between physical and digital realms. Cloud computing plays a pivotal role by offering scalable and cost-effective storage and computational power, allowing supply chain stakeholders to host, process, and analyze massive amounts of real-time data (Zhang et al., 2021). The flexibility of cloud platforms facilitates the integration of machine learning algorithms and data analytics tools that power predictive capabilities in digital twins. However, the rise of edge computing has complemented cloud computing by enabling data processing at the source—near sensors or smart devices—thus reducing latency and enhancing responsiveness, particularly in time-sensitive operations such as logistics and manufacturing (Shi et al., 2016). This hybrid architecture, combining centralized cloud resources with decentralized edge devices, ensures optimal system performance, efficient bandwidth usage, and higher system reliability.

Connectivity forms the lifeline of digital twins, making technologies such as the Internet of Things (IoT), 5G, and blockchain indispensable. IoT enables the real-time capture of physical asset conditions, environmental parameters, and operational data through a network of sensors and actuators embedded throughout the supply chain (Min et al., 2019). These interconnected devices serve as the sensory network of digital twins, providing dynamic inputs that keep the virtual models updated and responsive. The evolution of 5G technology introduces unprecedented advantages, including ultra-low latency, high-speed data transmission, and the ability to connect a massive number of devices simultaneously (Rao & Prasad, 2018). Such capabilities are critical in large-scale supply chain networks where real-time synchronization of multiple digital twins is essential.

Moreover, blockchain technology enhances the trustworthiness and transparency of data flows by providing an immutable ledger of transactions, which is particularly valuable in ensuring provenance and traceability in complex supply chains (Casino et al., 2019). When integrated into digital twin architectures, blockchain not only enhances data integrity but also supports automated smart contracts that can trigger actions in real-time based on digital twin simulations.

Interoperability and adherence to standards are fundamental to enabling the smooth integration of diverse systems and technologies across the digital twin ecosystem. Supply chains often comprise heterogeneous assets, platforms, and enterprise systems, necessitating the use of standardized data formats and communication protocols (Lu et al., 2020). Standards such as OPC UA (Open Platform Communications Unified Architecture) and ISO 23247 (Digital Twin Framework for Manufacturing) are gaining traction as they facilitate seamless data exchange and system integration across different domains and vendor systems. Interoperability ensures that digital twins are not siloed within individual organizations or departments but can function as part of an extended, cross-enterprise digital ecosystem. This holistic integration is particularly valuable for end-to-end visibility and collaboration among supply chain partners, enabling proactive responses to disruptions and opportunities.

Despite these technological advancements, cybersecurity and data privacy remain critical concerns that must be addressed in the architecture of digital twin systems. The continuous collection, transmission, and analysis of real-time operational data expose supply chains to various cyber threats, including data breaches, unauthorized access, and system sabotage (Khan et al., 2020). A multi-layered cybersecurity framework is essential, encompassing encryption, access controls, intrusion detection systems, and secure communication protocols. Additionally, compliance with data privacy regulations, such as the General Data Protection Regulation (GDPR), is essential, especially when handling personally identifiable information (PII) or sensitive customer data. Incorporating privacy-by-design principles into digital twin infrastructure helps organizations build trust with stakeholders while minimizing legal risks.

Scalability and cost considerations are also central to the implementation strategy of digital twins in supply chains. As organizations scale their digital twin initiatives from pilot projects to enterprise-wide deployments, they must ensure that the underlying architecture can support increased data volumes, device connections, and analytical complexity (Fuller et al., 2020). Cloud-native architectures and modular software design are increasingly adopted to enable elastic scaling and agile development cycles. However, the financial implications of digital twin deployment—covering hardware (sensors, edge devices), software (simulation engines, analytics platforms), integration services, and ongoing maintenance—can be substantial, particularly for small and medium-sized enterprises (SMEs). A thorough cost-benefit analysis is crucial, evaluating not only the upfront investment but also the long-term gains in efficiency, risk reduction, and strategic agility. Organizations can also explore "digital twin-as-a-service" models offered by technology providers, which reduce capital expenditures and enable quicker adoption through subscription-based pricing structures.

CASE STUDIES AND INDUSTRY APPLICATIONS

The integration of digital twin technology into Supply Chain 4.0 has significantly transformed various industries, driving efficiency, resilience, and sustainability. In the automotive and manufacturing sectors, digital twins are revolutionizing production and logistics by creating virtual replicas of physical assets and entire supply networks. Companies like BMW and General Electric have leveraged digital twins to optimize factory floor layouts, predict machine failures, and reduce downtime through predictive maintenance (Tao et al., 2018). These virtual models enable real-time monitoring and control, supporting lean manufacturing and enhancing quality assurance. In retail and consumer goods, digital twins are being employed to refine demand forecasting, personalize customer experiences, and streamline inventory management. Walmart and Amazon, for instance, use digital twins to model consumer behavior, optimize store layouts, and coordinate their vast logistical networks, especially during seasonal fluctuations (Ivanov & Dolgui, 2020). The ability to simulate supply and demand scenarios in real-time allows retailers to make agile decisions and reduce stockouts or overstock situations.

In the pharmaceutical and healthcare industry, digital twins play a pivotal role in ensuring the integrity and traceability of sensitive products across complex supply chains. Companies like Pfizer and Johnson & Johnson use digital twins to monitor temperature-sensitive shipments, simulate supply disruptions, and ensure compliance with regulatory standards such as Good Distribution Practices (GDP) (Min et al., 2019). Moreover, hospitals are exploring patient-specific digital twins to optimize medical logistics and reduce waste in drug distribution. Agriculture and food supply chains also benefit from digital twin applications, particularly in enhancing transparency, sustainability, and food safety. By modeling farm operations, weather patterns, and logistics flows, agritech firms like John Deere and Cargill can optimize yields, reduce spoilage, and respond to market demands more effectively (Kritzinger et al., 2018). Digital twins also facilitate traceability from farm to fork, ensuring that ethical and sustainable practices are maintained throughout the supply chain.

In the energy and utilities sector, digital twins are increasingly used to monitor infrastructure, manage asset life cycles, and integrate renewable energy sources into the grid. Companies such as Siemens and Shell utilize digital twin technology to simulate grid behavior, optimize energy distribution, and predict equipment degradation in oil refineries and wind farms (Fuller et al., 2020). These applications are critical in reducing downtime, enhancing operational safety, and meeting environmental targets. Across all sectors, the common thread lies in the ability of digital twins to provide end-to-end visibility, predictive insights, and data-driven decision-making capabilities. As industries continue to digitize and adapt to global uncertainties, digital twins are emerging as foundational tools for resilient and intelligent supply chain management.

SUSTAINABILITY AND RESILIENCE THROUGH DIGITAL TWINS

The integration of digital twin technology into supply chain management marks a transformative step toward achieving environmental sustainability and operational resilience. Digital twins—virtual replicas of physical assets, systems, or processes—allow organizations to model, monitor, and optimize supply chain operations in real time. One of the key sustainability applications of digital twins is environmental impact monitoring, where the technology facilitates real-time assessment of resource usage, energy consumption, and emissions throughout the value chain. This capability enables supply chain managers to identify inefficiencies, reduce environmental footprints, and ensure compliance with environmental regulations (Kritzinger et al., 2018).

Another critical function of digital twins is carbon footprint tracking. By integrating data from IoT sensors, enterprise systems, and external databases, digital twins provide a comprehensive and dynamic overview of greenhouse gas emissions associated with production, transportation, and warehousing. This granularity enables organizations to pinpoint emission hotspots and make informed decisions to reduce them—whether through route optimization, energy-efficient machinery, or switching to renewable energy sources (Negri et al., 2017). Moreover, predictive capabilities allow for scenario analysis, helping firms evaluate the environmental trade-offs of different operational strategies.

Digital twins also contribute to the circular economy and waste reduction by enabling end-to-end traceability and lifecycle monitoring. Companies can use digital twins to track product components and materials across their lifecycle, supporting reuse, remanufacturing, and recycling initiatives. This digital visibility allows for more efficient resource utilization and minimizes waste generation, aligning with circular economy principles (Tao et al., 2018). For instance, real-time tracking of materials can help identify excess inventory or expired goods, thereby reducing landfill waste and associated environmental harm.

In terms of resilience, digital twins enhance the ability of supply chains to anticipate and adapt to disruptions, whether due to climate events, geopolitical tensions, or pandemics. By simulating various risk scenarios and their impacts on supply chain performance, digital twins facilitate proactive contingency planning and real-time reconfiguration of logistics networks (Ivanov & Dolgui, 2020). This adaptability is crucial in an era of increasing volatility and environmental uncertainty. The combination of sustainability insights and resilient planning enables businesses to maintain service levels while reducing ecological harm.

Importantly, digital twins can play a vital role in advancing Sustainable Development Goal (SDG) 12: Responsible Consumption and Production, as well as other interlinked SDGs, including SDG 9 (Industry, Innovation, and Infrastructure) and SDG 13 (Climate Action). By promoting efficiency, transparency, and accountability in supply chain operations, digital twins support the global transition toward sustainable production systems (United Nations, 2015). Their ability to operationalize sustainability metrics ensures that environmental and social goals are embedded within day-to-day business decisions, fostering long-term ecological balance and economic competitiveness.

LEGAL, ETHICAL, AND REGULATORY CONSIDERATIONS

As Digital Twin technology becomes central to Supply Chain 4.0, legal, ethical, and regulatory frameworks must evolve to manage its complexities. One of the most pressing legal issues is data ownership and intellectual property (IP). Digital twins rely on a constant stream of real-time data from physical assets, often sourced from multiple stakeholders across the supply chain. Determining who owns the generated data—whether it is the manufacturer of the physical asset, the developer of the digital model, or the system integrator—poses a significant challenge. Furthermore, proprietary algorithms and modeling software used in digital twin creation raise questions about IP rights and licensing (Tao et al., 2019). The risk of data misuse or unauthorized replication of models further complicates enforcement, necessitating clearer contractual terms and legal precedents.

The issue of liability in autonomous decision-making also emerges as digital twins begin to drive automated responses, such as rerouting logistics or adjusting production schedules without human intervention. If such decisions result in financial loss or safety risks, attributing liability becomes legally murky. Traditional tort law may be inadequate to apportion blame when machine learning models act unpredictably or when decision chains are decentralized (Pagallo, 2020). This necessitates the development of new liability doctrines or the adaptation of existing ones to incorporate AI-driven systems, possibly applying concepts such as shared liability or mandatory risk insurance models for digital twin systems.

Compliance with international regulations adds another layer of complexity. Regulations such as the European Union's General Data Protection Regulation (GDPR) impose strict data protection obligations on organizations that collect and process personal data, even indirectly through supply chain operations (Voigt & Von dem Bussche, 2017). Since digital twins integrate data across multiple platforms and geographies, companies must ensure data flows comply with cross-border transfer rules, purpose limitation principles, and data subject rights. Failure to do so not only exposes firms to hefty fines but also reputational damage and legal injunctions. As digital twin applications expand into health, logistics, and smart infrastructure, the regulatory landscape will likely become more stringent.

Beyond legal compliance, the ethical use of predictive analytics embedded in digital twin systems is critical. These systems can perpetuate biases in data, leading to discriminatory outcomes in areas such as supplier selection, risk assessment, or workforce allocation (Mittelstadt et al., 2016). Ethical concerns also arise from over-surveillance of workers or suppliers and the use of data for purposes beyond the original intent. To mitigate these risks, developers and users of digital twins must implement ethical guidelines focused on transparency, explainability, and fairness in algorithmic decision-making. Ethics-by-design approaches—embedding ethical considerations into the development phase—can ensure that these technologies do not undermine trust or stakeholder rights.

Finally, robust governance and accountability frameworks are essential for ensuring the responsible deployment of digital twins in supply chains. Such frameworks should encompass data stewardship, risk management protocols, cybersecurity resilience, and stakeholder engagement mechanisms. Public-private partnerships and industry consortia can play a pivotal role in establishing interoperable standards and ethical benchmarks. Governance models should also be adaptive, capable of responding to emerging risks associated with new applications and evolving AI capabilities (Floridi et al., 2018). An integrated governance strategy, aligned with legal compliance and ethical responsibility, will be vital to harness the full potential of digital twins while safeguarding societal and organizational values.

CHALLENGES AND BARRIERS TO ADOPTION

The adoption of digital twin technology within Supply Chain 4.0 is not without significant challenges, many of which hinder its widespread implementation across industries. One of the primary barriers is the technological complexity and integration issues that accompany digital twin systems. These systems necessitate the seamless interplay of advanced technologies including IoT, artificial intelligence, cloud computing, and real-time analytics. Integrating digital twins with existing supply chain infrastructure often demands a complete overhaul or extensive modification of legacy systems, which is both technically demanding and time-consuming (Tao et al., 2018). Furthermore, ensuring real-time data synchronization between physical assets and their digital counterparts requires robust data pipelines and infrastructure, which many organizations lack.

Another major obstacle is the high initial investment and uncertain return on investment (ROI). Developing, deploying, and maintaining digital twins involve substantial financial outlays for hardware, software, skilled personnel, and cybersecurity measures. For small and medium-sized enterprises (SMEs), these costs can be prohibitive (Shao & Kibira, 2018). Moreover, since the benefits of digital twins—such as predictive maintenance, operational efficiency, and risk mitigation—often materialize over time, organizations may struggle to justify the expenditure without short-term tangible returns. This perceived financial risk can dissuade stakeholders from embracing the technology wholeheartedly.

Talent and skill gaps further compound the issue. The implementation and maintenance of digital twin systems demand interdisciplinary expertise in areas such as systems engineering, data science, AI, and domain-specific supply chain knowledge. However, there exists a notable shortage of professionals proficient in both digital technologies and supply chain operations (Jones et al., 2020). This talent deficit poses a significant barrier, particularly in regions or sectors where digital literacy remains low. Resistance to change and organizational inertia also hinder the successful adoption of digital twins. Many firms, especially those with long-established operational practices, exhibit cultural resistance to adopting novel technologies. Employees may perceive digital transformation as a threat to job security or fear the learning curve associated with new systems. This psychological and organizational resistance can impede the acceptance and full utilization of digital twin technologies (Kamble et al., 2020).

Lastly, interoperability and legacy system constraints present a technical and operational challenge. Existing supply chain systems often lack the ability to communicate effectively with new digital platforms due to differences in data formats, protocols, and system architectures. Without standardized frameworks, the integration of digital twins becomes a complex task requiring custom interfaces and middleware solutions, which increases the cost and complexity of adoption (Fuller et al., 2020). These legacy constraints limit scalability and reduce the flexibility of digital twin implementations across supply chain networks. Addressing these challenges requires a holistic strategy involving policy support, targeted investment in skills development, standardization initiatives, and the cultivation of a culture that embraces innovation. Only through such concerted efforts can the full potential of digital twins in Supply Chain 4.0 be realized.

FUTURE DIRECTIONS AND INNOVATIONS

The future of Supply Chain 4.0 is intrinsically linked to the evolution of enabling technologies, among which Artificial Intelligence (AI), the metaverse, quantum computing, and global standardization play pivotal roles. One of the most transformative developments is the integration of AI-augmented digital twins, which go beyond static models by enabling dynamic learning and decision-making through machine learning algorithms. AI allows digital twins to predict equipment failures, optimize operations autonomously, and adapt to changing market conditions in real-time (Tao et al., 2019). This synergy empowers organizations to simulate complex supply chain behaviors and mitigate risks with unprecedented precision. In parallel, the emergence of metaverse and immersive visualization tools promises to redefine how supply chains are designed, monitored, and optimized. These tools, incorporating extended reality (XR) technologies, allow supply chain managers to interact with digital twins in 3D virtual environments, enhancing situational awareness, collaboration, and training (Dwivedi et al., 2022). For instance, immersive platforms can simulate disruptions such as port delays or labor strikes, enabling stakeholders to visualize and test mitigation strategies in real-time.

Another promising frontier is the development of autonomous supply chain networks, wherein AI-driven digital twins communicate and coordinate without human intervention. These networks leverage edge computing, robotics, and distributed ledger technologies (e.g., blockchain) to facilitate decentralized decision-making and self-optimization (Queiroz et al., 2022). This shift toward autonomy fosters resilience by enabling supply chains to reconfigure routes, allocate resources, and manage demand fluctuations in response to real-time data, without centralized control. Equally transformative is the potential of quantum computing in enhancing digital twin simulations. Classical computing often falls short in modeling highly complex, multi-variable systems such as global supply chains. Quantum algorithms can process exponentially larger datasets and perform probabilistic simulations at unprecedented speed and accuracy (Preskill, 2018). This computational power may revolutionize scenario planning, supply chain design, and optimization models, offering a quantum leap in predictive analytics.

Lastly, evolving standards and global cooperation are crucial to ensuring interoperability, data integrity, and ethical governance of digital twin ecosystems. The lack of universal frameworks often impedes integration across heterogeneous systems. Efforts by organizations such as the International Organization for Standardization (ISO) and the Digital Twin Consortium are paving the way for standardized architectures and protocols (ISO, 2021). Moreover, global cooperation is essential in addressing data sovereignty, privacy, and cybersecurity risks, particularly as digital twins increasingly span national borders and involve sensitive supply chain intelligence. Collectively, these innovations signal a paradigm shift in supply chain management, where digital twins act not merely as passive mirrors but as intelligent, autonomous, and immersive orchestrators of complex global networks. As these technologies mature and converge, the vision of a responsive, sustainable, and resilient supply chain becomes increasingly attainable.

CONCLUSION

The evolution of Supply Chain 4.0 marks a significant milestone in the digital transformation of global logistics and production systems, with Digital Twin technology emerging as a cornerstone of this revolution. This book has unpacked the dynamic synergy between digital twins and smart supply chains, revealing how the fusion of real-time data, advanced analytics, and cyber-physical systems can enable unprecedented levels of visibility, agility, and optimization across the supply chain ecosystem. From demand forecasting and asset monitoring to sustainability tracking and risk mitigation, digital twins provide a powerful framework for simulating, analyzing, and enhancing every node and link in the value chain. The key insight that emerges is that digital twins are not just tools for operational excellence but strategic enablers for building resilient, responsive, and sustainable supply chains in a volatile global environment.

Strategically, implementing digital twins requires a multi-layered approach that integrates technological, organizational, and human dimensions. Organizations should begin with a clear assessment of their digital maturity and align digital twin initiatives with core business objectives. Investing in scalable infrastructure—such as IoT-enabled devices, cloud computing, and robust data platforms—is essential, as is fostering cross-functional collaboration between IT, operations, and data science teams. A phased approach—starting with pilot projects in high-impact areas like predictive maintenance or logistics—can help build internal capabilities and demonstrate value. Moreover, governance frameworks must be established to ensure data quality, cybersecurity, and ethical use of digital simulations, especially when decisions have real-world consequences.

On the policy front, governments and international bodies have a critical role in creating an enabling environment for digital twin adoption. This includes developing standards for data interoperability, offering incentives for digital infrastructure investments, and ensuring regulatory clarity around data privacy and intellectual property. Public-private partnerships can accelerate innovation and democratize access to digital twin technologies, particularly for small and medium-sized enterprises. In parallel, workforce development policies must address the growing demand for hybrid skills that blend engineering, analytics, and systems thinking, ensuring that the human capital gap does not become a bottleneck in the digital supply chain transformation.

Despite the progress, several research gaps remain. There is a need for more empirical studies on the ROI and long-term value of digital twins, particularly in developing economies. Interdisciplinary research is also required to explore the ethical and legal implications of autonomous decision-making in digital twin-enabled supply chains. Furthermore, the integration of emerging technologies such as quantum computing, edge AI, and the industrial metaverse with digital twins presents fertile ground for academic and industry exploration.

Ultimately, the Digital Twin Revolution in Supply Chain 4.0 is not just about technology—it is about reimagining how global value chains are designed, managed, and sustained. As we look to a future defined by climate risks, geopolitical shifts, and rapid technological change, digital twins offer a compass for navigating complexity and fostering innovation. By embracing this transformative paradigm with strategic foresight and collaborative effort, businesses and policymakers alike can unlock a smarter, greener, and more resilient future for global supply chains.

REFERENCES

Casino, F., Dasaklis, T. K., & Patsakis, C. (2019). A systematic literature review of blockchain-based applications: Current status, classification and open issues. *Telematics and Informatics*, *36*, 55–81. DOI: 10.1016/j.tele.2018.11.006

Christopher, M. (2016). *Logistics & supply chain management* (5th ed.).

Dwivedi, Y. K., Hughes, D. L., Ismagilova, E., Aarts, G., Coombs, C., Crick, T., & Williams, M. D. (2022). Metaverse for digital twins and immersive experiences: Opportunities and challenges. *International Journal of Information Management*, *66*, 102505.

Floridi, L., Cowls, J., Beltrametti, M., Chatila, R., Chazerand, P., Dignum, V., Luetge, C., Madelin, R., Pagallo, U., Rossi, F., Schafer, B., Valcke, P., & Vayena, E. (2018). AI4People—An ethical framework for a good AI society: Opportunities, risks, principles, and recommendations. *Minds and Machines*, *28*(4), 689–707. DOI: 10.1007/s11023-018-9482-5 PMID: 30930541

Fuller, A., Fan, Z., Day, C., & Barlow, C. (2020). Digital twin: Enabling technologies, challenges and open research. *IEEE Access : Practical Innovations, Open Solutions*, *8*, 108952–108971. DOI: 10.1109/ACCESS.2020.2998358

Glaessgen, E., & Stargel, D. (2012). *The digital twin paradigm for future NASA and U.S. Air Force vehicles*. In the 53rd *AIAA/ASME/ASCE/AHS/ASC Structures, Structural Dynamics and Materials Conference*. DOI: 10.2514/6.2012-1818

ISO. (2021). *Digital twin framework for manufacturing*. International Organization for Standardization. https://www.iso.org/standard/75066.html

Ivanov, D. (2020). Predicting the impacts of epidemic outbreaks on global supply chains: A simulation-based analysis on the coronavirus outbreak (COVID-19/SARS-CoV-2) case. *Transportation Research Part E, Logistics and Transportation Review*, *136*, 101922. DOI: 10.1016/j.tre.2020.101922 PMID: 32288597

Ivanov, D., & Dolgui, A. (2020). A digital supply chain twin for managing the disruption risks and resilience in the era of Industry 4.0. *Production Planning and Control, 32*(9), 775–788. DOI: 10.1080/09537287.2020.1768450

Ivanov, D., Dolgui, A., & Sokolov, B. (2022). *Digital supply chain twins: Managing the ripple effect, resilience, and disruption risks by data-driven optimization, simulation, and visibility*. Springer.

Ivanov, D., Dolgui, A., Sokolov, B., Ivanova, M., & Werner, F. (2019). A dynamic model and an algorithm for short-term supply chain scheduling in the smart factory industry 4.0. *European Journal of Operational Research, 274*(2), 425–443. DOI: 10.1016/j.ejor.2018.10.034

Jones, D., Snider, C., Nassehi, A., Yon, J., & Hicks, B. (2020). Characterising the digital twin: A systematic literature review. *CIRP Journal of Manufacturing Science and Technology, 29*, 36–52. DOI: 10.1016/j.cirpj.2020.02.002

Kamble, S. S., Gunasekaran, A., & Gawankar, S. A. (2020). Achieving sustainable performance in a data-driven agriculture supply chain: A review for research and applications. *Sustainable Production and Consumption, 23*, 60–79. DOI: 10.1016/j.spc.2020.04.005

Khan, R. A., McLaughlin, K., & Sezer, S. (2020). Cybersecurity considerations for digital twin systems. *Sensors (Basel), 20*(23), 6811. DOI: 10.3390/s20236811 PMID: 33260646

Kritzinger, W., Karner, M., Traar, G., Henjes, J., & Sihn, W. (2018). Digital Twin in manufacturing: A categorical literature review and classification. *IFAC-PapersOnLine, 51*(11), 1016–1022. DOI: 10.1016/j.ifacol.2018.08.474

Lu, Y., Liu, C., Kevin, I., Wang, K. I. K., Huang, H., & Xu, X. (2020). Digital Twin-driven smart manufacturing: Connotation, reference model, applications and research issues. *Robotics and Computer-integrated Manufacturing, 61*, 101837. DOI: 10.1016/j.rcim.2019.101837

Min, H., Zacharia, Z. G., & Smith, C. D. (2019). Defining supply chain analytics and its impact on supply chain operations. *Journal of Business Logistics, 40*(3), 147–152. DOI: 10.1111/jbl.12181

Mittelstadt, B. D., Allo, P., Taddeo, M., Wachter, S., & Floridi, L. (2016). The ethics of algorithms: Mapping the debate. *Big Data & Society*, *3*(2), 2053951716679679. Advance online publication. DOI: 10.1177/2053951716679679

Negri, E., Fumagalli, L., & Macchi, M. (2017). A review of the roles of Digital Twin in CPS-based production systems. *Procedia Manufacturing*, *11*, 939–948. DOI: 10.1016/j.promfg.2017.07.198

Pagallo, U. (2020). The Law and Ethics of AI and Robotics: A Literature Review. *Law, Innovation and Technology*, *12*(1), 115–137. DOI: 10.1080/17579961.2020.1724412

Preskill, J. (2018). Quantum Computing in the NISQ era and beyond. *Quantum : the Open Journal for Quantum Science*, *2*, 79. DOI: 10.22331/q-2018-08-06-79

Queiroz, M. M., Wamba, S. F., & Joshi, A. W. (2022). Blockchain adoption for supply chain resilience: Integrating behavioral and technical factors. *Industrial Marketing Management*, *105*, 55–68.

Rao, J., & Prasad, R. (2018). Impact of 5G technologies on smart cities: Technical challenges, security concerns and future prospects. *Journal of Urban Technology*, *25*(4), 3–28. DOI: 10.1080/10630732.2018.1455113

Schluse, M., Atorf, L., & Rossmann, J. (2018). The digital twin in industry 4.0: A cyber-physical approach to production control. *IFAC-PapersOnLine*, *51*(11), 131–136. DOI: 10.1016/j.ifacol.2018.08.474

Schrauf, S., & Berttram, P. (2016). *Industry 4.0: How digitization makes the supply chain more efficient, agile, and customer-focused.* PwC Strategy&. https://www.strategyand.pwc.com

Shao, G., & Kibira, D. (2018). Digital manufacturing: Requirements and challenges for implementing digital twin. *Proceedings of the ASME 2018 13th International Manufacturing Science and Engineering Conference*, 1–10. DOI: 10.1115/MSEC2018-6485

Shi, W., Cao, J., Zhang, Q., Li, Y., & Xu, L. (2016). Edge computing: Vision and challenges. *IEEE Internet of Things Journal*, *3*(5), 637–646. DOI: 10.1109/JIOT.2016.2579198

Tao, F., Zhang, H., Liu, A., & Nee, A. Y. C. (2018). Digital twin in industry: State-of-the-art. *IEEE Transactions on Industrial Informatics*, *15*(4), 2405–2415. DOI: 10.1109/TII.2018.2873186

Treiblmaier, H. (2018). The impact of blockchain on the supply chain: A theory-based research framework and a call for action. *Supply Chain Management*, *23*(6), 545–559. DOI: 10.1108/SCM-01-2018-0029

United Nations. (2015). *Transforming our world: The 2030 Agenda for Sustainable Development*. https://sdgs.un.org/2030agenda

Voigt, P., & Von dem Bussche, A. (2017). *The EU General Data Protection Regulation (GDPR): A practical guide*. Springer. DOI: 10.1007/978-3-319-57959-7

Wamba, S. F., & Queiroz, M. M. (2022). Industry 4.0 and the supply chain digitalization: A systematic review and a research agenda. *Annals of Operations Research*, *308*(1), 1–38. DOI: 10.1007/s10479-020-03620-0

Zhang, Y., Tao, F., Nee, A. Y. C., & Luo, Y. (2021). Digital twin-enabled smart manufacturing: Technologies and applications. *Journal of Manufacturing Systems*, *58*, 176–186. DOI: 10.1016/j.jmsy.2020.06.006

Chapter 4
Optimizing Last-Mile Delivery Using AI-Powered Route Optimization and Personalization

C. M. Prathik Raj

Dayananda Sagar College of Engineering, India

K. S. Ganesha

https://orcid.org/0000-0001-8181-2411

Dayananda Sagar College of Engineering, India

ABSTRACT

This study explores the literature that evaluates how to optimize last-mile delivery using AI-powered route optimization and personalization. This study provides a comprehensive view of the current state of optimizing last-mile delivery using AI-powered route optimization and personalization, identifying both the advances made and the gaps in the literature that require further attention. The results form a sound foundation for subsequent research aimed at exploring the real-world applications of

DOI: 10.4018/979-8-3373-2833-1.ch004

these technologies in various industrial and geographical environments, as well as for formulating policies encouraging a more equitable sharing of knowledge and resources within this new field.

INTRODUCTION

Last-mile delivery is a pressing and challenging supply chain and logistics management issue of the day, especially in our rapidly evolving digital economy. The last mile, or the delivery of products from a distribution center to the ultimate consumer, has direct-time implications on customer satisfaction, operational efficiency, and a company's competitiveness. While they travel more relatively short distances, the last mile is most typically the slowest, most costly, and most logistically difficult component of the entire delivery network (Al-Khatib et al., n.d.; Sorooshian et al., 2022). The explosive expansion of cross-border e-commerce has critically escalated these issues. With a valuation of USD 5.8 trillion in 2023, the worldwide e-commerce market is expected to grow to USD 8.1 trillion by 2026 (Statista, 2024). How to cite this paper. This boom, which is driven by the increasing demands of consumers for speed, reliability, and convenience, has exponentially increased package volumes, exerting unprecedented pressure on historical delivery infrastructures and forcing logistics providers to rethink their models at their very core (BACH & HOANG, 2025; Khalifa & Volkov, 2024). To address these needs, Artificial Intelligence (AI) is now the game-changer in logistics (Attah et al., 2023; El Makhloufi, 2023; Ponomarenko & Ponomarenko, 2023). AI introduces novel software solutions to manage the natural complexities of last-mile delivery (Muthukalyani, 2023), enabling companies to shatter last-century logistics conventionalism with novel solutions that spur performance, reduce costs, and stimulate higher customer satisfaction (Japiassu, 2022). Two of the most relevant applications of AI in this scenario are route optimization and delivery personalization. Route optimization utilizes AI-based algorithms that analyze real-time and past data—traffic flow, road conditions, weather, and time windows—to plan the most efficient delivery routes (Paul & Sarkar, 2021; Reyana & Kautish, 2024; Vaka, 2024). This not only makes the delivery faster but also saves fuel by a significant amount, maximizes fleet utilization, and minimizes greenhouse gas emissions, which ultimately results in improved delivery density, lower cost of operations, and cleaner operations (Kale, 2024). Personalization, however, is focused on maximizing the delivery experience from the customer's perspective (Patil, 2024; Wasilewski et al., 2025). With the help of customer behavior data, delivery patterns, and trends, AI systems can generate hypothesis-driven information to ascertain best-in-class delivery times, facilitate on-demand routing around stocks, and real-time communications channel optimization with consideration of user preference. These data-driven, customer-focused programs develop greater convenience, visibility, and trust, all of which matter most when establishing long-term customer loyalty. Despite making such unprecedented progress, however, the widespread embracement of AI in last-mile delivery remains uneven globally. While growth and penetration of AI solutions are being observed in more developed economies, others fall behind because of disruptions such as weak digital infrastructure, weak technical capabilities, and weak investment levels. This has contributed to a global research-practice gap. This recognition puts the imperative need for collaborative innovation and mutual information in high relief to bridge the gap between developing and developed world, enabling AI at last to make last-mile logistics smarter, more dynamic, and cleaner delivery systems around the world (Chen et al., 2024).

Evolution of AI Technology

The remarkable evolution of Artificial Intelligence (AI) technology is one of deep and enduring change, one that has irrevocably affected a complete spectrum of markets, not the least of which is the logistics industry, whose delicate subtleties of last-mile delivery have been transformed. AI. Its roots go all the way back to the mid-20th century with the likes of Alan Turing and John McCarthy. AI began as a rule-based paradigm designed to undertake certain tasks within fixed parameters without scope to respond to live, changing world events. It was a big shift in the 1980s and 1990s with the introduction of machine learning (ML)—a subdomain of AI in which machines are trained using data instead of pre-programmed instruction—applied to logistics for the identification of patterns such as delivery times, traffic flow, and customer interests, making improved predictions and improved prioritization of delivery planning possible. This innovation extended into the 21st century with the proliferation of deep learning (DL)—a deeper form of ML that uses stacked neural networks to recognize complex patterns in massive data sets—to enable applications like real-time imaging analysis for package recognition, adaptive routing planing, and autonomous navigation in autonomous delivery trucks, revolutionizing the ability of logistics systems to operate effectively in dynamic environments. The coordination of these technologies has transformed route optimization, formerly grounded in static modeling and past analysis, with present AI-driven models factoring in real-time traffic, customer behavior, precise geolocation, and other data streams to re-route deliveries in real time and tailor experiences to the needs of individual customers (Suraj et al., 2024) and, in the process, reduce delivery time and operational cost while enhancing customer satisfaction through timely and reliable service (Yerra). Other innovations include the convergence of AI with edge processing and IoT sensors, allowing for real-time tracking and proximate decision-making near the point of data origin (Kanyepe, 2025), and applications of autonomous drones and robots—powered by advanced computer vision and navigation software—enabling scalable, AI-driven last-mile delivery in urban and rural environments (Madhumithaa et al., 2024). Globally, adoption of AI in last-mile logistics is increasing (Takawale et al., 2024), though the differential gap between the developed economies and the developing economies still continues; however, open data sharing, tools, and best practice sharing and global collaboration to facilitate the democratization of AI have the prospects of filling such gaps. Improvements in areas such as computer vision, natural language processing, and reinforcement learning are bringing futuristic concepts such as self-driving delivery vehicles (Garikapati & Shetiya, 2024), drone deliveries (Gowsalya & Mayuri, 2025), and intelligent lockers not just feasible but ever more common, poised to be the cornerstone of efficient, responsive, and eco-friendly last-mile logistics (Fatorachian, 2024).

Last-Mile Delivery

Last-mile delivery, commonly forgotten in strategic thinking but central to operational implementation, is the last step of the logistics pipeline—getting the product from a distribution facility or local hub to the consumer's door. Though traversing the shortest physical distance throughout the supply chain, it contributes more than 50% towards the total delivery expense, and thus it is both the costliest and operationally complex segment. With consumers expecting greater speed, reliability, and convenience because of higher consumer expectations that have been driven by advances in e-commerce, their optimization is now a necessity for international businesses. Adoption of attributes like real-time tracking, precise delivery time slots, and day-of-delivery has exposed the weaknesses of legacy systems, which are more and more incapable of keeping up with this kind of complexity. Congested city centers, fluctuating fuel prices, failed delivery attempts, and customer availability uncertainties are also adding to last-mile inefficiencies and raising cost at the expense of service quality.

Historical Context and Traditional Challenges of Last-Mile Delivery

Before artificial intelligence implementation, last-mile delivery operations relied on manual or basic digital systems for route planning and scheduling. Static maps or GPS systems with no real-time updates were utilized by delivery managers, leading to inefficiencies. Real-time responses were not part of delivery assignments, and planning did not take into account dynamic variables like traffic congestion, weather patterns, or last-minute order cancellations. These limitations consistently led to missed delivery windows, fuel wastage, increased labor hours, and overall operational rigidity (Bowersox et al., 2013).

Specific Challenges

- Poor Route Planning: Legacy logistics infrastructure used rudimentary heuristics or predetermined routes, with little or no regard for real-time data. Drivers would double up or drive unnecessary miles, with resultant excessive fuel consumption, longer delivery times, and lower order density per trip (Toth & Vigo, 2014).

- Real-time Visibility: Prior to GPS integration and tracking based on IoT, the location of a package or delivery personnel was unknown to customers as well as managers. Such opacity led to poor customer service and rendered real-time reallocation of deliveries inefficient in most cases.
- Handling Returns: Reverse logistics were an afterthought and were typically handled through totally different systems or manual coordination. This caused delayed return processing, poor asset recovery rates, and additional warehouse congestion, all of which had a negative impact on profitability.
- Cost Burden: The "over 50%" ratio of total delivery costs in last-mile logistics comes from a confluence of operating costs. For instance, labor costs absorb 30–40% of the expense of last-mile delivery in the case of urban agglomeration. Maintenance of the vehicle and fuel absorb another 10–15%, and failed delivery efforts and return handling add to the cost another 5–10% (Gevaers et al., 2011). In New York or Mumbai, failed deliveries are the most expensive due to high traffic flow and opportunity costs per driver-hour.

Impact of E-commerce

The unprecedented growth of e-commerce in the last decade has rendered conventional delivery methods unviable. Customers now demand 24-hour or same-day deliveries, creating extreme pressure on logistics systems that are designed for 3–7 day delivery loops. The unprecedented rise in delivery frequency and quantity, fueled by Amazon and Flipkart, also puts extreme pressure on scalable and flexible systems capable of dynamically responding to peaks, rendering traditional systems redundant.

Foundational Logistics Theories and Their Limits Pre-AI

Before AI-based systems arrived, conventional logistics models were the backbone of last-mile planning:

- **Pinciples of Network Design:** These concerned ideal warehouse and distribution center location to minimize total transportation and handling costs (Simchi-Levi et al., 2008).
- **The Transportation Problem:** A linear programming method used to determine the minimum cost distribution schedule from one or more sources to one or more destinations with capacity restrictions (Hillier & Lieberman, 2014).
- **Vehicle Routing Problem (VRP):** A classic combinatorial optimization problem whose goal is to deliver products to various locations at the lowest aggregate cost of routes, time, or distance. Without AI, VRP was solved using stiff algorithms with low flexibility (Laporte, 2009).
- **Inventory Management's Impact:** Poor visibility in the inventory or decoupling of order fulfillment and inventory levels frequently derailed last-mile delivery. EOQ and ROP conventional models did not respond to real-time sales and spikes in demand, leading to stockouts or overstocking within local hubs (Chopra & Meindl, 2016).

THE MOVE TO AI-FOCUSED SOLUTIONS

In order to overcome such past limitations, Artificial Intelligence (AI) has emerged as a revolutionary force in last-mile logistics. AI-facilitated route optimization software now employs real-time variables of traffic, weather, delivery time slots, and driver whereabouts to devise emission-saving, cost-saving routes (Singh, 2025). Not only is this emission-saving and fuel-efficient, but it also increases delivery density and the productivity of workers (Khadem et al., 2023). AI also supports tailored delivery plans, offering customers with new delivery options, real-time updates, and anticipatory communication. These raise customer satisfaction, reduce missed delivery instances, and integrate brand loyalty (Oladele, 2025). Players like Amazon, FedEx, and Alibaba already use AI-based last-mile platforms, establishing efficiency and customer-centric service standards (Biswas, 2023). There are still challenges, however—particularly in emerging economies—due to infrastructural deficiencies, low digital literacy, and research intensity. The technology gap between advanced and emerging economies threatens to widen logistical disparities. The gap needs to be bridged through increased investment in digital infrastructure, greater research from academia, and a heightened level of global cooperation to make AI-powered logistics innovation more democratized (Attah et al., 2024). Closing this gap will provide access to effective, sustainable, and customer-focused last-mile delivery networks globally.

Data Analytics

Data analysis is central to transforming last-mile delivery networks through synergizing with artificial intelligence to optimize routes and deliver tailored customer experiences (Ramasamy et al., 2024; Abdullah, 2024). Driving this change is a myriad of data types—historical delivery history, GPS tracking, IoT sensor feeds, real-time traffic and weather conditions, and customer/order data—derived from telematics devices, mobile applications, CRM systems, and APIs (Oyetoro, 2024). Yet, the integration of such information is problematic, ranging from data silos in order, fleet, and customer service systems, non-standard data formats, real-time acquisition issues, to the sheer quantity and pace of data being acquired (Sundararajan et al., 2023; Al-Ghamdi et al., 2024). Resolution of these challenges requires sound data quality and governance processes because AI-driven intelligence is only as good as the information they operate on—paralleling the maxim of "garbage in, garbage out" and requiring standardized processes to support accuracy, completeness, and consistency (Zhou et al., 2024). When properly leveraged through sophisticated methods such as predictive analysis, clustering models, and real-time processing (Shaikh, 2025; Srinivasan et al., 2024; Abbey et al., 2024), this information facilitates dynamically improved routes, lower transit time, lower operational expenses (Krishnan et al., 2024), and higher customer satisfaction through personalization (Yaiprasert & Hidayanto, 2024) as well as enhanced resilience to disruptions through predictive modeling (Kanase et al., 2024).

Real Time Tracking

Real-time monitoring is a critical aspect of modern-day AI-based last-mile delivery solutions, which enable real-time tracking of the delivery process and therefore increase substantially the operational visibility and customer confidence. The union of AI algorithms elevates mere location tracking to an elite level, adding predictive analytics functionalities to predict arrival time, detect probable disruption, and real-time route reconfiguration (Sungheetha et al., 2023). This ability is vital for real-time route optimization based on real-time traffic, weather, and delivery restrictions to achieve efficient, timely deliveries while reducing operational expenses and fuel (Chaurasia et al., 2024). Additionally, the real-time data these systems gather is the power behind personalization initiatives, enabling customization of delivery options to individual customer preference, e.g., preferred delivery times and special requests. Within low-income nations, where infrastructure is limited, AI-driven real-time tracking can have the ability to revolutionize logistics and make cutting-edge delivery technology affordable. In addition to operational effectiveness, real-time tracking also increases customer control and visibility of their deliveries in terms of live locations, precise ETAs, and interactive rescheduling, ultimately designing a smoother, more interactive delivery process (Xu et al., 2024). This future-oriented logistics management facilitated through the integration of real-time tracking and artificial intelligence not only accelerates delivery speed and efficiency but also favors the global goals of sustainable logistics (Moghaddam & Karimzadeh, 2025) and improved customer satisfaction in the rapidly evolving context of delivery.

Predictive Tools

Machine learning (ML) and artificial intelligence (AI) powered predictive analytics are revolutionizing last-mile delivery operations in a major way by facilitating informed decisions based on precise, real-time information (Agarwal et al., 2021). These sophisticated systems scan enormous amounts of data—such as past delivery history, GPS and IoT-enabled real-time traffic flows (Kolasani, 2024), weather patterns, and customer behavioral trends—to make logistics operations more efficient and predict future delivery challenges. One of the fundamental methods applied in this shift is time series forecasting, whereby artificial intelligence models review past trends in parcel volume and delivery times to project future needs and possible delays. Delivery platforms, for instance, use recurrent neural networks (RNNs) and ARIMA models to forecast spikes in package volume during high-demand seasons like Black Friday or Diwali, making it possible for them to scale up fleet and employee capacity in advance (Hussain et al., 2024). Besides, regression models like linear and multivariate regressions have also been applied extensively to make estimates of delivery times given input parameters like delivery distance, time of day, number of delivery stops, traffic congestion levels, and weather disruptions. For example, Amazon and FedEx utilize regression algorithms to make estimated times of delivery by modeling the relationship between traffic density and travel speed so that dispatch systems can dynamically modify delivery routes (Dey et al., 2025). Specific uses of these technologies are the potential to predict parcel volumes on a daily basis in a given geography based on customers' order history and social media sentiment scores, or predict delivery delays by identifying real-time traffic congestion, accidents, or unplanned road closures through streaming feeds from city traffic APIs and IoT sensors deployed in vehicles. In addition, AI-powered customer profiling software improves personalization by forecasting customer availability windows, preferred communication media (e.g., SMS, email, or app message), and package acceptance probability. This minimizes failed delivery attempts and enhances both customer satisfaction and loyalty. Demand forecasting models are also combined with seasonal, demographic, and promotional data to drive scheduling of resources so that delivery personnel and fleets are best allocated in anticipation of local demand surges in the region. For instance, grocery delivery startups utilize AI to forecast higher weekend demand in residential locations and reallocate resources. Whereas the advantages of such innovations are already clear in developed economies, emerging markets are increasingly adopting such AI solutions in their logistics systems. Such change offers a potential path for inclusive innovation and co-development where AI enables more resilient and equitable delivery networks to bridge the digital divide at the global level (Dey et al., 2025).

AI- powered Route Optimization

AI-based route optimization has appeared as a game-changing solution to the rise in the complexity of last-mile delivery, a challenge fueled by the exponential rise of e-commerce and the expectations of customers for quick, consistent service (Zemanek Jr & Kros, 2024; Munuhwa & Chibaro, 2024). Traditional routing techniques based on static heuristics are unable to cope with the dynamic nature of urban logistics. Artificial Intelligence (AI) provides a more intelligent solution—adaptive, real-time route planning that maximizes delivery performance and minimizes operational drag (Odumbo & Nimma, 2025; Shobhana, 2024).

Advanced AI software utilizes sophisticated algorithms that better the performance of conventional heuristics:

- **Genetic Algorithms (GA)** mimic the evolutionary idea of natural selection. They create various routing solutions, assess them based on fitness criteria like cost, time, or fuel consumption, and iteratively develop these solutions through selection, crossover, and mutation. In the long run, this results in optimal or near-optimal routes for delivery (Kalkha et al., 2023).
- **Simulated Annealing (SA)** draws its inspiration from metallurgy's annealing process, in which metals are heated and slowly cooled to eliminate defects. In logistics, this algorithm has the capability of accepting worse solutions probabilistically in initial stages to avoid getting stuck in local optima, eventually converging to better global routing arrangements (Tamm et al., 2020).
- **Reinforcement Learning (RL)** enables an AI agent to learn best delivery policies through trial and error. The agent is rewarded for efficient action (e.g., early or timely delivery) and penalized for inefficiencies (e.g., delays), continually improving its decision-making strategy by interacting with the environment (Shen et al., 2025).

Such algorithms are context-aware and learn to incorporate multiple parameters, such as real-time traffic information, weather conditions, delivery time windows, driver availability, and vehicle capacity. For example, an RL-powered system can dynamically reallocate a driver in real time if IoT sensors find that there is congestion, re-routing the path in order to fulfill time-window commitments (Rane et al., 2024; Krishnan et al., 2024). Machine learning is also used by AI models to interpret past delivery data, detecting areas of congestion and making predictive corrections. These models continuously improve through feedback mechanisms—driver inputs, GPS trace data, and delivery success—thereby improving their performance in dense cityscapes (Gupta, 2025). Compatibility with IoT and telematics technologies enables recalibration of routes in real-time, allowing for accurate responses to roadblocks, weather disruptions, or last-minute customer shifts. Real-time alignment ensures uniform service even in the midst of turbulent conditions, especially crucial in high-density urban areas (Pugacheva, 2024). In addition, industry and academic research affirms the strategic benefits of AI-driven route optimization. Studies by Dhaliwal (2022) and Sohrabi (2023) identify its revolutionary effect, with keyword co-occurrence analysis demonstrating a strong correlation between AI integration and enhanced delivery KPIs of reliability, punctuality, and fuel efficiency (Ramasamy et al., 2024). Prescriptive analytics are also provided by AI systems—automatically grouping deliveries by location, assigning drivers by capacity and distance, and prioritizing emergency shipments. Not only do they save costs, but they also enhance customer satisfaction (Tabasum & Raghunandan, 2024).

AI- DRIVEN PERSONALIZATION

Artificial Intelligence (AI) is revolutionizing last-mile delivery operations from monolithic, one-size-fits-all to dynamic, hyper-personalized logistics solutions. The change is in the direction of making delivery services personalize and tailor according to individual customers' preferences—ranging from time and place to mode of communication—increasing customer satisfaction, operating performance, and brand loyalty in a competitive e-commerce landscape (Sarma et al., 2020; Johnpaul et al., 2025). Leading this revolution are sophisticated AI techniques such as machine learning (ML), data mining, natural language processing (NLP), and predictive analytics that allow logistics businesses to distill meaningful information from gigantic and dispersed data streams (Campbell et al., 2020). These are the foundation for customized delivery experiences tailored to the unique expectations of each customer.

Core AI Algorithms Enabling Personalization

1. Collaborative Filtering:

This algorithm anticipates customer preferences by monitoring behavioral patterns of comparable users. For instance, if users in a certain demographic group or area tend to choose evening time slots for delivery, collaborative filtering can provide recommendations of the same to new or repeat users in comparable scenarios. Amazon employs this technique to suggest delivery windows that statistically raise first-attempt success rates and minimize delivery friction (Reeyazati & Samizadeh, 2025).

2. Clustering Algorithms for Customer Segmentation

Clustering techniques like K-Means, DBSCAN, or Hierarchical Clustering allow businesses to segment customers based on factors such as delivery timing, population density, order frequency, and receptiveness to communication. These segments enable logistics companies to implement focused strategies—such as locker delivery for tech-friendly urban clients or doorstep service for senior citizens—thereby maximizing customer satisfaction and resource efficiency (Poornimathi et al., 2024).

Real-World Personalization Strategies

Time Window Personalization

AI models can learn preferred delivery time slots through the analysis of order history and delivery feedback and provide them automatically. FedEx and Amazon Flex have implemented similar features, enhancing delivery success rates and scheduling operations in sync with customer availability (Thaker & Parilkar, 2024).

Customized Communication Channels

AI utilizes NLP and engagement metrics to identify customers' native language and communication modes of choice—SMS, in-app notifications, email, or WhatsApp. Myntra, for example, employs AI to send updates in real time in the user's natural language, providing increased response and transparency (Rane et al., 2024).

Dynamic Delivery Spot Recommendations

AI can recommend other pick-up spots like parcel lockers, partner retail stores, or local hubs depending on geo-spatial conduct. Amazon Locker and InPost are excellent examples of this initiative, providing convenience and flexibility for busy customers on the move (Nasrudin, 2024).

Value-Added Preferences (Green & Secure Delivery)

Green delivery slots—composite deliveries or low-emission routes—can be availed by environmentally aware customers, while customers for shipping precious goods can be provided with advanced tracking and security services, all driven by AI knowledge of past purchase history and preference patterns (Shiddiqie, 2024).

Last-Mile Delivery Efficiency

The demand for enhanced last-mile delivery has become the number one priority of every company globally due to the stratospheric rise in e-commerce penetration and increasing consumers' expectations for quicker, guaranteed, and personalized delivery options (Thakur et al., 2024). This last leg of the supply chain, from shipment of merchandise from a hub to the end-user, is also typically the most expensive, timely, and complex leg, most frequently contributing to more than half of the expense of overall delivery. The intersection of increasing consumer expectations, increasing digital-first retailing, and the need for environmentally sustainable results has left businesses with even greater focus on optimizing their last-mile business, where inefficiency is greatest and most costly. This decision node in the logistics network is generally filled with such factors as traffic, urban infrastructure limitations, volatile fuel prices, and uncertainty of customers' opportunity windows, making conventional logistics strategies obsolete in their ability to maneuver this complex situation effectively (Sharma & Tripathi, 2024). And with the birth and widespread deployment of artificial intelligence (AI)-based technology, then, has come the revolution of last-mile delivery using innovative technologies to disintegrate deep-rooted inefficiencies that hitherto dominated traditional delivery patterns (Tabasum & Raghunandan, 2024). Pioneering this revolution is the use of AI-driven route optimisation, where real-time input data on traffic conditions, weather, delivery time, and truck capacity available are fed into dynamically computed most cost-effective delivery routes. They not only reduce delivery time and fuel expenses, and thus generate ginormous savings in operations, but also optimise driver productivity through auto-route and schedule optimisation. Additionally, AI systems learn from historical patterns of delivery, adapting the routing algorithms in real-time and adjusting to evolving realities of the urban landscape for optimal efficiency in the long run. In addition to the route optimization, personalization is another layer that is equally as important and where AI is streamlining the last-mile delivery efficiency, bound and leapfrogging the customer satisfaction and, at the same time, greatly minimizing failed delivery percentages (Kolasani, 2024). Thanks to the requirements of deep customers, delivery availability and delivery pattern, the AI platforms can offer strongly personalized up delivery windows as well as the best matching ones depending on one's requirement and timing. Predictive analytics also facilitate this hub through predictions of potential exceptions or delays in delivery and taking pre-emptive action with customers in advance, thereby creating transparency and trust. These tailor-made last-mile delivery systems also facilitate overall sustainability targets through trip surpluses removal and optimization of vehicle load capacity, greens the delivery process (Bedi et al., 2024). Last-mile delivery operational efficiency is greater than cost and speed, encompassing the entire end-to-end customer experience and environmental factors.AI enhances general operational effectiveness using smart scheduling applications, auto-dispatching tech, and live monitoring, altogether enhancing the quality and transparency of the entire delivery process (Venkateswaran et al., 2024). Besides, AI-decision-making portals allow logistics suppliers to quickly and effectively react to unforeseen downtime like traffic mishaps, barricades, or sudden increases in demand, preserve business continuity and reduce service intermissions. Driver scheduling, load balancing, and dispatch warehouse automation powered by AI minimizes human touch and error and produces leaner, more agile logistics centers. Predictive analytics, which anticipates pattern of demand, delivery volume, and likelihood of bottlenecks, allows the company to pre-book its facilities, balance the number of people in volume, and forecast peak delivery hours so as to deliver optimally and with ease. In fact, AI is more of a paradigm shift than a incremental improvement in last-mile logistics that will render it smarter, greener, more efficient, and ultimately more attuned to the changing priorities of the new consumer economy (Fu, 2025).

Level of Technological Access

The extent of technological access becomes a key driver in effective integration and wide coverage of AI-based solutions for last-mile delivery, especially in relation to route optimization and personalization. Access in this case extends beyond availability to encompass affordability, infrastructure, digital literacy, and institutional context for effective implementation and sustained use of advanced AI technology in different geographical and economic environments. In the developed world, numerous factors like good internet connectivity, high smartphone penetration, well-developed logistics infrastructure, and abundant computational resources provide fertile ground for the effective use of AI-based logistics (Prosper, 2021). These spaces are complemented with proven digital infrastructures that allow for real-time data analysis, precise GPS location monitoring, massive-scale cloud computing, and seamless integration with customer relationship management systems to allow businesses to utilize AI algorithms to intelligently optimize routes in real-time according to real-time traffic, advanced customer preferences, and evolving demand. This leads to enhanced operational effectiveness and enhanced, optimized customer experience. On the other hand, the majority of the developing world is plagued by unbalanced and predominantly restricted access to technology in the form of wide disparities between high-speed internet penetration, poorly developed transport infrastructures, and low levels of IoT-enabled equipment availability, all of which impact the slowdown in the uptake of advanced AI-driven logistics technologies. This constraint is then compounded by the absence of adequate numbers of skilled labor and underlying digital infrastructure required for effective collection, processing, and analysis of huge volumes of parcel-related data. Underrepresentation in the discussion of AI-based last-mile delivery of scientists and stakeholders from the developing world accentuates this broader digital divide, a disproportion not only in deployment but also in knowledge production and innovation. This technological deficit creates a two-tiered structure of progress where the technologically superior economies further drive the lead in innovation and the poorer economies find it hard to keep pace, sometimes even going back on less efficient hand-driven methods or rudimentary digital hardware more susceptible to human fallibility, with slow delivery rates, high operational expenses, and poor consumer satisfaction. Furthermore, the success of AI-driven personalization in last-mile delivery relies on its access to quality and availability of data and infrastructure for interpretation thereof. Low-penetration e-commerce markets and dispersed data environments face such huge challenges in aggregating coherent and pertinent information of users, affecting the quality of personalization and limiting potential for action-oriented feedback loops on which AI systems rely in order to learn and improve themselves on an ongoing basis. Closing these gaps requires joint action to close the technology gap through strategic public-private partnerships, consistent investment in building digital infrastructure, and concentrated efforts to ensure mass digital inclusion. Policymakers in developing nations can set this revolution rolling by actively facilitating foreign direct investment in technology-driven logistics, providing favorable incentives for digital innovation, and supporting massive capacity-building initiatives to improve the technological capabilities of small and medium enterprises. At the same time, international research networks and cross-border logistics companies can also promote a more inclusive technological ecosystem by engaging actively with institutions in lower-represented geographies so that the breakthrough benefits of AI-supported route planning and personalization of last-mile delivery are not just accessible to high-income nations but are equally accessible across different socio-economic and territorial contexts, creating a more inclusive and efficient global logistics ecosystem (Selvakumar et al., 2025; Karulkar et al., 2025).

Ethical and Societal Implications of AI in Last-Mile Delivery

In addition to the strategic and technical benefits of AI route optimization and personalization, it is also important to look at the wider social and ethical considerations of these technologies. As transformative as AI can be for last-mile delivery, its use also presents some urgent issues around work, equity, privacy, and sustainability (Wirtz et al., 2019).

Scenario

Suppose a large e-commerce business operator uses an AI-powered last-mile delivery solution in a city. The AI system utilizes real-time information and machine learning trends to route-optimize and personalize delivery experience based on customers' requirements.

Positive Impacts

Efficiency and Sustainability: The AI system maximizes total delivery time and minimizes fuel usage through dynamic route optimization, conserving greenhouse gases. It enhances urban sustainability and saves costs (Chen et al., 2021).

Improved Customer Experience: Customized delivery times improve customer satisfaction and reduce failed deliveries, leading to higher brand loyalty (Lim et al., 2018).

Negative Effects

Job Displacement: Autonomous delivery vans and autonomous dispatching reduce the need for human drivers and logistics staff needs, encouraging the specter of job displacement, especially in low-skilled markets (Frey & Osborne, 2017).

Upskilling Need: There is an urgent necessity of upskilling currently employed individuals to deal with, understand, and create AI systems. Without training programs, there is a likelihood of a digital divide hurting developing country workforces disproportionately (Bessen, 2019).

Data Privacy and Security: Customer behavior and location data and personal data harvesting for adjusting delivery processing constitute privacy concerns. Without robust data governance, abuse or misuse is possible (Zuboff, 2019).

Algorithmic Bias: Route optimization software inherently under-prioritizes some neighborhoods by history or perceived inefficiency, perpetuating service disparities and exacerbating socioeconomic disparities (Eubanks, 2018).

Since route optimization saves fuel, AI powers power-hungry data centers with ridiculous power needs. The second-order environmental cost must be accounted for on net savings in sustainability (Strubell et al., 2019).

Case Study 1

Optimizing Last-Mile Logistics with AI and ML (https://www.linkedin.com/pulse/optimizing-last-mile-logistics-ai-ml-case-study-india-rachelkar/)

India's booming online shopping business led to a blowout in the demand for reliable last-mile delivery, which the company Delhivery overcame by strategic infusions of Machine Learning (ML) and Artificial Intelligence (AI). By making use of analytics, Delhivery optimizes delivery routes, predicts time of arrival, and minimizes deliveries that do not reach their targets. Machine learning software goes through massive data from GPS traces, delivery history, and customer profiles to yield accurate ETAs and optimal routes to ensure on-time delivery. Customer service is enhanced with AI-based chatbots that solve questions and complaints at the click of a button, keeping the human support minimal. Apart from that, computer vision is also employed in auto-sorting machines by Delhivery to ensure that parcels can be efficiently sorted quickly and precisely, hence increasing processing levels and operational effectiveness. Such an extensive adoption of AI and ML technologies has helped improve significantly Delhivery's delivery effectiveness, lowered operating costs, raised client satisfaction, and established itself among leaders in India's active logistics landscape.

Positive Impacts

- AI and ML assist in providing reliable ETAs and choosing best routes, minimizing delays and failed deliveries
- Automation via ML and computer vision saves human effort and human mistakes, lowering operational expenditures by a huge margin.
- Chatbots powered by AI provide instant assistance, promoting customer satisfaction and minimizing human intervention.
- Real-time analysis assists in anticipatory decision-making for fleet management, stock, and delivery planning.

Negative Impacts

- Deploying AI, ML, and computer vision involves huge capital, which may not be possible for small logistics companies.
- An overdependence on technology might lead to operational lockup in cases of system crashes, cyber attacks, or software malfunctions.
- Customer data and GPS tracking can pose data security and privacy issues, particularly under rigorous data protection laws.

Challenges

- ML and AI machines require clean, organized, and pertinent data, which is often difficult to obtain or consolidate from various sources.
- Constant upgradation and maintenance of AI models, hardware (such as auto-sorters), and software systems must be done in order to remain competitive.
- Staff must be trained for working with AI systems. There is usually resistance to change from established workforces.

- With increasing adoption of AI, adherence to changing laws pertaining to AI ethics, data usage, and labor laws becomes an increasing issue.

Case Study 2

Omdena's AI-Enhanced Route Optimization for Last-Mile Delivery (https://www.omdena.com/blog/ai-enhanced-route-optimization-for-last-mile-delivery-at-omdena)

Omdena collaborated with Latin American logistics company Carryt to overcome last-mile delivery inefficiencies within Bogotá, among other cities. For eight weeks, an international group of 50+ AI engineers and data scientists developed an AI route optimization platform from remote work. The system compared delivery habits, geographical factors, and current traffic patterns in suggesting efficient routes to reduce travel time and fuel consumption. Overcoming issues such as unstructured addresses and underdeveloped infrastructure, the team leveraged geospatial data, clustering, and predictive analytics to develop a dynamic model. The solution drastically lowered delivery times, enhanced fleet efficiency, and enhanced customer satisfaction. The successful pilot in Bogotá set the stage for scaling to other key Latin American cities, illustrating the strength of global AI collaboration to address local challenges and drive sustainable logistics.

Positive Impacts

- AI-based algorithms greatly enhanced delivery efficiency by recognizing the shortest and most efficient routes, reducing delivery time and delays.
- More efficient routes meant less fuel use and lower carbon emissions, contributing to environmentally friendly logistics in heavily congested cities.
- The Omdena model highlighted the strength of global AI collaboration in pooling together multiple expertise to efficiently address localized challenges.

Negative impacts

- Long-term AI deployment may result in decreased demand for manual planning and logistics jobs, affecting employment.
- Over-reliance on AI systems may result in exposure if the system crashes or is hacked.
- Unless properly designed, AI models may inadvertently favor some routes or neighborhoods, resulting in service imbalances.

Challenges

- Poor internet connectivity, outdated digital infrastructure, and traffic unpredictability made real-time data collection difficult.
- Recurring updates in traffic movement, road closure, and climate necessitated that the AI model be extremely flexible and reactive.
- Insufficient historical delivery and traffic data of quality limited the initial training and validation of the AI models.

Case Study 3

DoorDash's Machine Learning Solutions for Last-Mile Connectivity (https://analyticsindiamag.com/it-services/how-doordash-uses-ml-to-solve-last-mile-connectivity)

DoorDash uses machine learning to coordinate the intricacies of last-mile food delivery. Their AI software forecasts demand, estimates restaurant cooking times, and considers real-time traffic to determine best delivery routes. The system adaptively allocates Dashers by location, history, and expected demand, dynamically reallocating for surges in orders to avoid backlogs. This data-driven methodology has optimized operations, reduced delivery times and improved customer satisfaction, and optimized resource allocation. Through ongoing learning from each delivery, DoorDash has turned a problematic logistical process into a smooth and seamless experience for both restaurants and customers.

Positive Impacts

- Precise order volume predictions enable optimal assignment of Dashers to reduce wait times and maximize operational efficiency.
- Smart assignment of drivers based on location, experience, and demand patterns maximizes productivity and minimizes downtime.
- Real-time adjustment for kitchen slowdowns, traffic, and order spikes maintains a seamless and predictable delivery experience.

Negative Impacts

- Excessive use of algorithms can miss exceptional circumstances needing human intuition or local know-how.
- Drivers might sense the system as opaque or biased, particularly if they are assigned difficult routes or reduced orders as a result of algorithmic judgments.

Challenges

- Reliable AI forecasting depends on gigantic quantities of tidy, high-quality data—which is tricky to maintain across all territories uniformly.
- Making adjustments for erratic variables such as abrupt weather fluctuations, demonstrations, or road blocks continues to be a technical challenge
- AI can maximize efficiency, but it also sets up expectations—any failure can result in discontent and public outrage.

FUTURE DIRECTIONS

The application of AI in last-mile delivery has the potential to make dramatic improvements in efficiency, cost reduction, and customer satisfaction in retail. But implementation is successful only if data quality, regulation, and existing systems are given careful consideration. Future research must explore new AI algorithms for dynamic cityscapes and autonomous delivery systems. It is crucial to create AI to handle real-world complexity and address ethical issues like data privacy and bias. Synergies with blockchain for transparency and IoT monitoring also hold potential. Real-world implementation challenges in a range of global environments, including infrastructure limitations and digital divides, also need consideration. Research should also study the scalability and adaptability of AI solutions, their impact on the workforce and the necessity of upskilling, and the development of ethics to provide data security, transparency, and positive societal impacts for a sustainable last-mile delivery transformation worldwide.

CONCLUSION

This chapter has offered a critical and academic analysis of the revolutionary role of Artificial Intelligence (AI) in last-mile delivery in the retail and e-commerce supply chain. It has explained the evolution of AI from its early rule-based systems to the current machine learning, deep learning, and reinforcement learning algorithms and how these have revolutionized logistics by enabling real-time, data-driven decision-making in activities such as route optimization and delivery customization. With meticulous examination of route optimization using AI application, real-time locationing, segmentation of customers, predictive analytics, and automated dispatching, the chapter shows how AI has made a behemoth leap in maximizing the efficiency of operations, reducing delivery times, minimizing fuel consumption, and enhancing customer satisfaction levels to all-time highs. This revolution has its limitations and drawbacks. Although the encouraging advancements are welcome, actual deployment of AI-driven solutions still depends on a set of enabling conditions: quality and mass data, robust digital infrastructure, regulatory environments, and organizational readiness. The gap between developing and advanced economies, and other moral concerns such as job displacement, data protection, and discrimination through algorithms, are issues that need immediate attention if AI is to provide sustainable and inclusive logistic innovation. Also, the social implications that span from environmental conservation to labor reorganization highlight the need for logical and ethical uptake of these technologies. Synthesizing these findings, it is clear that AI does not exist in an isolation chamber; rather, it is a component of larger logistical, technological, and societal systems. Its effect is amplified when integrated with other technologies like Internet of Things (IoT), edge computing, and cloud infrastructure and supported with strategic leadership, ethical governance, and customer orientation. The chapter also illustrates with some examples from around the world how AI already begun reshaping delivery models so that big players in the logistics sector and local players can take advantage of agility, resilience, and scalability against growing customer requirements and complexity in the market.The potential for AI in last-mile delivery is gigantic but yet to get underway. Subsequent research will have to explore the convergence of new technologies such as autonomous transport vehicles, drone delivery systems, and blockchain openness for further optimization of last-mile logistics. Special focus must be given to developing adaptive models of AI able to perform in low-data, poor-infrastructure situations common in emerging economies. Research must also focus on the human factor—how AI impacts work, justice, and community resilience—and develop roadmaps for ethics-driven AI regulation, workforce re-skilling, and policy convergence. Moreover, geographically differentiated innovation in AI solutions based on local cultural, infrastructural, and regulatory differences by geography will be critical in inducting growth inclusively.

REFERENCES

Abbey, A. B. N., Eyo-Udo, N. L., & Olaleye, I. A. (2024). Implementing Advanced Analytics for Optimizing Food Supply Chain Logistics and Efficiency.

Abdullah, S. S. (2024). THE IMPACT OF THE ON-DEMAND ECONOMY ON MALAYSIAN LOGISTICS. *PIONEERING THE FUTURE: DELVING INTO E-LEARNING'S LANDSCAPE*, 35.

. Al-Khatib, A., Saif, D. A., Al-Husseini, O., Al-Tamimi, L., Al-Qawasmeh, Y., Batan, A., & Al-Najjar, H. Last-Mile Delivery with Artificial Intelligence: Dynamic Routing, Predictive Analytics, and Sustainable Logistics Solutions in the E-Commerce Era.

Attah, R. U., Garba, B. M. P., Gil-Ozoudeh, I., & Iwuanyanwu, O. (2024). Enhancing supply chain resilience through artificial intelligence: Analyzing problem-solving approaches in logistics management. *International Journal of Management & Entrepreneurship Research*, *5*(12), 3248–3265.

Attah, R. U., Ogunsola, O. Y., & Garba, B. M. P. (2023). Revolutionizing logistics with artificial intelligence: Breakthroughs in automation, analytics, and operational excellence. *Iconic Research and Engineering Journals*, *6*(12), 1471–1493.

Bach, N. H. A., & Hoang, C. C. (2025). Exploring the Evolution of Distribution in E-Commerce: A Bibliometric Analysis. *Journal of Distribution Science*, *23*(1), 79–93.

Bedi, P., Das, S., Goyal, S. B., Rajawat, A. S., & Kautish, S. (2024). Revolutionizing sustainability: the role of robotics in supply chains. In *Computational Intelligence Techniques for Sustainable Supply Chain Management* (pp. 225–273). Academic Press. DOI: 10.1016/B978-0-443-18464-2.00007-8

Bessen, J. E. (2019). *AI and Jobs: The Role of Demand.* NBER Working Paper No. 24235.

Biswas, S. (2023). Assimilation of 'Artificial Intelligence'(AI) in 'Amazon': An in depth Research Case Study. *Globsyn Management Journal, 17.*

Campbell, C., Sands, S., Ferraro, C., Tsao, H. Y. J., & Mavrommatis, A. (2020). From data to action: How marketers can leverage AI. *Business Horizons*, *63*(2), 227–243. DOI: 10.1016/j.bushor.2019.12.002

Chaurasia, A., Parashar, B., & Kautish, S. (2024). Applications of artificial intelligence in Echo Global Logistics. In *Computational Intelligence Techniques for Sustainable Supply Chain Management* (pp. 405–428). Academic Press. DOI: 10.1016/B978-0-443-18464-2.00009-1

Chen, W., Men, Y., Fuster, N., Osorio, C., & Juan, A. A. (2024). Artificial intelligence in logistics optimization with sustainable criteria: A review. *Sustainability (Basel)*, *16*(21), 9145. DOI: 10.3390/su16219145

Chen, Z., Pan, S., Zhong, R. Y., & Liu, D. (2021). Managing last-mile delivery through intelligent optimization and planning: A review. *Transportation Research Part E, Logistics and Transportation Review*, *151*, 102400.

Dey, A. K., Mukherjee, D., Ghosh, A. K., Satsangi, A., & Mandal, B. K. (2025). AI and Sustainable E-commerce.

Dhaliwal, A. (2022, December). Towards AI-driven transport and logistics. In *Workshop on e-Business* (pp. 119-131). Cham: Springer Nature Switzerland.

El Makhloufi, A. (2023). AI application in transport and logistics: opportunities and challenges (An Exploratory Study).

Eubanks, V. (2018). *Automating Inequality: How High-Tech Tools Profile, Police, and Punish the Poor*. St. Martin's Press.

Fatorachian, H. (2024). Leveraging Artificial Intelligence for Optimizing Logistics Performance: A Comprehensive Review. *Global Journal of Business Social Sciences Review (GATR-GJBSSR)*, *12*(3).

Frey, C. B., & Osborne, M. A. (2017). The future of employment: How susceptible are jobs to computerisation? *Technological Forecasting and Social Change*, *114*, 254–280. DOI: 10.1016/j.techfore.2016.08.019

Fu, R. J. (2025). The Future of AI, ML, and Robotics in Business and Beyond. *Artificial Intelligence, Machine Learning, &. Robotics in Business, 1*(1), 8–22. DOI: 10.32473/aimlrb.1.1.138290

Garikapati, D., & Shetiya, S. S. (2024). Autonomous vehicles: Evolution of artificial intelligence and the current industry landscape. *Big Data and Cognitive Computing*, *8*(4), 42. DOI: 10.3390/bdcc8040042

Gowsalya, M., & Mayuri, K. N. (2025). Revolutionizing the Sustainable Supply Chain of Medical Product With AI-Driven Drone Delivery: Innovations in Supply Chain Management Through Autonomous UAV Technology in Healthcare. In *Ecological and Human Dimensions of AI-Based Supply Chain* (pp. 69-96). IGI Global Scientific Publishing.

Gupta, V. (2025). Leveraging AI and ML for Logistics Excellence: Case Studies and Success Strategies. In *Supply Chain Transformation Through Generative AI and Machine Learning* (pp. 313-346). IGI Global Scientific Publishing.

Japiassu, N. (2022). *AI-Powered Logistics and Mobility as a Service (MaaS)*. Driving the Future of Autonomous Vehicles and Smart Transportation.

Johnpaul, M., Miryala, R. S. B., Mazurek, M., Jayaprakashnarayana, G., & Miryala, R. K. (2025). Artificial Intelligence and Machine Learning in eCommerce. In *Strategic Innovations of AI and ML for E-Commerce Data Security* (pp. 31–58). IGI Global.

Kale, A. A. (2024). Modern AI in Green Logistics: Smart Systems for Sustainability and Carbon Reduction.

Kalkha, H., Khiat, A., Bahnasse, A., & Ouajji, H. (2023). The rising trends of smart e-commerce logistics. *IEEE Access : Practical Innovations, Open Solutions*, *11*, 33839–33857. DOI: 10.1109/ACCESS.2023.3252566

Kanase, R., Chitnis, A., & Priyadarshi, R. (2024, May). Assessing the feasibility of last-mile delivery alternatives using fuzzy AHP in the Indian Urban Context. In *2024 2nd International Conference on Advancement in Computation & Computer Technologies (InCACCT)* (pp. 547-552). IEEE. DOI: 10.1109/InCACCT61598.2024.10551042

Kanyepe, J. (2025). Data-Driven Logistics Optimization: Powering the Digital Supply Chain. In Impacts of Technology on Operations Management: Adoption, Adaptation, and Optimization (pp. 63-96). IGI Global.

Rane, N., Choudhary, S., & Rane, J. (2024). Artificial intelligence and machine learning for resilient and sustainable logistics and supply chain management. Available at *SSRN* 4847087.

Karulkar, Y., Shah, A., & Naik, R. (2025). AI-Powered Business Evolution: Transformative Strategies for Success of Evolving Industries. In *Creating AI Synergy Through Business Technology Transformation* (pp. 39-72). IGI Global.

Khadem, M., Khadem, A., & Khadem, S. (2023). Application of artificial intelligence in supply chain revolutionizing efficiency and optimization. *International journal of industrial engineering and operational research, 5*(1), 29-38.

Khalifa, L., & Volkov, N. (2024). E-commerce Supply Chain Strategies: Meeting the Demands of Online Retail. *Social Dynamics Review, 7*(1), 1–9.

Kolasani, S. (2024). Connected cars and autonomous vehicles: personalizing owner/customer experiences and innovation using AI, IoT, Blockchain, and Big Data. *International numeric journal of machine learning and robots, 8*(8), 1-17.

Krishnan, R., Perumal, E., Govindaraj, M., & Kandasamy, L. (2024). Enhancing Logistics Operations Through Technological Advancements for Superior Service Efficiency. In *Innovative Technologies for Increasing Service Productivity* (pp. 61–82). IGI Global. DOI: 10.4018/979-8-3693-2019-8.ch004

Lim, S. F. W. T., Jin, X., & Srai, J. S. (2018). Consumer-driven e-commerce: A literature review, design framework, and research agenda on last-mile logistics models. *International Journal of Physical Distribution & Logistics Management, 48*(3), 308–332. DOI: 10.1108/IJPDLM-02-2017-0081

Madhumithaa, N., Elangovan, G., Sridharan, S., & Karthick, L. ul Islam, A., & Venkatesh, R. P. (2024). Cutting-Edge AI-Powered Driverless Delivery Solution. In *Trends and Applications in Mechanical Engineering, Composite Materials and Smart Manufacturing* (pp. 129-145). IGI Global.

Moghaddam, G. K., & Karimzadeh, M. (2025). AI-Driven Digital Transformation and Sustainable Logistics: Innovations in Global Supply Chain Management.

Munuhwa, S., & Chibaro, M. (2024). E-Commerce Logistics Unleashed: Automation, Artificial Intelligence Challenges, and Triumphs. In *Applications of New Technology in Operations and Supply Chain Management* (pp. 145-163). IGI Global.

Muthukalyani, A. R. (2023). Optimizing Last-Mile Delivery in Retail Through AI-Powered Routing and Scheduling. [IJCET]. *International Journal of Computer Engineering and Technology, 14*(2).

Nasrudin, M. F. (2024). Integrating Advance Technology and Logistics Customer Service for Optimal Logistics Performance: A Study at Shopee Express Pangalengan Branch. *Integrating Advance Technology and Logistics Customer Service for Optimal Logistics Performance: A Study at Shopee Express Pangalengan Branch.*

Odumbo, O. R., & Nimma, S. Z. (2025). Leveraging Artificial Intelligence to Maximize Efficiency in Supply Chain Process Optimization. *Int J Res Publ Rev, 6*(1), 3035–3050. DOI: 10.55248/gengpi.6.0125.0508

Oladele, O. K. (2025). AI in Retail: Personalized Shopping Experiences, Inventory Management, and Supply Chain Optimization.

Oyetoro, A. (2024). *The Application of Technology in Logistics.*

Patil, D. (2024). Artificial Intelligence In Retail And E-Commerce: Enhancing Customer Experience Through Personalization, Predictive Analytics, And Real-Time Engagement. *Predictive Analytics, And Real-Time Engagement (November 26, 2024).*

Paul, R. K., & Sarkar, B. (2021). AI-powered forecasting algorithms to optimize last mile delivery. *Journal ID, 2811*, 6201.

Ponomarenko, I., & Ponomarenko, D. (2023). AI-Powered Logistics and Digital Marketing for Business Optimisation. *Economics & Education, 8*(4), 27–33. DOI: 10.30525/2500-946X/2023-4-4

Poornimathi, K., Kumar, A. D., & Srinithi, A. (2024, April). ROUTESENSE–An AI powered solution to Car pooling systems. In *2024 10th International Conference on Communication and Signal Processing (ICCSP)* (pp. 1168-1174). IEEE. DOI: 10.1109/ICCSP60870.2024.10543353

Prosper, J. (2021). Scalable AI Architectures for E-Commerce and Retail.

Pugacheva, O. (2024). Basic directions for the use of artificial intelligence technologies in the transportation and logistics sector. In *Competitivitatea şi inovarea în economia cunoaşterii* (pp. 89-98).

Ramasamy, I., Natarajan, S., & Sathyamoorthy, V. K. P. (2024). Does disruptive technology and AI (Artificial Intelligence) influence logistics management? *Multidisciplinary Science Journal, 6*(12), 2024259–2024259. DOI: 10.31893/multiscience.2024259

Rane, N., Choudhary, S., & Rane, J. (2024). Artificial intelligence and machine learning for resilient and sustainable logistics and supply chain management. *Available at SSRN* 4847087. DOI: 10.2139/ssrn.4847087

Reeyazati, A., & Samizadeh, R. (2025). Targeted and Personalized Online Advertising in the Age of Artificial Intelligence (AI): A Literature Review and Research Agenda. *International Journal of Supply and Operations Management, 12*(1), 105–122.

Reyana, A., & Kautish, S. (2024). Machine learning techniques for route optimizations and logistics management description. In *Computational Intelligence Techniques for Sustainable Supply Chain Management* (pp. 197–224). Academic Press. DOI: 10.1016/B978-0-443-18464-2.00010-8

Sarma, W., Nagavalli, S. P., & Sresth, V. (2020). Leveraging AI-Driven Algorithms to Address Real-World Challenges in E-Commerce: Enhancing User Experience, Fraud Detection, and Operational Efficiency. *International Journal of Research and Analytical Reviews, 7*, 2348–1269.

Selvakumar, P., Shanthi, M., Pitchiah, R., Sharma, M., Dahake, P. S., & TC, M. (2025). The Role of Artificial Intelligence in Business Model Innovation: Overview of AI Technologies. *AI-Driven Business Model Innovation*, 219-246.

Shaikh, Z. P. (2025). Supply Chain Processes Through Artificial Intelligence and Machine Learning: Application of Demand Planning, Reinforcement Learning, and Product Clustering. In *Supply Chain Transformation Through Generative AI and Machine Learning* (pp. 379-408). IGI Global Scientific Publishing.

Sharma, D., & Tripathi, K. (2024). Navigating the digital age: smart manufacturing and logistics. In *Recent Trends in Artificial Intelligence Towards a Smart World: Applications in Industries and Sectors* (pp. 99–144). Springer Nature Singapore. DOI: 10.1007/978-981-97-6790-8_4

Shen, B., Dong, C., & Chan, H. L. (2025). Operational Research Models for E-Commerce Platforms: New Technology Innovation. *Asia-Pacific Journal of Operational Research*, •••, 2502001. DOI: 10.1142/S0217595925020014

Shiddiqie, S. R. A. (2024). Artificial Intelligence-driven Supply Chain Management: Exploring Adoption and Implications in the Turkish Context. *İKTİSAT VE İŞLETME*, 111.

Shobhana, N. (2024). AI-powered supply chains towards greater efficiency. In *Complex AI Dynamics and Interactions in Management* (pp. 229–249). IGI Global. DOI: 10.4018/979-8-3693-0712-0.ch011

Singh, B. (2025). Revolutionizing Supply Chains for Optimized Demand Planning, Inventory Management, and Logistics: An In-Depth Analysis of AI and ML Solutions in the Modern Era. In *Supply Chain Transformation Through Generative AI and Machine Learning* (pp. 103-128). IGI Global Scientific Publishing.

Sohrabi, M. (2023). Artificial Intelligence in Logistic Industry. *Implementation of disruptive technologies in supply chain management, 73.*

Sorooshian, S., Khademi Sharifabad, S., Parsaee, M., & Afshari, A. R. (2022). Toward a modern last-mile delivery: Consequences and obstacles of intelligent technology. *Applied System Innovation*, *5*(4), 82. DOI: 10.3390/asi5040082

Srinivasan, K., Chauhan, G. S., Jadon, R., Budda, R., Gollapalli, V. S. T., & Garikipati, V. (2024). AI-DRIVEN OPTIMIZATION MODELS FOR E-COMMERCE SUPPLY CHAINS: INTEGRATING HMO, MAXENT RL, TS, AND MDVRP FOR ENHANCED DEMAND FORECASTING, INVENTORY MANAGEMENT, AND DELIVERY EFFICIENCY.

Strubell, E., Ganesh, A., & McCallum, A. (2019). *Energy and policy considerations for deep learning in NLP*. *Proceedings of the 57th Annual Meeting of the Association for Computational Linguistics*, 3645–3650. DOI: 10.18653/v1/P19-1355

Sungheetha, A., Bharathi, B., Ganesan, D., Karthikeyan, T., & Madhavi, N. B., & KR, C. L. (2023, November). E-Commerce Business Model Analysis and Success in Urban Areas Using AI-Distributed Machine Learning. In *2023 International Conference on Research Methodologies in Knowledge Management, Artificial Intelligence and Telecommunication Engineering (RMKMATE)* (pp. 1-6). IEEE. DOI: 10.1109/RMKMATE59243.2023.10369718

Suraj, P., Shetty, P. P., Suhas, B. E., & Pranav, H. M. (2024, November). Predictive Analytics and AI in Logistics: Driving Operational Excellence and Cost Reduction. In *2024 8th International Conference on Computational System and Information Technology for Sustainable Solutions (CSITSS)* (pp. 1-6). IEEE.

Tabasum, H., & Raghunandan, G. (2024). FUTURE TRENDS AND INNOVATIONS IN AI COMMERCE. *Applications of Artificial Intelligence in Commerce and Mathematics*, 98.

Takawale, P. S., Omkar, K., Maitery, K., & Kale, A. (2024). DeliveRite AI Hub: A Review of Innovations in AI-Powered Logistics and Delivery Systems. *ITSI Transactions on Electrical and Electronics Engineering*, *13*(2), 41–46.

Tamm, K., Leht, R., Vaher, M., Rebane, K., Poder, A., Batan, A., & Kask, L. (2020). Transformative Impacts of Artificial Intelligence on E-Commerce Supply Chain Management: Enhancing Transparency, Mitigating Risks, and Advancing Adaptive Logistics Strategies.

Thaker, B., & Parilkar, S. (2024). UNDERSTANDING CUSTOMER PERCEPTION: EXPLORING THE ROLE OF ARTIFICIAL INTELLIGENCE IN PERSONALIZED SERVICE FOR Q-COMMERCE BUSINESS MODEL.

Thakur, S., Sandhu, S., & Yehuwalashet, F. (2024). E-Commerce and Trade: The Role of Artificial Intelligence. In *Handbook of Artificial Intelligence Applications for Industrial Sustainability* (pp. 232-248). CRC Press.

Vaka, D. K. (2024). From Complexity to Simplicity: AI's Route Optimization in Supply Chain Management. *Journal of Artificial Intelligence. Machine Learning and Data Science*, *2*(1), 386–389.

Venkateswaran, P. S., Sriramkumar, M., Vaddy, R. K., Kotagiri, A., Rajest, S. S., & Regin, R. (2024). Applications of Artificial Intelligence and Robots in Service Industries. In *Advancing Intelligent Networks Through Distributed Optimization* (pp. 61–80). IGI Global. DOI: 10.4018/979-8-3693-3739-4.ch004

Wasilewski, A., Chawla, Y., & Pralat, E. (2025). Enhanced E-commerce Personalization Through AI-Powered Content Generation Tools. *IEEE Access : Practical Innovations, Open Solutions*, *13*, 48083–48095. DOI: 10.1109/ACCESS.2025.3550956

Wirtz, B. W., Weyerer, J. C., & Geyer, C. (2019). Artificial Intelligence and the Public Sector—Applications and Challenges. *International Journal of Public Administration*, *42*(7), 596–615. DOI: 10.1080/01900692.2018.1498103

Xu, S., Zhang, X., Kim, R., & Su, M. (2024). Anthropomorphic last-mile robots and consumer intention: An empirical test under a theoretical framework. *Journal of Retailing and Consumer Services*, *81*, 104028. DOI: 10.1016/j.jretconser.2024.104028

Yaiprasert, C., & Hidayanto, A. N. (2024). AI-powered in the digital age: Ensemble innovation personalizes the food recommendations. *Journal of Open Innovation, 10*(2), 100261. DOI: 10.1016/j.joitmc.2024.100261

Yerra, S. IMPROVING CUSTOMER SATISFACTION WITH PREDICTIVE ANALYTICS IN LOGISTICS AND DELIVERY SYSTEMS.

Zemanek Jr, J. E., & Kros, J. F. (2024). Risk-Mitigation Strategies for Autonomous Delivery Vehicles in the Last Mile: A Comprehensive Overview of the Current State and Future Potential of Autonomous Delivery Technologies in the Supply Chain. *Journal of Comprehensive Business Administration Research.*

Zuboff, S. (2019). *The Age of Surveillance Capitalism: The Fight for a Human Future at the New Frontier of Power.* PublicAffairs.

Chapter 5 Demand Forecasting and Optimized Inventory Management in E-Grocery Last-Mile Delivery: Leveraging Predictive Analytics

Venkatesh Ganapathy

https://orcid.org/0000-0001-7500-2877

ICFAI Business School, India

ABSTRACT

The e-grocery industry faces unique challenges in demand forecasting and inventory management due to the perishable nature of many products and the complexity of last-mile delivery. Leveraging predictive analytics offers a transformative solution by harnessing AI-driven algorithms to forecast consumer demand with high accuracy. These tools analyze historical sales data, consumer behaviors, and external factors, such as weather or regional events, to anticipate future demand patterns. Predictive analytics allows businesses to optimize inventory levels, ensuring that products are available without overstocking or waste, which is particularly crucial for perishable goods like fresh produce. Additionally, predictive analytics

DOI: 10.4018/979-8-3373-2833-1.ch005

plays a key role in optimizing last-mile delivery by enabling real-time route planning and minimizing delivery costs. As the industry continues to expand, integrating predictive analytics will be crucial for maintaining competitiveness, sustainability, and customer satisfaction, marking a step toward supply chain optimization in e-grocery services.

INTRODUCTION

The e-grocery industry faces unique challenges in managing perishable goods and navigating the complexities of last-mile logistics. Traditional forecasting methods, which primarily rely on historical data and basic predictive models, often struggle to accurately predict demand for perishable items like fresh produce, dairy, and meats. These goods are sensitive to factors such as changing customer preferences, seasonality, shelf life, and local demand variations. Consequently, inaccurate forecasts can lead to stock outs, excessive spoilage, and inefficient inventory management, all of which contribute to significant financial losses and poor customer experiences.

In addition to the forecasting difficulties, last-mile delivery for e-groceries is highly dynamic, affected by real-time variables like traffic patterns, weather conditions, and unpredictable order volumes. These factors further complicate the timely delivery of perishable goods, resulting in delays, food quality degradation, and increased operational costs.

As a result, traditional forecasting approaches in e-grocery supply chains often lead to errors in the range of 30-50%, necessitating a more sophisticated and adaptive solution to optimize demand prediction and last-mile delivery operations.

The objective of this study is to explore how Artificial Intelligence (AI) and Machine Learning (ML) can address the inherent limitations of traditional forecasting methods in e-grocery supply chains. By integrating AI/ML techniques, this research aims to significantly reduce forecasting errors by 30-50%, resulting in more accurate demand predictions for perishable goods and optimized last-mile logistics. Through the application of AI/ML models, we seek to enhance inventory management, reduce food waste, and ensure that customers receive their grocery orders on time, all while improving cost-efficiency and customer satisfaction.

E-Grocery Industry: An Overview

The global e-grocery industry is undergoing unprecedented growth, projected to expand from $595.58 billion in 2024 to $3.61 trillion by 2033 at a 22.17% compound annual growth rate. This surge is particularly evident in the U.S., where the market is expected to reach $715.54 billion by 2033, driven by 77.8 million active online grocery households. Key growth drivers include consumer demand for convenience, with 72% of users favoring single fulfillment methods like curbside pickup, alongside rapid technological adoption of AI-powered personalization engines and automated reordering systems. Infrastructure advancements, such as strategically located dark stores and micro-fulfillment centers, further support this expansion by enabling 10-minute delivery windows in urban areas.

Challenges in Managing Perishable Goods

Managing perishable goods presents unique challenges, accounting for 30% of global food waste. Shelf-life constraints require precise FIFO/FEFO inventory rotation, particularly for fresh produce and dairy, while maintaining strict temperature controls between 2-8°C for pharmaceuticals and 4°C for fresh items (Kumar et al, 2020).

FIFO (First In, First Out) and FEFO (First Expired, First Out) are inventory rotation methods critical for managing perishable goods and minimizing waste. FIFO ensures that the oldest stock (first received) is used or sold first, regardless of expiration dates. This method is ideal for non-perishable items or products without strict shelf-life requirements, such as electronics or textiles. It simplifies warehouse organization by arranging items chronologically, reducing the risk of obsolescence for goods with longer shelf lives. FEFO prioritizes items with the earliest expiration dates, even if they were received later. It is mandatory in regulated industries like pharmaceuticals and food, where product safety and compliance are paramount. For example, vaccines or fresh produce are managed using FEFO to prevent distribution of expired goods and ensure sufficient remaining shelf life for end users (Imran et al, 2025).

Demand volatility compounds these issues, with fresh goods experiencing 40% demand fluctuations due to weather and seasonal patterns. This delicate balance between overstocking and stockouts contributes significantly to the $218 billion annual food waste in the U.S. alone. Technological solutions like warehouse management systems with real-time batch tracking and IoT temperature sensors are becoming critical, complemented by AI-driven forecasting tools that have demonstrated 95% error reduction in SKU-level predictions through advanced LSTM networks.

Advanced Long Short-Term Memory (LSTM) networks are a type of recurrent neural network (RNN) specifically designed to address the limitations of traditional RNNs in capturing long-range dependencies in sequential data. LSTM networks are equipped with specialized memory units that enable them to retain information over extended periods, making them particularly effective for time-series forecasting, sequence prediction, and tasks where context from previous time steps is crucial. Advanced LSTM models often incorporate variations such as bidirectional LSTMs (which process data in both forward and backward directions) or stacked LSTMs (multiple layers of LSTM units) to enhance model performance. These enhancements allow LSTMs to better capture complex patterns and trends in data, making them ideal for applications in dynamic and volatile environments, such as demand forecasting in e-grocery supply chains or last-mile logistics. Additionally, advancements like attention mechanisms and hybrid LSTM models further improve the ability to focus on relevant time periods, increasing predictive accuracy and overall model efficiency (Hochreiter & Schmidhuber, 1997; Graves, 2013; Bai, Zhan, & Zhang, 2018; Vaswani et al., 2017).

Complexities in Last Mile Delivery

Last-mile delivery complexities remain the industry's most formidable obstacle, representing 53% of total shipping costs. Operational inefficiencies manifest through first-attempt delivery failures that increase costs by 15-20%, necessitating dynamic routing algorithms that adapt to real-time traffic and weather conditions. Customer expectations have escalated, with

67% of consumers demanding mid-route delivery changes and 2-hour delivery windows becoming standard in urban markets. Sustainability pressures are driving innovation in electric vehicle adoption, projected to reach 35% of metro fleets by 2025, alongside reusable packaging systems and route optimization strategies that reduce fuel consumption by 10-15% (Nandy & Padhy, 2025; Tudisco et al ., 2025).

INTEGRATED SOLUTIONS FRAMEWORK

Leading operators are implementing integrated solutions combining predictive analytics stacks with automated fulfillment systems. These include demand-sensing algorithms that incorporate weather and event data, voice-picking warehouse technologies, and drone delivery systems for urgent pharmaceutical shipments. Customer-centric innovations like AR-powered quality verification during delivery and carbon-neutral checkout options are reshaping consumer expectations. Looking ahead, the industry is moving toward hyperlocal 15-minute delivery networks powered by neighborhood dark stores, blockchain-enabled freshness traceability systems, and autonomous robotic picking systems capable of handling 200+ SKUs per hour. As food e-commerce penetration reaches 15-20% in major markets, success will depend on harmonizing AI-driven inventory optimization with agile logistics frameworks to simultaneously address profitability and sustainability challenges (Shuaibu, Mahmoud, & Sheltami, 2025).

Last-mile delivery (LMD) remains a critical component of modern logistics, significantly influencing operational costs, efficiency, and customer experience. This review examines key optimization strategies, emphasizing AI-driven decision-making systems, IoT-enabled real-time tracking, and hybrid delivery models combining autonomous and traditional vehicles. AI enhances predictive analytics and dynamic route adjustments, while IoT sensors improve fleet monitoring and exception management. Hybrid networks integrating drones, ground robots, and conventional fleets demonstrate potential to reduce energy consumption and expand delivery coverage in congested urban areas. Sustainable solutions, such as electric vehicle adoption and shared delivery hubs, further address environmental concerns. However, challenges persist, including scalability limitations, regulatory hurdles for autonomous systems, and infrastructure gaps for green technologies. Economic feasibility remains a barrier to widespread implementation of advanced solutions like drone deliveries. This analysis highlights evolving trends in LMD optimization, advocating for updated regulatory frameworks, cross-sector collaborations, and innovation in scalable technologies to balance cost-efficiency with sustainability. The integration of AI, IoT, and hybrid networks offers a pathway to resilient, eco-friendly logistics systems, though strategic investments and policy alignment are essential for overcoming adoption barriers (Shuaibu, Mahmoud, & Sheltami, 2025).

The e-grocery sector has undergone transformative growth since the COVID-19 pandemic, driven by shifting consumer preferences toward faster and more sustainable delivery options. A critical innovation in this space involves integrating third-party logistics (3PLs) through on-demand vehicle networks to address last-mile delivery challenges. Recent research by Tudisco et al. (2025) proposes an optimization model that redefines traditional vehicle routing by incorporating on-demand fleet design alongside delivery scheduling, balancing cost efficiency with environmental sustainability. Their extended vehicle routing problem with time windows (VRPTW) framework introduces three objective functions: cost-minimization, emission-reduction, and a balanced cost-environmental approach. Through an Italian case study, the authors demonstrate that prioritizing environmental objectives can reduce emissions by over 90% while maintaining service quality, with only marginal increases in annual operational costs (Tudisco et al., 2025). The model enables retailers to dynamically adjust fleet composition using 3PL partnerships, eliminating the need for large capital investments in dedicated delivery vehicles. Key contributions include actionable insights into sustainable fleet optimization, a mathematical framework for joint route-fleet design, and empirical validation using real-world data. These findings emphasize how environmental considerations can fundamentally reshape fleet composition strategies while maintaining profitability in fast-moving e-grocery markets (Tudisco et al., 2025).

Last-mile delivery (LMD) remains a critical component of modern logistics, significantly influencing operational costs, efficiency, and customer experience. This review examines key optimization strategies, emphasizing AI-driven decision-making systems, IoT-enabled real-time tracking, and hybrid delivery models combining autonomous and traditional vehicles. AI enhances predictive analytics and dynamic route adjustments, while IoT sensors improve fleet monitoring and exception management. Hybrid networks integrating drones, ground robots, and conventional fleets demonstrate potential to reduce energy consumption and expand delivery coverage in congested urban areas. Sustainable solutions, such as electric vehicle adoption and shared delivery hubs, further address environmental concerns. However, challenges persist, including scalability limitations, regulatory hurdles for autonomous systems, and infrastructure gaps for green technologies. Economic feasibility remains a barrier to widespread implementation of advanced solutions like drone deliveries. This analysis highlights evolving trends in LMD optimization, advocating for updated regulatory frameworks, cross-sector collaborations, and innovation in scalable technologies to balance cost-efficiency with sustainability. The integration of AI, IoT, and hybrid networks offers a pathway to resilient, eco-friendly logistics systems, though strategic investments and policy alignment are essential for overcoming adoption barriers (Jahnke, Ulrich, Pesch, Senge, & Langrock, 2025).

AI/ML Models for Reducing Forecasting Errors in E-Grocery Supply

AI/ML models have become crucial in addressing the challenges of forecasting demand in the e-grocery supply chain, particularly in the context of perishable goods and last-mile delivery. Traditional methods often fall short when it comes to accounting for dynamic factors such as seasonal demand shifts, promotions, customer behavior changes, and disruptions in supply chains. AI-driven predictive analytics use historical data to create more accurate demand forecasts by incorporating numerous influencing factors that traditional models may miss. Machine learning algorithms, such as decision trees, support vector machines, and neural networks, allow for the identification of complex patterns and nonlinear relationships in data, which are often present in e-grocery demand. Specifically, neural networks, including deep learning architectures like Convolutional Neural

Networks (CNN) and Long Short-Term Memory (LSTM) networks, are highly effective in handling large volumes of data and identifying trends over long periods. By applying deep learning to demand forecasting, e-grocery businesses can make real-time predictions, adjust inventory levels proactively, and reduce spoilage for perishable goods.

In addition to predictive models, reinforcement learning (RL) has emerged as a powerful technique for dynamic decision-making in the supply chain. RL models are capable of continuously improving their predictions and actions through feedback from the environment, which is essential in highly volatile and unpredictable e-grocery markets. For instance, an RL-based approach can optimize delivery routes, manage fleet deployment, and dynamically adjust to disruptions such as traffic, weather, or last-minute changes in demand. The integration of AI/ML algorithms in both forecasting and delivery optimization leads to significant reductions in forecasting errors, improving inventory management, and minimizing waste in perishable goods. Furthermore, these technologies can enhance last-mile delivery efficiency by enabling more accurate demand predictions and real-time adjustments in logistics operations (Elvas, Tokkozhina, Martins, & Ferreira, 2023).

Inventory Optimization Mechanics

Effective inventory optimization is a critical aspect of supply chain management, particularly within the e-grocery industry, where demand is dynamic and perishable goods require special attention. To streamline inventory management and improve supply chain efficiency, it is necessary to implement stock-level formulations that accommodate the complexities of perishable goods, safety stock calculations, and last-mile synchronization. These key factors help e-grocery businesses strike a balance between having sufficient stock and minimizing waste, ultimately leading to better service delivery and cost management (Fernandez Vazquez-Noguerol, 2021).

One of the central challenges in inventory optimization for e-grocery operations is the differentiation between perishable items, such as fresh produce, and non-perishable packaged goods. Perishable items have a limited shelf life and must be handled with much more care than packaged products. Inventory management for fresh produce must take into account spoilage rates, temperature sensitivity, and the need for frequent replenishment. A well-optimized system uses demand forecasting models and real-time data to predict when items will sell out or expire, ensuring that stock levels are aligned with actual consumer demand.

For packaged goods, which are more durable and have longer shelf lives, the inventory optimization mechanics are less stringent. However, they still benefit from AI-driven tools that forecast demand accurately, minimizing overstocking and ensuring that items are always available to customers. By applying different stock-level formulations based on perishability, businesses can more effectively manage inventory for both types of products. This approach is particularly crucial in reducing waste and increasing profitability in the e-grocery sector, where unsold fresh produce can lead to significant losses (Do & Omdahl, 2018).

Safety stock is a crucial component of inventory optimization, designed to buffer against uncertainties in demand and supply chain disruptions. In the context of e-grocery, safety stock calculations must be dynamic to account for the rapid changes in consumer demand, especially for perishable goods. Traditional static safety stock models often fall short in the face of unpredictable fluctuations, leading to either excessive inventory levels or stockouts.

AI-driven dynamic buffer adjustments address this issue by leveraging machine learning algorithms to continuously monitor and adjust safety stock levels in real-time based on factors like historical sales data, seasonal trends, and external variables such as weather patterns or regional events. This dynamic approach allows for more accurate safety stock levels, ensuring that businesses maintain an optimal inventory balance without overstocking or understocking. As a result, AI-driven systems not only minimize waste but also ensure that customer demand is met promptly, improving service levels and operational efficiency (Calzavara et al., 2023).

Last-mile synchronization is a vital element in the optimization of the e-grocery supply chain, ensuring that deliveries are made in a timely, cost-effective manner. One of the key aspects of last-mile synchronization is delivery window optimization. With the aid of AI and predictive analytics, businesses can optimize the timing of deliveries by using demand heatmaps, which provide insights into when and where specific products are likely to be in high demand.

By analyzing historical order data and real-time information, predictive routing systems can adjust delivery schedules to ensure that items are delivered at the most optimal time. For example, demand heatmaps can reveal peak delivery windows for certain regions or specific customer segments, allowing delivery drivers to plan their routes more efficiently. This helps to minimize delivery delays, reduce transportation costs, and enhance overall customer satisfaction by ensuring that products arrive within the designated time frame (Cagliano et al., 2017).

Dark stores, which are retail facilities dedicated solely to fulfilling online orders without serving customers on-site, have become an increasingly important part of e-grocery logistics. The proper allocation of inventory across these dark stores is essential for maintaining supply chain efficiency and meeting customer expectations. Neural network-based inventory positioning systems are an effective solution to optimize dark store allocations.

These AI-powered systems use deep learning techniques to analyze sales patterns, inventory levels, and other relevant factors to determine the best placement of products within dark stores. By optimizing inventory positioning, businesses can reduce picking time, improve order fulfillment speed, and ensure that the most popular items are stocked at the appropriate locations. This approach also helps to manage inventory more effectively, minimizing the risk of stockouts and reducing the need for last-minute replenishments.

Neural network-based inventory positioning is particularly effective in complex multi-echelon systems, where goods are stored across various locations and fulfillment centers. By incorporating data from multiple sources, such as customer demand, product type, and geographic region, these systems can ensure that inventory is distributed in a way that maximizes efficiency and customer satisfaction (Calzavara et al., 2023).

Inventory optimization in e-grocery supply chains requires the implementation of sophisticated strategies that consider perishability constraints, dynamic safety stock adjustments, and efficient last-mile synchronization. AI-driven tools, such as predictive demand forecasting, machine learning-based dynamic buffer adjustments, and neural network-powered inventory positioning, are revolutionizing how businesses manage inventory and deliver products to customers. By addressing the specific needs of perishable goods, optimizing delivery windows, and improving dark store allocations, e-grocery companies can enhance operational efficiency, reduce waste, and ensure a seamless customer experience. As the e-grocery sector continues to grow and evolve, leveraging these advanced technologies will be crucial for staying competitive and meeting the ever-increasing demand for fast, reliable, and sustainable deliveries (Fernandez Vazquez-Noguerol, 2021; Cagliano et al., 2017).

CASE STUDIES: AI/ML APPLICATIONS IN E-GROCERY SUPPLY CHAIN OPTIMIZATION

The application of AI and machine learning (AI/ML) in e-grocery supply chains has become a game-changer, transforming various aspects of operations from demand forecasting to last-mile delivery optimization. Several real-world case studies illustrate the tangible benefits of AI/ML technologies in the e-grocery sector, particularly in improving demand forecasting accuracy, reducing waste, and enhancing overall delivery performance.

A notable example of AI/ML's impact can be seen in Walmart's use of AI for demand forecasting. Walmart, one of the largest e-grocery players globally, has leveraged machine learning models to improve its demand forecasting, especially for perishable goods. Traditionally, demand forecasting in retail has relied heavily on historical sales data, which can often be outdated or insufficient for capturing short-term fluctuations, particularly in the context of perishable goods. By integrating AI/ML algorithms such as deep learning and neural networks, Walmart is now able to predict demand with much greater accuracy, factoring in not only historical data but also external factors like weather, local events, and consumer sentiment. This improved forecasting has led to a significant reduction in waste, particularly for perishable items like fresh produce and dairy, as well as better stock replenishment decisions that reduce out-of-stock situations. Walmart's AI-driven system uses both predictive analytics and reinforcement learning to dynamically adjust forecasts as new data becomes available, helping the company stay agile in a fast-moving market.

Another key case study comes from Instacart, an on-demand grocery delivery service that serves as a prime example of how AI/ML technologies can streamline delivery performance. Instacart has implemented machine learning algorithms to optimize its delivery network, focusing on improving route planning and delivery time predictions. Using real-time data from traffic, weather, and order volumes, Instacart's AI models can dynamically adjust routes for drivers, ensuring that deliveries are made as efficiently as possible. This is particularly important in the context of last-mile delivery, where delays due to unforeseen circumstances, such as traffic congestion or weather disruptions, can significantly impact customer satisfaction. By using machine learning to optimize delivery times and route choices, Instacart has been able to improve its operational efficiency, reduce fuel consumption, and ultimately deliver a more reliable service to customers. Furthermore, AI models have allowed Instacart to improve the accuracy of delivery time windows, leading to greater customer satisfaction and repeat business (Ciger et al., 2022)

Amazon Fresh, Amazon's own e-grocery division, provides another example of how AI/ML technologies have been implemented to enhance supply chain optimization. Amazon Fresh uses advanced machine learning algorithms to predict the demand for specific products at a granular level, even within specific geographic locations. These predictions enable Amazon to allocate resources more efficiently, ensuring that warehouses are stocked with the right amount of products at the right time. In addition, Amazon's use of AI extends to its last-mile delivery optimization, where machine learning models optimize routes and schedules to ensure timely delivery to customers. By predicting demand fluctuations in real time and adjusting delivery strategies dynamically, Amazon has been able to significantly reduce delivery costs, improve customer experience, and minimize waste. Additionally, Amazon has integrated AI-powered robotics into its fulfillment centers, automating the picking and packing processes, which accelerates delivery times and enhances operational efficiency (Mkansi & Masilela, 2025)

Ocado, a UK-based online-only grocery retailer, has also made significant strides in AI/ML adoption. Ocado uses machine learning algorithms to predict demand at the level of individual items and customer preferences. This allows for precise stock management and the reduction of waste, particularly in perishable goods. In addition, Ocado employs AI-powered robotic systems within its warehouses to pick and pack orders with exceptional speed and accuracy. This not only reduces the need for human labor but also minimizes errors in the picking process, leading to a more efficient and cost-effective supply chain. Ocado's AI-based route optimization models for its delivery fleet further improve last-mile delivery by predicting traffic patterns, optimizing delivery schedules, and reducing the overall environmental impact of the delivery process (Elvas et al., 2023)

Sainsbury's, another UK-based supermarket chain, has also incorporated AI/ML into its supply chain to optimize demand forecasting and reduce waste. Sainsbury's uses machine learning algorithms to analyze data from its stores and online channels to predict demand for both non-perishable and perishable goods. The system uses a range of variables, including customer purchasing history, product seasonality, and external data like weather forecasts, to improve its forecasts and adjust stock levels accordingly. As a result, Sainsbury's has been able to reduce waste and improve its inventory management, especially for perishable items like fruits and vegetables, which are more sensitive to fluctuations in demand. Moreover, the integration of AI-driven demand forecasting with delivery route optimization has allowed Sainsbury's to make its logistics more efficient, ensuring that deliveries are made in a timely and cost-effective manner.

Finally, Tesco, one of the largest grocery retailers in the UK, has developed an advanced AI/ML-driven system to reduce food waste and optimize supply chain performance. Tesco uses machine learning models to predict demand fluctuations and ensure that fresh produce is delivered to its stores and customers at the right time. The system also helps Tesco optimize its last-mile delivery operations, using real-time traffic data, weather conditions, and customer preferences to ensure timely deliveries. By improving forecasting accuracy and operational efficiency, Tesco has managed to reduce food waste, lower costs, and improve customer satisfaction, making it one of the leaders in AI adoption in the e-grocery space (Elvas et al., 2023)

In conclusion, the integration of AI/ML models into the e-grocery supply chain has already demonstrated tangible benefits in demand forecasting, waste reduction, and delivery performance optimization. As evidenced by the case studies of Walmart, Instacart, Amazon Fresh, Ocado, Sainsbury's, and Tesco, AI/ML applications are not only enhancing operational efficiency but also creating more sustainable and customer-centric business models. By leveraging the power of predictive analytics, machine learning, and real-time data, these companies are transforming the way e-grocery operations are managed, with AI-driven solutions providing a competitive edge in an increasingly complex and dynamic market. As e-grocery continues to grow, the role of AI/ML technologies will only become more critical in driving efficiencies, enhancing customer satisfaction, and reducing the environmental impact of last-mile delivery (Singh & Kaur, 2023).

IMPLEMENTATION STRATEGIES FOR AI/ML IN E-GROCERY SUPPLY CHAINS

The application of artificial intelligence (AI) and machine learning (ML) in e-grocery supply chains has become a transformative force, providing solutions for demand forecasting, inventory management, and delivery optimization. With the ever-growing complexity of consumer expectations, the volatility of demand, and the pressure to reduce costs while improving service quality, AI/ML technologies offer a promising avenue for enhancing e-grocery operations. However, the adoption of these technologies requires a strategic approach to ensure effective implementation. This article outlines the practical steps for implementing AI/ML solutions in e-grocery supply chains, covering data collection, model development, training, and integration into existing systems for forecasting demand and optimizing delivery logistics.

The first step in implementing AI/ML solutions in the e-grocery supply chain is the collection of high-quality, relevant data. AI and ML models rely heavily on data for both training and prediction. In the e-grocery sector, data can come from various sources, including customer transactions, inventory levels, historical demand, delivery times, and external factors such as weather or local events (Masi, Ciccullo, & Pero, 2021).

Data collection in e-grocery is often more challenging compared to other industries due to the dynamic and perishable nature of the products involved. Grocery products have varying shelf lives, and their demand can fluctuate based on factors like seasonality, promotions, and even social media trends. Therefore, e-grocery companies must ensure they have robust systems in place for collecting data from all stages of the supply chain, including supplier data, point-of-sale (POS) systems, logistics data, and customer feedback. Integrating Internet of Things (IoT) sensors, RFID tags, and GPS technology into the supply chain can also provide valuable real-time data on the condition and location of products, which is particularly important for perishable items (Jackson et al., 2024).

For example, AI/ML models can use data from temperature sensors in the cold chain to ensure products like frozen or chilled items are stored and transported under optimal conditions. This integration of real-time data will allow AI systems to predict not just demand but also potential risks in the supply chain, such as delays or temperature breaches, that may affect the quality and availability of products (Jackson et al., 2024).

Once data has been collected, the next step is to develop the AI/ML models that will be used to forecast demand and optimize delivery logistics. The choice of model depends on the specific use case, the type of data available, and the objectives of the supply chain optimization. Common AI/ML models used in e-grocery supply chains include time-series forecasting models, regression models, neural networks, and reinforcement learning algorithms (Masi, Ciccullo, & Pero, 2021).

For demand forecasting, traditional statistical methods like ARIMA (AutoRegressive Integrated Moving Average) or more advanced models such as LSTMs (Long Short-Term Memory networks) can be used to predict future demand based on historical data. However, more advanced AI/ML algorithms like deep learning models can provide superior accuracy by capturing complex patterns in data that may be missed by traditional models (Masi, Ciccullo, & Pero, 2021). These models are particularly useful in the highly variable and dynamic environment of e-grocery, where demand can change rapidly due to various factors like promotions, weather, or regional events.

For last-mile delivery optimization, reinforcement learning (RL) algorithms are particularly effective. RL models can learn to optimize delivery routes dynamically by receiving feedback from the environment in the form of rewards and penalties. This allows them to improve their decision-making over time and adapt to changing conditions, such as traffic or last-minute changes in delivery schedules. A model can be trained to minimize costs, reduce delivery time, and even reduce carbon emissions by considering factors such as optimal route planning, vehicle capacity, and fuel efficiency (Jackson et al., 2024).

Once the AI/ML model has been developed, it needs to be trained using historical data. Training the model involves feeding it a large volume of data to allow it to learn patterns and make predictions. During the training phase, it is essential to ensure that the model is not overfitting or underfitting. Overfitting occurs when a model is too closely aligned to the training data and performs poorly on unseen data, while underfitting occurs when the model fails to capture the complexity of the data (Masi, Ciccullo, & Pero, 2021).

One of the best practices for model training is the use of cross-validation techniques, where the data is split into multiple subsets to evaluate the model's performance on different portions of the dataset. For instance, in demand forecasting, cross-validation can help assess how well the model predicts future demand by testing it on data that was not part of the training set. Additionally, it is important to regularly retrain the models as new data is collected to ensure the model adapts to changes in consumer behavior, market conditions, and other factors that may affect demand (Masi, Ciccullo, & Pero, 2021).

For e-grocery companies, incorporating real-time data into the training process is vital. With continuous data from multiple sources—such as sales, inventory, and customer behavior—AI/ML models can evolve over time to become more accurate. For instance, integrating real-time data from delivery fleets or IoT sensors in the cold chain helps the system learn to adjust for unforeseen disruptions, such as traffic delays or temperature fluctuations in the supply chain (Jackson et al., 2024).

Implementing AI/ML solutions successfully requires seamless integration with existing e-grocery systems. This can be a significant challenge, as many e-grocery companies rely on legacy systems that may not be designed to support advanced AI/ML algorithms. Therefore, the integration process must be carefully planned to ensure that new AI/ML models complement existing processes, rather than disrupting operations.

One key area for integration is with inventory management systems. AI/ML models for demand forecasting can provide valuable insights to help inventory managers make more informed decisions about stock levels. However, these models need to be integrated with warehouse management systems (WMS) to ensure that the forecasted demand translates into optimal stock replenishment orders. Similarly, AI/ML-driven delivery optimization models need to be integrated with existing routing and dispatch systems to provide real-time updates to delivery drivers (Masi, Ciccullo, & Pero, 2021).

To facilitate this integration, e-grocery companies can adopt cloud-based platforms that support flexible and scalable AI/ML solutions. Cloud platforms allow for the easy exchange of data between different systems, and their scalability enables companies to expand their AI/ML capabilities as their operations grow. Furthermore, APIs (Application Programming Interfaces) can be used to link AI/ML models with other enterprise systems, ensuring that data flows seamlessly between demand forecasting, inventory management, and delivery logistics systems (Jackson et al., 2024).

After implementing AI/ML solutions, it is crucial to continuously monitor their performance and make adjustments as needed. AI/ML models are not static; they need to be continually updated and improved to account for new data, market conditions, and changes in consumer behavior. This is especially important in the dynamic e-grocery environment, where consumer preferences and external factors can shift rapidly (Masi, Ciccullo, & Pero, 2021).

Performance monitoring can be done using key performance indicators (KPIs) such as forecast accuracy, inventory turnover rates, order fulfillment times, and delivery efficiency. Regular performance reviews and audits can help identify areas where the models are not performing as expected and highlight areas for improvement. For instance, if a demand forecasting model consistently underestimates the demand for certain products, it can be retrained with updated data or adjusted to account for seasonal trends and market conditions (Jackson et al., 2024).

Furthermore, the feedback loop from the AI/ML models should be used to fine-tune the algorithms. As the system receives new data from the supply chain, it can adjust its predictions and decisions. For example, a delivery optimization system that uses real-time traffic data can learn from past delivery outcomes to make better route decisions over time, leading to continuous improvement in delivery efficiency (Jackson et al., 2024).

The implementation of AI/ML in e-grocery supply chains represents a powerful tool for enhancing operational efficiency, reducing waste, and improving customer satisfaction. By following a structured approach that involves data collection, model development, training, integration, and continuous monitoring, e-grocery companies can harness the potential of AI/ML to optimize demand forecasting and last-mile delivery logistics. However, the successful implementation of AI/ML technologies requires careful planning and execution to ensure that these solutions integrate smoothly with existing systems and adapt to changing market conditions. As demonstrated by Jackson et al. (2024), the benefits of AI/ML in optimizing cold chain management and Masi et al. (2021) in advancing the digitalization of supply chains, AI/ML technologies have the potential to revolutionize the e-grocery sector and drive future growth.

EVALUATION AND IMPACT ASSESSMENT OF AI/ML SOLUTIONS IN E-GROCERY SUPPLY CHAINS

The integration of artificial intelligence (AI) and machine learning (ML) in e-grocery supply chains has shown remarkable promise in addressing longstanding challenges such as demand forecasting inaccuracies, inventory management inefficiencies, and the complexity of last-mile delivery optimization. However, the true impact of these technologies can only be understood through a detailed evaluation that assesses their effectiveness in real-world applications. This assessment should focus on the measurable results they generate in key areas such as reducing forecasting errors, improving inventory control, and enhancing delivery efficiency.

Demand forecasting is a critical component in e-grocery supply chains, particularly because grocery products are perishable and subject to fluctuating demand patterns. Traditional forecasting methods, such as moving averages or simple regression models, often fail to capture the dynamic nature of consumer demand, leading to either stockouts or excess inventory. AI/ML technologies, particularly deep learning and reinforcement learning algorithms, have demonstrated significant improvements in reducing forecasting errors by capturing complex patterns in data and making real-time adjustments based on new inputs.

AI-driven models, such as Long Short-Term Memory (LSTM) networks, have shown particular promise in demand forecasting. LSTMs are capable of analyzing long-term dependencies in time-series data, which is essential for understanding seasonal demand variations and the impact of events (e.g., holidays, promotions, weather) on customer behavior (Jahnke et al., 2025). Studies have revealed that these models can reduce forecasting errors by up to 30-50%, improving accuracy in predicting product demand at granular levels (Jackson et al., 2024). Such improvements help e-grocery retailers optimize stock levels, reducing both stockouts and waste, which is critical when dealing with perishable goods.

In addition to LSTMs, reinforcement learning (RL) has also proven effective in adapting forecasts based on real-time market conditions. For instance, an RL-based forecasting model might adjust predictions dynamically based on real-time data from sales transactions, weather reports, or shifts in customer purchasing behavior (Masi, Ciccullo, & Pero, 2021). This adaptive capability allows the model to better anticipate fluctuations in demand, leading to more accurate stock management and fewer forecasting errors, which has a direct impact on profitability and customer satisfaction.

One of the core challenges in e-grocery supply chains is maintaining optimal inventory levels. Overstocking leads to higher holding costs and potential product spoilage, especially for perishable goods, while understocking results in stockouts and missed sales opportunities. AI/ML models significantly improve inventory management by providing data-driven insights that allow for better stock control, optimal replenishment strategies, and effective demand planning.

AI solutions can help optimize inventory in various ways. For example, predictive analytics powered by AI can forecast demand patterns not only at the product level but also across different locations and time periods, ensuring that inventory levels are adjusted accordingly. This helps e-grocery retailers avoid overstocking or understocking products and improve the flow of goods through their distribution centers and last-mile delivery networks. AI-driven inventory management systems use real-time data to trigger automatic restocking orders, ensuring that products are available when needed without unnecessarily tying up capital in excess inventory (Elvas et al., 2023).

In addition, machine learning algorithms can help optimize the distribution of products across various warehouses and delivery hubs, taking into account regional demand fluctuations and transportation efficiency. By using historical sales data and predictive models, AI solutions can allocate products to specific warehouses or stores based on anticipated demand in different geographic areas (Jahnke et al., 2025). This dynamic inventory allocation helps minimize transportation costs and speeds up the replenishment process, ultimately leading to cost savings and faster delivery times.

Furthermore, AI/ML algorithms can help identify slow-moving products that may need to be discounted or removed from the inventory to reduce waste. In the case of perishable goods, AI models can prioritize the sale of products approaching their expiration dates, ensuring that they are sold before they become unsellable, thus minimizing food waste and maximizing revenue.

The last-mile delivery process in e-grocery supply chains is one of the most costly and challenging aspects of the operation. It is highly complex due to the need for timely deliveries, handling perishables with care, and navigating traffic-congested urban environments. AI/ML solutions, particularly in route optimization, autonomous delivery technologies, and real-time fleet management, have significantly enhanced the efficiency of last-mile delivery in e-grocery logistics.

AI-powered route optimization algorithms use real-time traffic data, historical delivery patterns, and customer preferences to determine the most efficient delivery routes for drivers. By constantly adjusting to changing conditions, such as traffic jams or last-minute order additions, these models help reduce delivery times and fuel consumption. Reinforcement learning models can further enhance delivery efficiency by continuously learning and optimizing delivery routes over time, adjusting for variables such as weather conditions, peak traffic times, and customer delivery windows (Elvas et al., 2023).

For example, a study of AI-powered delivery systems in an urban e-grocery environment found that route optimization algorithms resulted in a 15-20% reduction in delivery time and a corresponding decrease in fuel usage (Jackson et al., 2024). The ability to optimize delivery routes in real-time also reduces the environmental footprint of e-grocery deliveries, aligning with sustainability goals that many e-grocery companies are striving to achieve.

In addition to route optimization, the integration of autonomous vehicles, drones, and robots into last-mile delivery networks has shown significant potential for enhancing delivery efficiency. AI models that control autonomous delivery vehicles can reduce reliance on human drivers, cut labor costs, and improve scalability, particularly in dense urban environments where traffic congestion can severely impact delivery efficiency. For instance, drone-based delivery models have been shown to provide faster deliveries in areas where traditional vehicle-based systems struggle to meet the demand (Masi, Ciccullo, & Pero, 2021). Autonomous systems can also provide more precise scheduling, helping to further reduce delivery windows and increase the predictability of delivery times, which is vital for customer satisfaction.

Additionally, AI can help optimize fleet management by predicting vehicle maintenance needs and scheduling repairs before problems occur. This proactive approach minimizes downtime and ensures that delivery vehicles are operating at peak efficiency, reducing delays and operational costs. AI systems can also track the status of deliveries in real-time, providing updates to both customers and delivery teams, thus improving communication and enhancing the overall customer experience (Elvas et al., 2023).

The success of AI/ML solutions in e-grocery supply chains can be measured by assessing key performance indicators (KPIs) such as forecasting accuracy, inventory turnover rates, order fulfillment time, delivery efficiency, and customer satisfaction. Implementing AI/ML technologies in demand forecasting and inventory management has been shown to increase the accuracy of product availability predictions, reducing waste and stockouts. For instance, AI-driven demand forecasting models can achieve up to a 50% reduction in forecasting errors, which leads to better stock availability and fewer missed sales opportunities (Jackson et al., 2024).

In terms of last-mile delivery, AI-powered optimization has resulted in a significant reduction in delivery time and operational costs. Route optimization algorithms can reduce delivery times by up to 20%, while autonomous vehicles and drones offer additional cost-saving opportunities by reducing the need for human labor and increasing delivery capacity (Elvas et al., 2023). Furthermore, AI models can improve customer satisfaction by providing accurate delivery time windows and reducing the frequency of delayed deliveries.

On the environmental side, AI/ML solutions in e-grocery supply chains contribute to sustainability by optimizing delivery routes and reducing energy consumption. As more companies adopt electric vehicles (EVs) and green technologies, the impact of AI-driven logistics solutions becomes even more significant, helping e-grocery businesses lower their carbon footprint and contribute to sustainable supply chain practices (Elvas et al., 2023).

The integration of AI/ML technologies in e-grocery supply chains has had a profound impact on improving forecasting accuracy, optimizing inventory management, and enhancing last-mile delivery efficiency. These technologies have proven to be effective in reducing forecasting errors, lowering operational costs, improving delivery times, and enhancing the customer experience. As e-grocery businesses continue to face pressure to meet customer expectations while maintaining profitability, the role of AI/ML in driving supply chain optimization will only grow more important. The results from real-world applications have demonstrated that AI/ML solutions not only improve supply chain performance but also contribute to sustainability goals, making them a crucial tool in the future of e-grocery logistics.

CONCLUSION

The e-grocery industry has undergone significant transformation in recent years, driven largely by advances in artificial intelligence (AI) and machine learning (ML). As the demand for online grocery shopping continues to grow, the efficiency of the supply chain becomes even more critical. For e-grocery businesses, achieving precise demand forecasting, effective inventory management, and timely last-mile delivery are essential to meeting customer expectations while maintaining profitability. This is where AI and ML technologies have shown immense potential, transforming traditional approaches and optimizing complex, dynamic processes in e-grocery supply chains.

Throughout this exploration of AI/ML applications in the e-grocery sector, several key findings have emerged that underscore the transformative power of these technologies.

AI plays a crucial dual role in both demand sensing and achieving inventory leanness within the e-grocery supply chain. By leveraging advanced algorithms, AI can analyze historical data, customer behavior, and real-time market fluctuations to predict future demand with remarkable accuracy. This enables businesses to anticipate consumer needs more effectively, leading to smarter purchasing and stock management decisions. Furthermore, AI-driven demand sensing helps minimize excess inventory, reducing waste, especially for perishable goods, and supporting leaner, more cost-efficient operations. The industry-wide implication of this shift is profound, marking a move from traditional, reactive supply chains to more proactive, predictive systems. Instead of merely responding to demand after it arises, AI-powered systems allow e-grocery businesses to anticipate and plan for demand spikes or drops in advance. This predictive capability enables better allocation of resources, smoother operations, and enhanced customer satisfaction by ensuring products are available without overstocking or understocking. The adoption of predictive supply chains also lays the groundwork for more agile and resilient business models, capable of adjusting quickly to market shifts, consumer preferences, and disruptions, ultimately transforming how businesses engage with customers and optimize their logistics.

AI and ML have revolutionized demand forecasting in e-grocery by enabling businesses to make more accurate predictions based on historical data, consumer trends, and real-time information. Traditional forecasting models, such as moving averages or exponential smoothing, have proven inadequate in the fast-paced, volatile world of e-grocery, especially when dealing with perishable goods. AI models, including deep learning techniques like Long Short-Term Memory (LSTM) networks, have proven capable of accounting for the long-term dependencies in demand patterns, reducing forecasting errors by significant margins. These improvements not only help businesses optimize stock levels but also minimize waste, reduce stockouts, and ensure the timely availability of products.

Another major benefit of AI/ML technologies is in inventory management. The use of predictive analytics, machine learning algorithms, and real-time data feeds has enabled better inventory control and stock management across multiple locations. AI models can dynamically adjust stock levels based on predicted demand fluctuations, optimizing stock distribution across warehouses and reducing instances of overstocking or understocking. These advancements have been particularly useful for perishable goods, which require more precise management to prevent spoilage and loss. AI-driven inventory systems also contribute to sustainability by helping businesses manage resources more efficiently and reduce food waste.

Last-mile delivery is arguably the most critical and expensive segment of the e-grocery supply chain. AI and ML have significantly enhanced the efficiency of this process by optimizing routes, reducing delivery times, and lowering operational costs. Advanced algorithms can adjust delivery routes in real-time based on traffic conditions, weather patterns, and other variables, ensuring that products reach customers quickly and with minimal delays. The integration of autonomous vehicles, drones, and robots into last-mile delivery networks has further streamlined the process, offering the potential for cost savings and increased scalability. In addition, AI-driven systems can forecast and manage delivery windows more accurately, improving the customer experience and boosting satisfaction levels.

AI and ML have also shown promise in helping e-grocery businesses achieve their sustainability goals. By optimizing routes, reducing delivery distances, and enhancing the use of electric vehicles or green technologies, AI/ML applications contribute to reducing the carbon footprint of delivery operations. The integration of sustainable technologies, such as electric delivery vehicles, coupled with AI-based route optimization, can help reduce fuel consumption and minimize emissions, which aligns with the growing demand for eco-friendly supply chain practices. Furthermore, better inventory management and waste reduction directly support environmental sustainability by reducing the amount of perishable goods that go unsold or are discarded.

Emerging Trends in E-Grocery Forecasting and Logistics

As AI/ML continues to evolve, several emerging trends are shaping the future of e-grocery supply chains. These trends not only promise to improve operational efficiency but also offer new ways to address the industry's challenges.

1. AI-Driven Predictive Analytics

The use of predictive analytics in e-grocery is expected to expand further, particularly with the advent of more sophisticated AI models capable of learning from vast amounts of data. As AI systems become more adept at analyzing historical data, customer behavior patterns, and external variables, businesses will be able to anticipate demand fluctuations with even greater accuracy. Predictive analytics will allow e-grocery retailers to better align inventory with expected demand, minimizing waste and optimizing the distribution process. This will be especially important as e-grocery providers expand their product offerings and enter new markets.

2. Advanced Automation in Last-Mile Delivery

Automation will continue to play a pivotal role in the evolution of last-mile delivery. AI-powered autonomous vehicles, drones, and robots are increasingly being integrated into logistics networks to provide faster, more efficient, and cost-effective delivery solutions. Drones, for example, can bypass traffic congestion and deliver products directly to customers, especially in urban areas. Similarly, autonomous vehicles equipped with AI algorithms can reduce human intervention, cut labor costs, and improve scalability. These automation technologies, coupled with AI-driven optimization tools, will make it possible to handle higher volumes of deliveries while maintaining high standards of service.

3. Integration of Internet of Things (IoT) with AI/ML

The integration of IoT with AI and ML is another area poised for growth in the e-grocery supply chain. IoT sensors can provide real-time data on product conditions (e.g., temperature, humidity), allowing businesses to monitor the status of perishable goods throughout the supply chain. When combined with AI/ML analytics, this data can be used to improve demand forecasting, optimize storage conditions, and minimize spoilage. Additionally, IoT-enabled smart shelves and automated inventory tracking systems will provide real-time updates on stock levels, improving inventory management and reducing the risk of stockouts.

4. Personalized Customer Experiences

AI/ML technologies are also opening new avenues for creating personalized customer experiences. By analyzing purchase histories, preferences, and browsing behaviors, AI algorithms can generate personalized recommendations and promotions tailored to individual customers. This level of personalization enhances the shopping experience, increases customer satisfaction, and encourages repeat purchases. Furthermore, AI models can predict when customers are likely to reorder specific items, helping businesses anticipate demand more accurately and stock the right products in advance.

5. Blockchain and AI Integration for Transparency

Blockchain technology, combined with AI, has the potential to significantly enhance transparency and traceability in the e-grocery supply chain. Blockchain can provide a secure, decentralized record of every transaction and movement of goods, ensuring that customers and retailers have access to real-time information about the origins of products, their journey through the supply chain, and their quality. This integration will enhance the credibility of the e-grocery industry and improve consumer trust, particularly in areas such as food safety, sustainability, and ethical sourcing.

Future Technologies in E-Grocery Logistics

The future of e-grocery logistics will likely be shaped by the continued advancement of AI/ML technologies, alongside other cutting-edge innovations. As the demand for online grocery shopping grows, the need for more advanced, scalable solutions will increase.

Edge AI integration, combined with 5G-enabled devices, holds transformative potential for real-time prediction updates in the e-grocery supply chain. By processing data at the edge, closer to where it is generated, AI models can make faster, more responsive decisions. In e-grocery logistics, this can significantly enhance demand forecasting, inventory management, and last-mile delivery, reducing delays and improving operational efficiency. With the speed and low latency of 5G, real-time adjustments to inventory levels, customer demand, and delivery routes can be executed instantaneously, ensuring that products are always available when needed, especially for time-sensitive and perishable goods. Additionally, the integration of sustainability initiatives within e-grocery operations has become a key area of focus, particularly in reducing waste through more accurate forecasting of perishable goods.

AI models that incorporate real-time data, weather forecasts, and demand trends can optimize stock levels, reducing spoilage and ensuring that food waste is minimized. This waste reduction strategy aligns with growing environmental concerns and consumer demand for more sustainable business practices. Furthermore, the potential of quantum computing is gaining traction in the e-grocery sector, offering hyper-optimization of multi-echelon inventories. Quantum computing's ability to process vast amounts of data at unprecedented speeds could enable next-level inventory management strategies, particularly in multi-echelon networks that involve several layers of distribution, storage, and delivery. By optimizing the flow of goods through these complex systems, quantum computing could improve supply chain agility, reduce costs, and ensure that products are delivered in the most efficient manner possible, enhancing both operational performance and customer satisfaction. Collectively, these technologies—Edge AI, sustainability efforts, and quantum computing—represent the next frontier of innovation in e-grocery, driving efficiencies, reducing waste, and fostering a more sustainable, agile supply chain.

1. Quantum Computing in AI Models

Quantum computing holds the potential to revolutionize AI applications in logistics by enabling faster data processing and more sophisticated predictive analytics. The massive computational power of quantum computers could allow for real-time optimization of complex supply chain networks, from demand forecasting to delivery routing. This could greatly enhance the scalability of AI/ML systems in e-grocery, enabling them to handle exponentially larger datasets and more intricate logistics problems with higher accuracy and speed.

2. Edge Computing for Real-Time Data Processing

Edge computing will play an increasingly important role in AI/ML applications by enabling faster data processing at the source, reducing latency and improving real-time decision-making. In e-grocery logistics, edge computing can facilitate the rapid processing of data from IoT devices, allowing for immediate adjustments in inventory management, delivery routing, and order fulfillment. By decentralizing data processing, edge computing can ensure that AI models remain responsive and adaptable in dynamic environments, such as fluctuating demand or unexpected disruptions in the supply chain.

3. AI-Enhanced Customer Service

AI-powered chatbots and virtual assistants will continue to improve customer service in the e-grocery sector. These tools can handle a wide range of customer interactions, from answering questions about product availability to assisting with order modifications. Machine learning models will enable these virtual assistants to learn from customer interactions and improve their responses over time. As a result, customer service will become more efficient, freeing up human agents to focus on more complex issues and ensuring that customers receive timely and accurate assistance.

The integration of AI and ML into e-grocery supply chains has the potential to revolutionize the industry, addressing longstanding challenges such as demand forecasting, inventory management, and last-mile delivery optimization. As AI/ML models continue to improve and new technologies emerge, the e-grocery sector will benefit from even more accurate forecasting, better customer experiences, and increased operational efficiency. Future innovations, such as quantum computing, edge computing, and AI-enhanced customer service, will further expand the capabilities of e-grocery supply chains, allowing for more personalized, scalable, and sustainable operations. As these technologies evolve, the role of AI/ML in transforming the e-grocery industry will only become more critical, reshaping the way businesses deliver products to customers and manage their supply chains.

REFERENCES

Bai, S., Zhan, X., & Zhang, L. (2018). A survey on LSTM and its variants in time series forecasting. *IEEE Access : Practical Innovations, Open Solutions*, *6*, 36573–36583. DOI: 10.1109/ACCESS.2018.2848007

Cagliano, A. C., De Marco, A., & Rafele, C. (2017). E-grocery supply chain management enabled by mobile tools. *Business Process Management Journal*, *23*(1), 47–70. DOI: 10.1108/BPMJ-01-2016-0002

Calzavara, M., Finco, S., Persona, A., & Zennaro, I. (2023). A cost-based tool for the comparison of different e-grocery supply chain strategies. *International Journal of Production Economics*, *262*, 108899. DOI: 10.1016/j.ijpe.2023.108899

Ciger, G., Ess, A., Hart, J., Hürtgen, H., & Goldrick, M. (2022). Navigating the market headwinds: The state of grocery retail 2022.

Do, V. C., & Omdahl, K. (2018). Efficiency of e-grocery: Challenges and suggestions (Master's thesis, University of Stavanger, Norway).

Elvas, L. B., Tokkozhina, U., Martins, A. L., & Ferreira, J. C. (2023). Implementation of disruptive technologies for the last mile delivery efficiency achievement. *Transportation Research Procedia*, *72*, 32–39. DOI: 10.1016/j.trpro.2023.11.319

Fernandez Vazquez-Noguerol, M. (2021). Modeling and optimization of the supply chain in e-groceries (Doctoral dissertation, Organización de empresas e márketing).

Graves, A. (2013). Supervised sequence labelling with recurrent neural networks. In *Studies in Computational Intelligence* (Vol. 385, pp. 1–35). Springer., DOI: 10.1007/978-3-642-36876-0_1

Hochreiter, S., & Schmidhuber, J. (1997). Long short-term memory. *Neural Computation*, *9*(8), 1735–1780. DOI: 10.1162/neco.1997.9.8.1735 PMID: 9377276

Imran, M., Kang, H., Lee, S. G., Kim, E. H., Park, H. M., & Oh, S. W. (2025). Current trends and future prospects in onion production, supply, and demand in South Korea: A comprehensive review. *Sustainability (2071-1050), 17*(3).

Jackson, I., Namdar, J., Saénz, M. J., Elmquist, R. A.III, & Dávila Novoa, L. R. (2024). Revolutionize cold chain: An AI/ML driven approach to overcome capacity shortages. *International Journal of Production Research*, •••, 1–23.

Jahnke, H., Ulrich, M., Pesch, R., Senge, R., & Langrock, R. (2025). Distributional Regression for Demand Forecasting in e-grocery.

Kumar, A., Mangla, S. K., Kumar, P., & Karamperidis, S. (2020). Challenges in perishable food supply chains for sustainability management: A developing economy perspective. *Business Strategy and the Environment, 29*(5), 1809–1831. DOI: 10.1002/bse.2470

Masi, A., Ciccullo, F., & Pero, M. (2021, June). Digitalizing agri-food supply chains to achieve Sustainable Development Goals: A systematic literature review. In *2021 IEEE International Conference on Engineering, Technology and Innovation (ICE/ITMC)* (pp. 1-8). IEEE. DOI: 10.1109/ICE/ITMC52061.2021.9570237

Mkansi, M., & Masilela, P. (2025). Green Purchasing as a Catalyst for Suppliers' Compliance to Environmental Standards: E-grocery Perspective. *Procedia Computer Science, 253*, 1–12. DOI: 10.1016/j.procs.2025.01.064

Nandy, I., & Padhy, R. (2025). From traditional to consumer-centric: The evolution of themes in technology-focused last mile delivery. *Global Knowledge, Memory and Communication*. Advance online publication. DOI: 10.1108/GKMC-03-2024-0167

Shuaibu, A. S., Mahmoud, A. S., & Sheltami, T. R. (2025). A Review of Last-Mile Delivery Optimization: Strategies, Technologies, Drone Integration, and Future Trends. *Drones (Basel), 9*(3), 158. DOI: 10.3390/drones9030158

Singh, S., & Kaur, H. (2023, September). Analyzing the Impact of UPI on Supply Chain Performance: A Natural Language Processing Approach with Generative Pre-trained Transformers. In *International Conference on Entrepreneurship, Innovation, and Leadership* (pp. 107-122). Singapore: Springer Nature Singapore.

Tudisco, V., Perotti, S., Ekren, B. Y., & Aktas, E. (2025). Sustainable e-grocery home delivery: An optimization model considering on-demand vehicles. *Computers & Industrial Engineering*, *201*, 110874. DOI: 10.1016/j.cie.2025.110874

Vaswani, A., Shazeer, N., Parmar, N., Uszkoreit, J., Jones, L., Gomez, A. A., Kaiser, Ł., & Polosukhin, I. (2017). Attention is all you need. In *Advances in neural information processing systems* (Vol. 30). Curran Associates, Inc. Top of Form Bottom of Form

KEY TERMS AND DEFINITIONS

Predictive Analytics: A branch of AI that uses historical data and machine learning algorithms to identify patterns and trends, helping businesses forecast future demand and make data-driven decisions for inventory management and supply chain optimization (Jackson et al., 2024).

Last-Mile Optimization: Refers to the strategies and AI tools used to minimize costs in the final stage of the delivery process. It involves optimizing delivery routes and stock management to ensure timely, cost-effective deliveries while maximizing customer satisfaction (Masi et al., 2021).

Perishability Index: A metric used to quantify the rate at which fresh produce and other perishable goods decay over time. It helps in understanding the optimal shelf life of products and is critical in managing stock levels to reduce waste and ensure product freshness (Fernandez Vazquez-Noguerol, 2021).

Demand Elasticity Forecasting: Involves predictive models that estimate how sensitive consumer demand is to changes in price. These models allow businesses to understand price elasticity and make informed pricing decisions to optimize revenue and demand fulfillment (Do & Omdahl, 2018).

Dark Store Allocation: Refers to the AI-driven process of positioning inventory within dark stores—retail outlets dedicated to fulfilling online orders. These systems optimize product placement based on demand patterns and sales forecasts to improve order fulfillment speed and minimize picking time (Cagliano et al., 2017).

Chapter 6
Reducing Delivery Delays and Improving Customer Satisfaction in Indian Heavy Commercial Vehicle Logistics

R. Venkateshkumar
https://orcid.org/0009-0001-3735-0341
Hindustan Institute of Technology and Science, India

Dennis Amirtharaj S. M.
Hindustan Institute of Technology and Science, India

ABSTRACT

On-time delivery in India's heavy commercial vehicle logistics sector is critical for operational efficiency and customer satisfaction. However, issues like poor infrastructure, traffic congestion, regulatory delays, driver shortages, and end-of-month invoicing disruptions contribute to frequent delivery delays. This book examines strategies to address these challenges using emerging technologies, data-driven decision-making, optimized route planning, predictive analytics, and end-to-end delivery

DOI: 10.4018/979-8-3373-2833-1.ch006

management. Telematics tracking & digital documentation enhance transparency and responsiveness across the logistics value chain. Effective collaboration among logistics providers, government agencies, and tech firms can streamline operations. Faster payment processing cycles for service providers are crucial for timely deliveries. HCV logistics firms can improve delivery timelines, reduce costs, and increase customer satisfaction. This research offers practical insights to enhance reliability and competitiveness in India's evolving logistics sector.

1. INTRODUCTION

India's logistics sector, valued at over $250 billion, plays a pivotal role in supporting the country's economic development, industrialization, and trade competitiveness (Tiwari & Mohan, 2022). Within this ecosystem, heavy commercial vehicle (HCV) logistics forms the backbone of road freight transport, accounting for over 60% of cargo movement across the nation (Kumar & Bansal, 2020; Rao & Patel, 2022). However, despite its indispensable nature, the sector continues to grapple with delivery delays, inefficient infrastructure, driver-related issues, and low customer satisfaction—challenges that hinder India's ambitions to become a global manufacturing and logistics hub (Jha & Singh, 2020; Sharma & Sharma, 2019).

In the context of rising consumer expectations and booming e-commerce, customer satisfaction in logistics has evolved from being a competitive differentiator to a strategic imperative (Lin et al., 2023; Sumrit & Sowijit, 2023). Timely delivery is now directly correlated with customer loyalty, brand perception, and operational cost efficiencies (Świtała et al., 2019; Lee & Woo, 2019). The inefficiencies prevalent in Indian HCV logistics—ranging from unpredictable travel times and uncoordinated loading schedules to bottlenecks at inter-state borders—have made delivery reliability a growing concern for stakeholders across the supply chain (Verma & Das, 2022; Srivastava & Chatterjee, 2022).A substantial body of research points toward multi-dimensional factors causing delivery delays, including poor road conditions, fragmented trucking operations, outdated fleet management systems, and frequent vehicle breakdowns (Ghosh &

Jha, 2016; Mahajan & Kumar, 2023; Harshitha et al., 2024). Kumar and Bansal (2020) conducted a qualitative investigation highlighting unsafe driver behavior and regulatory non-compliance as significant contributors to delivery inefficiencies. Meanwhile, Naik and Sharma (2022) emphasized the importance of time-series modeling to predict truck movements in urban areas and reduce congestion-led delays.

Digital transformation has emerged as a potential game-changer. Studies on the adoption of Internet of Things (IoT), Blockchain, Artificial Intelligence, and E-logistics platforms suggest these innovations significantly enhance visibility, real-time tracking, and predictive logistics planning (Shakeel & Baskar, 2024; Tijan et al., 2019; Tian et al., 2021). Yet, their integration into India's traditional HCV logistics ecosystem remains limited, especially among small and medium freight operators (Reddy, 2023; Joseph & Thomas, 2022).

Customer satisfaction in HCV logistics is determined not just by delivery speed, but also by communication, service responsiveness, reliability, and the ability to handle exceptions such as rerouting or cargo damage (Lang, 2020; Wareewanich et al., 2019; Uvet, 2020). Recent models developed in emerging markets reveal that logistics service quality (LSQ) directly influences repeat purchasing behavior and long-term trust in freight carriers (Choi et al., 2019; Umair et al., 2019; Prastyorini et al., 2023). India's road logistics also faces systemic structural challenges, including fragmented ownership patterns in trucking, poor coordination between supply chain actors, inadequate investment in infrastructure, and regulatory inefficiencies (Cantarelli et al., 2018; Koul & Mehta, 2020). Carrier collaboration models and multi-modal integration have been proposed as viable strategies to tackle such inefficiencies (Bhatnagar & Rao, 2021; Choudhary & Iyer, 2022). However, their large-scale implementation has been constrained by lack of standardization and technological literacy.

The study is structured as follows: Section 2 presents a comprehensive literature review of academic work on delivery performance, logistics service quality, and customer satisfaction in freight transport. Section 3 outlines the background and operational characteristics of Indian HCV logistics. Section 4 examines current challenges and bottlenecks. Section 5 discusses the role of digitalization, automation, and emerging technologies. Section 6 highlights case studies and comparative analyses, while Section

7 outlines actionable policy implications, managerial recommendations, and future research directions. Ultimately, the goal of this research is to assist logistics firms, policymakers, and technology providers in redesigning Indian HCV freight systems to be more reliable, efficient, and customer-centric.

2. SIGNIFICANCE OF STUDY

India's logistics sector, particularly the heavy commercial vehicle (HCV) segment, is a cornerstone of national economic activity, facilitating the movement of goods across vast geographies. Despite rapid industrialization and infrastructural advances, persistent challenges related to delivery delays and customer dissatisfaction hinder the sector's efficiency and growth potential. The significance of this study lies in its comprehensive exploration of these challenges and its emphasis on integrating advanced technologies and strategic interventions to enhance service quality and customer satisfaction in Indian HCV logistics.

The Indian logistics market is expected to grow significantly in the coming years, driven by the rise of e-commerce, manufacturing, and infrastructural development (Soni & Shukla, 2023). However, logistical inefficiencies such as poor road infrastructure, traffic congestion, and inadequate fleet management contribute substantially to delivery delays (Tiwari & Mohan, 2022; Kumar & Bansal, 2020). These delays adversely impact customer satisfaction, especially in time-sensitive industries like FMCG and automotive (Jha & Singh, 2020; Shinde & Bansode, 2022). Therefore, understanding the root causes of these delays and their impact on end-users is critical for designing responsive and resilient logistics systems.

Digitalization and technological innovations are transforming the logistics industry globally. In India, the integration of technologies such as IoT, blockchain, and AI-driven tools holds promise for optimizing route planning, vehicle tracking, and delivery schedules (Shakeel & Baskar, 2024; Tijan et al., 2019). These tools can help reduce delays by providing real-time visibility into logistics operations and enabling data-driven decision-making. However, the adoption of such technologies remains inconsistent across the Indian logistics landscape, particularly in the HCV segment. This study seeks to bridge the gap between technology availability and practical implementation by identifying the enablers and barriers of digital transformation in logistics.

In summary, this study is significant because it integrates multiple perspectives—operational, technological, customer-centric, and policy-driven—to provide a holistic understanding of the factors affecting delivery performance and customer satisfaction in Indian HCV logistics. Its findings are expected to benefit logistics companies, policymakers, and researchers by offering actionable insights and strategic recommendations aimed at building a more efficient, reliable, and customer-focused logistics ecosystem in India.

3. BENEFITS OF REDUCING DELIVERY DELAYS AND IMPROVING CUSTOMER SATISFACTION

India's logistics sector, particularly the heavy commercial vehicle (HCV) segment, is a cornerstone of national economic activity, facilitating the movement of goods across vast geographies. Despite rapid industrialization and infrastructural advances, persistent challenges related to delivery delays and customer dissatisfaction hinder the sector's efficiency and growth potential. The significance of this study lies in its comprehensive exploration of these challenges and its emphasis on integrating advanced technologies and strategic interventions to enhance service quality and customer satisfaction in Indian HCV logistics.

The Indian logistics market is expected to grow significantly in the coming years, driven by the rise of e-commerce, manufacturing, and infrastructural development (Soni & Shukla, 2023). However, logistical inefficiencies such as poor road infrastructure, traffic congestion, and inadequate fleet management contribute substantially to delivery delays (Tiwari & Mohan, 2022; Kumar & Bansal, 2020). These delays adversely impact customer satisfaction, especially in time-sensitive industries like FMCG and automotive (Jha & Singh, 2020; Shinde & Bansode, 2022). Therefore, understanding the root causes of these delays and their impact on end-users is critical for designing responsive and resilient logistics systems.

Furthermore, customer-centric approaches such as CRM and service personalization can significantly enhance satisfaction levels (Wareewanich et al., 2019). The study also acknowledges the importance of reverse logistics and sustainable practices in achieving long-term customer engagement and operational efficiency (Ezura & Jalil, 2019; Tian et al., 2021).

In summary, this study is significant because it integrates multiple perspectives—operational, technological, customer-centric, and policy-driven—to provide a holistic understanding of the factors affecting delivery performance and customer satisfaction in Indian HCV logistics. Its findings are expected to benefit logistics companies, policymakers, and researchers by offering actionable insights and strategic recommendations aimed at building a more efficient, reliable, and customer-focused logistics ecosystem in India.

4. LITERATURE REVIEW

The table below shows a summary for the literature review, capturing key findings and relevance of study.

Table 1. Literature review summary

S.no	Author(s)	Year	Title	Methodology	Key Findings	Relevance to Study
1	Kumar & Bansal	2020	Qualitative investigation of the influential factors behind unsafe trucking behaviours in India	Qualitative interviews with truck drivers	Unsafe driving behavior linked to time pressure and poor logistics planning	Highlights how unsafe practices due to delays affect logistics reliability
2	Tiwari & Mohan	2022	Freight traffic impacts and logistics inefficiencies in India	Policy analysis and conceptual modelling	Policy gaps, infrastructure bottlenecks lead to inefficiencies	Suggests systemic causes of delays and how policy reforms can help improve satisfaction
3	Shakeel & Baskar	2024	IoT in courier services: Impact on customer satisfaction and supply chain sustainability	Empirical quantitative survey	IoT improves tracking and transparency, boosting satisfaction	Demonstrates tech use to reduce delay uncertainty and improve trust

continued on following page

Table 1. Continued

S.no	Author(s)	Year	Title	Methodology	Key Findings	Relevance to Study
4	Reddy	2023	Study of faults in transportation management as a reason for delays	Case study and document analysis	Poor planning and miscommunication cause delivery delays	Directly connects delay causes to customer dissatisfaction
5	Soni & Shukla	2023	A study on the impact of logistics management on customer satisfaction	Survey and statistical analysis	Timely delivery and information sharing crucial to satisfaction	Reinforces importance of delivery timelines
6	Sharma & Sharma	2019	Assessment of lean supply chain practices in Indian automotive industry	Survey of supply chain managers	Lean practices reduce lead times and variability	Suggests process improvements to cut delay and enhance service
7	Bhatnagar & Rao	2021	Benefits of carrier collaboration under incomplete demand information	Simulation modelling	Collaboration reduces delays and improves service predictability	Highlights operational changes to minimize logistics uncertainty
8	Jha & Singh	2020	Examining freight performance of 3PLs in the automotive industry	Survey and SEM	Sustainability and timely service drive 3PL performance	Underscores logistics performance's role in customer satisfaction
9	Mahajan & Kumar	2023	Performance analysis of signalized intersections from truck drivers' perspective	Observational and survey data	Intersection delays are major contributors to delivery delays	Infrastructure-level delay contributor
10	Ghosh & Jha	2016	Determinants of safe and productive truck driving	Quantitative regression analysis	Driving hours, rest, and route planning impact delay and safety	Operational behavior as key delay influence

5. BACKGROUND

The Heavy Commercial Vehicle (HCV) industry plays a critical role in economic development, especially in large and growing economies like India, where goods transportation depends heavily on road networks. Here's a structured overview of the industry's background:

5.1 Definition and Scope

Heavy Commercial Vehicles (HCVs) typically refer to trucks and buses with a gross vehicle weight (GVW) exceeding 16.2 tons. These include:

- Long-haul trucks
- Tippers and dumpers (used in construction and mining)
- Trailers
- Heavy-duty buses (for intercity and industrial transport)

5.2 Key Segments in India

- Freight Transport: Over 65% of freight in India moves by road, and HCVs form the backbone for transporting industrial goods, construction materials, food grains, fuel, and automotive components.
- Construction & Mining: Tippers and multi-axle vehicles are heavily used in infrastructure projects.
- Public Transport: Heavy buses are used for intercity and intra-city transport by both private and state transport undertakings.

5.3 Major Players in the Indian HCV Market

- Tata Motors – Market leader in the HCV segment.
- Ashok Leyland – Strong in southern and eastern India, especially in buses.
- Eicher Motors (VE Commercial Vehicles) – Competing in both medium and heavy-duty trucks.
- Bharat Benz (Daimler India Commercial Vehicles) – Focus on premium HCVs.
- Mahindra Truck and Bus Division – Gaining traction in cargo transport.

5.4 Industry Drivers

- Infrastructure Development: National highway projects, Smart Cities, and logistics parks boost demand.
- E-commerce and Retail: Need for long-haul and last-mile delivery solutions.
- Make in India & Industrial Growth: Increased production and interstate logistics.

- Vehicle Scrappage Policy: New emission norms (BS-VI) and scrappage policy encourage fleet modernization.

5.5 Challenges

- Delivery Delays: Due to poor infrastructure, traffic congestion, border checks, and driver shortages.
- Fuel Costs: High diesel prices impact operating margins.
- Underdeveloped Cold Chain & Warehousing: Affects sectors like pharmaceuticals and perishables.
- Driver Availability and Welfare: Shortage of trained drivers, poor facilities at truck stops.

5.6 Digital Transformation Trends

- Telematics & Fleet Management Systems: Improve route planning, fuel efficiency, and maintenance.
- IoT & GPS Tracking: Enable real-time shipment tracking and customer visibility.
- E-Logistics Platforms: Streamline demand-supply match-making (e.g., Blackbuck, Rivigo).
- Electrification & Sustainability: Growing interest in electric and alternative fuel HCVs.

5.7 Policy and Regulation

- BS-VI Emission Standards: Implemented in April 2020, reducing vehicle emissions.
- GST & E-Way Bill System: Streamlined interstate logistics and documentation.
- National Logistics Policy (2022): Focus on reducing logistics costs (targeting 8% of GDP from the current ~14%).

6. KEY TRENDS IN LOGISTICS

6.1 Rapid Growth in Road Freight and Its Implications

The Indian logistics sector has witnessed a consistent increase in freight movement, primarily dominated by road transport, which carries over 65% of the country's cargo (Tiwari & Mohan, 2022; Verma & Das, 2022). The rise of e-commerce, retail expansion, and infrastructure development (such as dedicated freight corridors and Bharatmala projects) has accelerated the demand for timely and efficient deliveries.

However, this surge in freight traffic has not been matched by proportional infrastructure development, especially in urban and semi-urban areas (Naik & Sharma, 2022). This has led to bottlenecks, increased transit times, and delivery variability, especially for HCVs involved in long-haul and last-mile connectivity.

6.2 Unbalanced Model Mix and Fleet Fragmentation

Multiple studies (e.g., Sharma & Sharma, 2019; Bhatnagar & Rao, 2021) have flagged concerns regarding the unbalanced use of vehicle types. Rigid trucks are overutilized even for consignments better suited for articulated or multi-axle vehicles, leading to suboptimal efficiency and overloading.

Furthermore, fleet ownership is highly fragmented in India—over 70% of trucking companies operate less than five vehicles (Kumar & Bansal, 2020). This fragmentation leads to:

- Poor economies of scale
- Limited investment in telematics or route optimization
- Challenges in standardizing service quality

Such fleet imbalances reduce adaptability and cause operational inefficiencies, ultimately impacting delivery times and customer satisfaction.

6.3 Delivery Delays: Root Causes and Patterns

Many papers (e.g., Jha & Singh, 2020; Reddy, 2023; Ghosh & Jha, 2016) have empirically identified the main causes of delivery delays:

- Traffic congestion and poor road conditions
- Border check-post delays due to compliance and documentation
- Vehicle breakdowns due to aging fleets
- Lack of multimodal coordination

The absence of real-time visibility in cargo movements further compounds these issues, especially when delivery performance is measured against tight customer expectations. These delays have a direct negative impact on customer satisfaction, particularly in industries like automotive, construction, and FMCG logistics (Soni & Shukla, 2023).

6.4 Digitalization and Real-Time Tracking

A prominent trend observed is the increasing adoption of digital tools such as:

- IoT and GPS for real-time tracking (Shakeel & Baskar, 2024)
- Transport Management Systems (TMS)
- E-way bill systems and automated route planning

Digitalization is being driven by both cost pressures and customer demand for visibility. However, adoption remains uneven. Large fleet operators and 3PL providers are more likely to invest in such technologies, while smaller operators often lag due to cost and skill barriers (Shinde & Bansode, 2022).

Despite the challenges, digitization has been shown to:

- Reduce idle time and fuel consumption
- Improve customer communication and delivery accuracy
- Enable better decision-making based on analytics

6.5 Customer-Centric Logistics and Service Quality

Multiple studies highlight the shift towards customer-oriented logistics, where timely delivery, tracking updates, communication, and flexibility are crucial to satisfaction (Soni & Shukla, 2023; Shakeel & Baskar, 2024).

Factors influencing customer satisfaction include:

- On-time delivery rate
- Condition of goods upon arrival
- Ease of interaction with logistics providers
- Transparency and complaint resolution

Reddy (2023) and Sharma & Sharma (2019) note that service quality is often inconsistent due to a lack of performance measurement systems in many Indian logistics firms. This inconsistency erodes trust and reduces the chances of repeat business.

6.6 Environmental and Sustainability Pressures

Environmental concerns are increasingly influencing logistics decisions. As Jha & Singh (2020) observed, there is growing awareness about the carbon footprint of road freight, especially HCVs.

India's BS-VI emission norms and Vehicle Scrappage Policy are efforts to modernize fleets and reduce emissions. Electrification of commercial vehicles, though in early stages, is gaining policy support.

However, challenges remain:

- High initial cost of green vehicles
- Lack of charging/refuelling infrastructure for electric/H2 trucks
- Limited incentives for logistics companies to decarbonize voluntarily

6.7 Regulatory and Policy Shifts

Recent policies such as the National Logistics Policy (2022), PM Gati Shakti, and the E-Way Bill system aim to formalize and streamline logistics operations.

Key impacts:

- Reduced transit time due to fewer documentation stops
- Encouragement for multimodal integration (road-rail-air)
- Push for logistics parks and warehousing clusters

However, the policy impact is yet to fully materialize, particularly at the grassroots level, where operators still struggle with legacy compliance burdens (Srivastava & Chatterjee, 2022).

6.8 Urban Freight Challenges

As cities grow, urban freight demand increases, but city infrastructure isn't designed for HCVs. Key issues include:

- Lack of loading/unloading zones
- Daytime entry restrictions
- Poor last-mile connectivity (Choudhary & Iyer, 2022)

Urban freight contributes significantly to air pollution and congestion, especially during peak hours. Integrated planning and the use of smaller, cleaner vehicles for last-mile deliveries are being proposed.

6.9 Workforce and Driver-Related Issues

Several papers (e.g., Ghosh & Jha, 2016; Mahajan & Kumar, 2023) have identified driver fatigue, low wages, and inadequate rest infrastructure as contributors to inefficiency and accidents.

India faces a severe shortage of skilled HCV drivers, especially for long-haul routes. This shortage:

- Limits vehicle utilization
- Increases delays due to driver availability
- Affects safety and insurance costs

Investment in driver welfare, training, and digital upskilling is essential for sustainable logistics growth.

6.10 Reverse Logistics and Sustainability

While under-researched in India, reverse logistics—especially in e-commerce and automotive sectors—is gaining relevance. Efficient handling of returns, repairs, and recycling can reduce costs and improve customer loyalty (Shinde & Bansode, 2022).

7. CURRENT CHALLENGES IN LOGISTICS

7.1 Poor Road Infrastructure and Congestion

One of the most critical factors affecting delivery timelines is inadequate road infrastructure. Despite rapid highway development under projects like Bharatmala, many state and rural roads remain in poor condition, especially in key industrial and agricultural zones. Potholes, narrow roads, and incomplete bypasses reduce average speed and damage vehicles.

In urban areas, congestion is a daily challenge, especially near ports, industrial hubs, and city entry points. Commercial vehicles often get stuck in bottlenecks, construction zones, or restricted corridors, leading to delays in both long-haul and last-mile deliveries. A lack of dedicated freight lanes and insufficient traffic management exacerbate the issue.

7.2 Regulatory and Compliance Delays

While GST and the E-Way Bill have improved interstate freight movement, frequent inspections, documentation issues, and border delays still persist in several regions. Vehicles may be stopped for tax checks, vehicle fitness verification, or overloading inspections—each causing unpredictable waiting times.

Additionally, compliance with new norms (e.g., BS-VI emission standards, fitness certification, FASTag) often involves downtime due to paperwork or maintenance requirements. Digital systems aren't always integrated across states, leading to inconsistent implementation.

7.3 Driver Shortages and Workforce Issues

India faces an acute shortage of trained, professional HCV drivers. The profession is considered low-paying, physically demanding, and lacks basic amenities such as rest stops, toilets, and safety.

Delays occur when:

- Assigned drivers are unavailable
- Replacement drivers are unskilled or delayed
- Driver fatigue leads to slower movement or accidents

Driver absenteeism during festivals or agricultural seasons also affects the delivery schedule. A lack of standard working hours and poor welfare discourages long-term retention, further aggravating the issue.

7.4 Fragmented Fleet Ownership and Limited Technology Use

Over 70% of Indian trucking companies operate with fleets of fewer than five vehicles. This highly fragmented ownership model limits investment in digital solutions like GPS tracking, route planning, or predictive maintenance tools.

Without real-time tracking, logistics coordinators cannot anticipate delays or reroute shipments efficiently. Manual planning and lack of system integration lead to miscommunication between carriers, suppliers, and customers.

In contrast, large logistics providers using TMS and IoT-based tools have better on-time delivery performance, highlighting the digital divide within the sector.

7.5 Unpredictable Demand and Poor Inventory Coordination

Commercial vehicle deliveries are often tied to OEM production schedules, dealer requests, and customer financing cycles. Any change in manufacturing output, transport availability, or documentation delays (e.g., RTO registration, insurance) can stall deliveries.

Further, the lack of coordination between OEMs, third-party logistics (3PL) providers, and dealers results in last-minute dispatch requests, idle fleet time, and poor inventory visibility. During peak demand (e.g., fiscal year-end, harvest seasons), vehicle availability becomes erratic.

7.6 Weather and Seasonal Disruptions

India's logistics system is heavily impacted by monsoons, floods, fog, and extreme heat, which delay transit, damage roads, or reduce driver visibility. Natural disasters like cyclones or landslides also disrupt routes and require last-minute rerouting, often without updated digital mapping or alerts.

Transporters face increased vehicle breakdowns, safety concerns, and temporary route closures—all contributing to delivery delays that are hard to predict and mitigate in real time.

7.7 Inefficient Payment Cycles and Financial Constraints

Many logistics firms—especially small or regional carriers—face delayed payments from clients, including OEMs or dealers. These delayed payment cycles affect their ability to:

- Maintain vehicle health (leading to breakdowns)

- Pay drivers on time
- Manage toll, fuel, and permit costs up front

Cash flow uncertainty causes dispatch delays, poor driver retention, and even vehicle unavailability during urgent deliveries. Larger firms with better financial backing are often able to absorb these shocks, but smaller operators struggle to stay consistent.

8. ROLE OF TECHNOLOGY IN AVOIDING DELIVERY DELAYS AND ENHANCING CUSTOMER

8.1 Satisfaction in Commercial Vehicle Logistics

Technology is transforming the Indian logistics landscape, particularly in the commercial vehicle (CV) segment. As freight volumes increase and customer expectations rise, logistics providers are increasingly turning to digital tools to ensure timely deliveries, reduce variability, and build customer trust. Insights from recent research underscore how specific technologies address key operational challenges and elevate logistics service quality.

8.2 Real-Time Vehicle Tracking and Visibility

Papers by Shakeel & Baskar (2024), Kumar & Bansal (2020), and Soni & Shukla (2023) highlight the widespread adoption of GPS tracking and telematics systems in commercial vehicle fleets. These technologies allow logistics managers to:

- Monitor vehicle location in real time
- Identify and reroute vehicles around traffic or disruptions
- Provide live delivery updates to customers

By reducing uncertainty, real-time visibility helps avoid miscommunication, proactively manage delays, and assure customers about the status of their deliveries—directly impacting satisfaction scores.

8.3 Transport Management Systems (TMS)

Many large logistics providers have implemented TMS platforms that automate route planning, dispatch scheduling, load optimization, and delivery tracking (Shinde & Bansode, 2022; Mahajan & Kumar, 2023). These systems:

- Identify the fastest and most cost-efficient routes
- Prevent under-utilization of fleet capacity
- Enable centralized dispatch control across regions

By improving operational efficiency, TMS adoption leads to more predictable delivery timelines, minimizing idle time and detours, especially for long-haul HCV movements.

8.4 Predictive Maintenance and IoT Sensors

As Ghosh & Jha (2016) and Reddy (2023) point out, vehicle breakdowns are a major contributor to delivery delays in India. By deploying IoT-enabled sensors, operators can monitor:

- Engine health
- Tire pressure
- Fuel usage
- Brake condition

This allows for predictive maintenance, where vehicles are serviced proactively based on performance data rather than reactive breakdowns. Result: fewer unexpected halts, greater fleet reliability, and enhanced customer confidence in service consistency.

8.5 Digital Documentation and Compliance Automation

Several papers (e.g., Sharma & Sharma, 2019; Srivastava & Chatterjee, 2022) emphasize how digital paperwork, such as e-way bills, FASTag tolling, and electronic proof of delivery (e-POD), has streamlined regulatory processes. These technologies reduce time lost at:

- State borders
- Toll booths
- Delivery validation points

By eliminating manual verification and long wait times, deliveries become faster and more seamless—reducing the friction that traditionally frustrated customers and drivers alike.

8.6 Data Analytics and Delivery Forecasting

Advanced analytics, discussed in Naik & Sharma (2022) and Bhatnagar & Rao (2021), allows companies to forecast delivery times more accurately and measure performance through KPIs such as:

- On-time delivery rate
- Vehicle turnaround time
- Delay frequency by route or region

By turning data into insights, logistics firms can identify bottlenecks, optimize delivery windows, and improve their Service Level Agreements (SLAs)—leading to measurable customer satisfaction gains.

8.7 Warehouse Management and Load Planning Tools

For vehicle manufacturers and their logistics partners, load consolidation and timely dispatch from factories or stockyards is critical. Studies such as Verma & Das (2022) show how Warehouse Management Systems (WMS) and digital load planning reduce:

- Dispatch errors
- Loading delays
- Manual paperwork at the dock

These tools ensure that commercial vehicles are dispatched on time, fully loaded, and with the right documents—preventing cascading delays throughout the distribution network.

9. CUSTOMER SATISFACTION OF LOGISTICS PROVIDERS' SERVICES

9.1 Overview of Satisfaction Theme

In today's fast-paced global economy, logistics performance plays a central role in determining both the efficiency of supply chains and the satisfaction of end customers. For the heavy commercial vehicle (HCV) logistics sector in India, delivery delays pose critical challenges, impacting customer retention, operational costs, and overall competitiveness. Drawing insights from over 40 academic sources, this section explores how reducing delivery delays improves customer satisfaction by examining the role of logistics cost structures, performance metrics, and global benchmarking practices.

9.2 The Strategic Importance of Delivery Time in Logistics

Delivery time is one of the most influential attributes in shaping customer satisfaction, particularly in B2B logistics settings involving commercial vehicles. According to Reddy (2023), delays often stem from transportation management faults, including route inefficiencies, inadequate infrastructure, and driver behavior issues. Kumar & Bansal (2020) further highlight that unsafe trucking practices and lack of training contribute to both delays and safety risks.

In the automotive logistics domain, Soni & Shukla (2023) found that timely delivery directly correlates with customer loyalty, especially among commercial buyers who rely on HCVs for industrial operations. Shakeel & Baskar (2024) demonstrate that IoT implementation significantly improves courier service timeliness, showcasing how digital transformation helps minimize uncertainties in logistics operations.

9.3 Cost Implications of Delivery Delays

Logistics costs account for approximately 13-14% of India's GDP, significantly higher than the global average of 8–10% (Tiwari & Mohan, 2022). A major component of these elevated costs stems from inefficiencies such as delivery delays, long turnaround times, and vehicle underutilization. Jha & Singh (2020) assert that third-party logistics (3PL) providers in India face elevated costs when delays cascade through the supply chain, particularly in the automotive sector.

Mahajan & Kumar (2023) examined the impact of signalized intersections on truck drivers' wait times, revealing that such systemic inefficiencies add to fuel and labor costs while causing delivery time variances. Choudhary & Iyer (2022) support this view by linking logistics outsourcing models to better cost control, as insourced models struggle with scale and flexibility in handling last-mile disruptions.

Key performance indicators (KPIs) like on-time delivery rate, vehicle turnaround time, and freight damage rate offer quantifiable metrics for assessing logistics service quality. Lin et al. (2023) suggest that logistics service quality (LSQ) directly influences customer satisfaction and re-use intention, reinforcing the need for performance-based logistics strategies.

In India's freight sector, Ghosh & Jha (2016) point out that driver productivity, rest time compliance, and vehicle maintenance are crucial for reducing delivery delays. Sharma & Sharma (2019) emphasize lean supply chain practices, including route optimization and inventory visibility, as enablers of faster and more reliable deliveries.

From a customer-facing perspective, Lang (2020) found that logistics firms that actively measure and act on feedback across delivery, packaging, and communication touchpoints are better positioned to improve performance and satisfaction.

9.4 Global Best Practices and Benchmarks

Globally, leading logistics providers have established stringent benchmarks to reduce delays. For instance, Choi et al. (2019) illustrate how Chinese e-commerce firms leverage AI and smart warehousing to ensure rapid last-mile fulfillment. Tijan et al. (2019) discuss the role of blockchain in enhancing supply chain transparency and reducing administrative delays across customs and distribution centers.

Comparatively, Uvet (2020) shows that European logistics firms maintain 98–99% on-time delivery rates by integrating transport management systems (TMS) and predictive analytics. In contrast, Indian firms often operate in fragmented markets with multiple intermediaries, reducing visibility and control.

The World Bank's Logistics Performance Index (LPI) offers a framework for global benchmarking. Rao & Patel (2022) use expenditure-based freight segmentation to suggest that India's freight market inefficiencies can be addressed through improved policy and investment in multimodal infrastructure.

9.5 Digitalization as a Catalyst for Reducing Delays

One of the most consistent themes across literature is the transformational potential of digitalization. Shinde & Bansode (2022) analyze the FMCG sector, showing that digital dashboards, GPS-enabled tracking, and cloud-based order management systems improve logistics distribution performance. Tian et al. (2021) propose a blockchain-based evaluation model to monitor and improve customer delivery satisfaction in urban logistics.

Wareewanich et al. (2019) advocate the integration of CRM systems in logistics to track complaints and proactively resolve delivery-related issues. Waseem-Ul-Hameed et al. (2018) emphasize ICT as a mediator between e-logistics performance and customer satisfaction, particularly in emerging economies like Pakistan and India.

9.6 Customer-Centric Logistics and Service Differentiation

Meeting or exceeding customer expectations in delivery services is no longer optional; it is a competitive imperative. Lee & Woo (2019) argue that power dynamics within logistics triads—comprising carriers, shippers, and end customers—affect trust and satisfaction levels. Świtała et al. (2019) suggest that performance in outsourced logistics relationships must be regularly audited to avoid service degradation.

Sumrit & Sowijit (2023) apply the three-factor theory to understand what logistics service attributes drive satisfaction versus those that merely prevent dissatisfaction. Speed, communication, and reliability emerged as critical enablers. Umair et al. (2019) show that even in traditional retail settings, improved logistics performance directly increases in-store sales and customer perception.

9.7 Policy Interventions and Infrastructure Investment

Infrastructure bottlenecks like congested highways, limited warehouse capacity, and outdated vehicle fleets are long-standing causes of delays in India. Verma & Das (2022) and Naik & Sharma (2022) model freight movements of agricultural commodities and urban truck traffic, respectively, calling for infrastructure upgrades to handle rising demand.

Cantarelli et al. (2018) raise concerns over cost overruns in transport infrastructure projects globally, stressing the need for better project planning and execution. Hsu et al. (2018) propose a stochastic optimization model for logistics planning in modular construction, demonstrating how project-based freight can benefit from real-time scenario modeling.

10. CHANGES IN LOGISTICS STRATEGY AND FREIGHT NEEDS FOR HIGHER CUSTOMER DELIGHT

Customer expectations in the logistics sector have evolved dramatically in recent years. In today's highly competitive and digitized environment, speed, reliability, flexibility, and transparency have become critical factors that influence customer satisfaction. Traditional logistics strategies focused primarily on cost optimization and operational efficiency are now being transformed to meet new demands driven by customer delight. Based on an extensive review of 40 academic papers, this document explores the major strategic shifts and freight planning transformations required to deliver consistent, delay-free logistics services that maximize customer satisfaction.

10.1 Shift from Cost-Driven to Customer-Centric Logistics

Historically, logistics strategies emphasized minimizing transportation and warehousing costs while maximizing asset utilization. However, customer demands for real-time delivery updates, customized delivery windows, and sustainable logistics have necessitated a redefinition of priorities. As noted by Umair et al. (2019) and Lin et al. (2023), customer satisfaction is now a critical competitive differentiator, prompting organizations to prioritize customer experience over pure cost savings. Companies are increasingly investing in technologies such as route optimization software, IoT devices, and customer relationship management tools to improve last-mile delivery performance. Logistics is no longer just a backend support function but a direct contributor to brand reputation and customer loyalty.

10.2 Integration of Digital Technologies

The digital transformation of logistics has been a game-changer. Tools such as GPS-enabled tracking, blockchain, automated warehouses, and AI-powered decision systems have transformed how freight is planned, executed, and monitored. Shakeel & Baskar (2024) demonstrated that

IoT in courier services improves transparency and customer satisfaction, while Tijan et al. (2019) showed that blockchain implementation enhances trust and reduces disputes in logistics. Companies are also using mobile apps and digital platforms to provide customers with real-time shipment tracking, delivery notifications, and two-way communication channels. These innovations foster trust and reduce anxiety associated with uncertain delivery timelines.

10.3 Strategic Role of 3PLs and Freight Consolidation

Third-party logistics (3PL) providers play a critical role in meeting the evolving freight needs of businesses. With rising demand volatility and expanding geographic coverage, organizations are increasingly outsourcing logistics functions to experts. Bhatnagar & Rao (2021) identified collaboration with carriers and 3PLs as a key strategy to reduce delivery delays through better vehicle utilization and dynamic scheduling. Freight consolidation has emerged as another effective strategy to balance cost and speed. Combining multiple shipments into fewer loads helps reduce transportation expenses while still maintaining high service levels. It also contributes to environmental sustainability, which is becoming an important factor in customer satisfaction, especially in B2B contexts.

10.4 Multimodal and Sustainable Freight Strategies

To mitigate risks associated with a single mode of transportation, companies are adopting multimodal freight strategies. According to Verma & Das (2022), combining rail, road, and air transport allows businesses to choose the optimal mode based on urgency, cost, and carbon impact. This flexibility supports on-time delivery commitments and enhances overall logistics resilience. Furthermore, green logistics is gaining traction as sustainability becomes a priority for consumers. Hsu et al. (2018) and Tian et al. (2021) highlighted the growing demand for low-emission freight options and recyclable packaging materials. Companies that offer eco-friendly logistics solutions not only comply with regulations but also appeal to environmentally conscious customers, creating an emotional value layer in customer delight.

10.5 Role of Customer Feedback and Personalization

Modern logistics strategies increasingly incorporate customer feedback mechanisms. According to Hui et al. (2021), actively collecting and analysing customer reviews helps logistics providers identify pain points and service gaps. Personalized delivery options, such as time-slot selection and delivery rerouting, increase customer convenience and satisfaction. CRM systems are now integrated with logistics platforms to synchronize customer preferences with operational decisions. As Wareewanich et al. (2019) emphasized, personalized logistics solutions result in higher customer engagement and reduce complaint rates.

10.6 Data-Driven Decision Making and Performance Metrics

Quantitative performance measurement is vital for continuously improving logistics strategies. Key performance indicators (KPIs) such as on-time delivery rate, order accuracy, return rate, and net promoter score (NPS) are being tracked rigorously. Shinde & Bansode (2022) demonstrated how digital dashboards and analytics tools help managers make real-time decisions that enhance logistics efficiency and customer experience. Koul & Mehta (2020) applied double-bootstrap DEA to evaluate intercity freight efficiency, showing that data-backed strategy formulation results in more balanced cost and service outcomes.

10.7 Challenges and Future Outlook

Despite these advancements, several challenges remain. Infrastructure limitations, regulatory hurdles, and talent shortages continue to affect freight efficiency, particularly in developing regions like India (Tiwari & Mohan, 2022). However, the shift toward data-centric, customer-first logistics strategies is irreversible.

Future trends include the rise of autonomous supply chains, real-time supply-demand matching, and AI-powered customer communication. Investment in infrastructure, policy reforms, and public-private partnerships will also play a pivotal role in aligning freight strategies with the goal of customer delight.

11. CASE STUDY 1: INVESTIGATING UNSAFE TRUCKING BEHAVIOURS AND ITS IMPACT ON DELIVERY DELAYS IN INDIA

Background

Unsafe trucking behaviours in India are a major cause of delays in freight transport. The trucking industry in India is plagued by factors like poorly trained drivers, road safety negligence, driver fatigue, and a lack of traffic discipline. The poor road infrastructure further exacerbates this issue, leading to frequent accidents and delays in the delivery of goods.

Analysis

Kumar and Bansal's study highlights that unsafe driving behaviours—such as speeding, tailgating, and driving under the influence—are widespread among truck drivers in India. These behaviours often result in accidents, traffic jams, and vehicle breakdowns, all of which contribute to delays in logistics operations. The authors also emphasize the lack of training programs for drivers on road safety and the poor enforcement of traffic laws in many regions of India.

Unsafe behaviours also stem from the demanding work schedules of truck drivers, who often face long hours on the road with minimal rest. This fatigue impairs decision-making, leading to dangerous driving practices that contribute to accidents.

Strategy

To tackle this problem, the study suggests the following strategies:

- **Enhanced Driver Training**: Investing in comprehensive driver safety training programs that focus on defensive driving, fatigue management, and safe driving practices.
- **Technology Adoption**: Use of telematics and GPS tracking systems to monitor driving behavior in real-time, detect dangerous driving practices, and provide instant feedback to drivers.
- **Stricter Law Enforcement**: Stronger enforcement of traffic laws, including penalties for unsafe driving behaviours such as over-speeding and driving under the influence of alcohol.

Outcome

By implementing these strategies, trucking companies can expect a reduction in the number of accidents, improving the overall safety and efficiency of deliveries. With better-trained drivers and real-time monitoring systems, trucking companies can ensure that their fleet operates safely, leading to fewer delays and lower accident-related costs.

Impact

The outcome of adopting these strategies would be a significant reduction in delays caused by accidents and vehicle breakdowns. Timely deliveries would improve, leading to higher customer satisfaction and better logistical performance. Safer road conditions would also lower insurance costs for logistics providers.

Recommendations

- Establish mandatory safety training programs for truck drivers and ensure ongoing education on safe driving.
- Integrate GPS tracking and telematics in trucks to monitor driving behavior and ensure adherence to safety standards.
- Work with local authorities to improve the enforcement of traffic regulations and ensure penalties for unsafe practices.

12. CASE STUDY 2: LEVERAGING IOT FOR IMPROVED CUSTOMER SATISFACTION IN COURIER SERVICES

Background

The logistics and courier services industry is increasingly adopting technology to enhance customer satisfaction and operational efficiency. One key innovation is the integration of the Internet of Things (IoT) in the logistics process. Shakeel and Baskar's study focuses on how IoT can improve service delivery, provide real-time tracking, and contribute to sustainability in the supply chain.

Analysis

The use of IoT technologies in logistics, especially in courier services, allows for real-time monitoring of shipments, efficient routing of delivery vehicles, and better inventory management. By embedding sensors in packages and vehicles, logistics providers can offer customers precise delivery times, track the exact location of their packages, and provide real-time updates via mobile apps.

Moreover, IoT-based systems can help logistics companies predict potential delays by analysing traffic patterns, weather conditions, and historical data. This predictive capability allows companies to proactively adjust their routes or notify customers in advance if a delay is expected.

Strategy

To optimize customer satisfaction and operational performance, the study recommends the following strategies:

- **Real-time Tracking and Updates**: Implement IoT-based systems to provide real-time visibility of packages in transit. This enhances transparency and builds trust with customers.

- **Predictive Analytics**: Leverage IoT data to predict and mitigate potential delays by adjusting delivery routes or schedules based on real-time data.
- **Sustainability Practices**: Use IoT to optimize fuel consumption and reduce the carbon footprint of logistics operations by enabling smarter route planning and vehicle management.

Outcome

By adopting these strategies, courier service providers can ensure timely deliveries, minimize delays, and reduce customer complaints. The ability to predict delays in advance and communicate with customers proactively improves the customer experience and builds loyalty. Additionally, optimizing routes and vehicle management reduces operational costs and environmental impact.

Impact

The integration of IoT technologies leads to increased operational efficiency, faster deliveries, and enhanced customer satisfaction. Customers benefit from real-time tracking and timely updates, which are crucial for industries requiring high reliability, such as e-commerce. The reduced operational costs and environmental footprint also contribute to the sustainability goals of logistics providers.

Recommendations

- Invest in IoT-enabled tracking systems to provide real-time updates to customers.
- Use predictive analytics to identify potential delays and inform customers in advance.
- Implement environmentally friendly practices by optimizing fuel usage through IoT-based route planning.

13. CASE STUDY 3: FREIGHT TRAFFIC AND LOGISTICS INEFFICIENCIES IN INDIAN CITIES

Background

India's urban centres face significant freight traffic congestion, which results in delays and inefficiencies in logistics operations. Tiwari and Mohan's paper explores how urban freight impacts logistics performance and discusses potential policy interventions to address these issues.

Analysis

The study identifies congestion as a key issue affecting the timely movement of goods within cities. With growing urban populations and increasing demand for goods, freight vehicles are often stuck in traffic, resulting in significant delays. The inefficiency of current road infrastructure, particularly in highly populated areas, leads to unpredictable delivery times.

The authors argue that better urban freight planning is necessary to reduce congestion and improve logistics performance. They suggest several strategies, including dedicated freight corridors and the use of alternative transport modes like electric vehicles (EVs).

Strategy

- **Dedicated Freight Corridors**: Developing exclusive routes for freight vehicles to reduce congestion in city centres and improve delivery times.
- **Urban Freight Planning**: Integrating logistics into urban development plans to create infrastructure that facilitates the efficient movement of goods.
- **Use of EVs**: Promoting the use of electric vehicles in logistics to reduce pollution and improve the sustainability of freight transportation.

Outcome

The implementation of these strategies is expected to reduce traffic congestion, improve delivery times, and reduce the environmental impact of logistics. By providing a more structured and sustainable framework for freight movement, logistics companies can offer more reliable and efficient services.

Impact

Reducing congestion and improving infrastructure directly leads to reduced delivery delays, which enhances customer satisfaction. In addition, the use of sustainable practices like EVs can improve the corporate social responsibility (CSR) profile of logistics companies and appeal to environmentally conscious consumers.

Recommendations

- Invest in dedicated freight corridors to reduce congestion and enhance delivery efficiency.
- Plan urban logistics with a focus on long-term sustainability and scalability.
- Adopt green logistics solutions, including the use of electric vehicles, to reduce environmental impact and improve operational efficiency.

14. FUTURE RESEARCH DIRECTIONS IN LOGISTICS: REDUCING DELIVERY DELAYS AND ENHANCING CUSTOMER SATISFACTION

The logistics sector, particularly in emerging markets like India, faces unique challenges in ensuring timely deliveries and meeting customer expectations. As technology evolves and customer demands become more complex, future research should focus on addressing the following areas to reduce delays, improve efficiency, and enhance customer satisfaction:

14.1 Integration of Advanced Technologies in Logistics Operations

The integration of emerging technologies such as Artificial Intelligence (AI), Machine Learning (ML), Blockchain, and the Internet of Things (IoT) has already begun to transform logistics. However, there is still much to be explored in terms of their full potential in reducing delivery delays and enhancing customer satisfaction.

- **AI and ML for Predictive Analytics**: Research can focus on developing AI-based models that predict demand, optimize routes, and forecast potential delays based on historical data, weather conditions, and real-time information. These models can help logistics providers proactively manage disruptions and streamline operations.
- **Blockchain for Transparency and Security**: As blockchain technology offers transparency and security, future research can explore its use in tracking deliveries, verifying transactions, and ensuring that customer data is handled securely and transparently, thus improving trust and satisfaction.
- **IoT for Real-Time Monitoring and Automation**: IoT-enabled devices, such as smart sensors and GPS systems, can continuously monitor goods in transit, providing real-time updates on delivery status. Research into how to scale and integrate IoT devices into the broader logistics network could provide significant advancements in reducing delays and improving customer satisfaction.

14.2 Sustainability in Logistics

As environmental concerns become more significant, sustainability has become a top priority in logistics operations. Future research should explore how green logistics practices can be integrated into logistics networks to reduce delays while minimizing environmental impact.

- **Electric and Autonomous Vehicles**: The development and adoption of electric and autonomous vehicles for logistics purposes can potentially reduce fuel consumption, cut costs, and lower the carbon footprint. Research into how these technologies can be scaled and integrated into existing logistics networks is essential for future sustainability.

- **Green Supply Chain Management**: Future studies should examine how sustainable practices in logistics, such as energy-efficient warehouse management and optimized route planning, can help reduce delays while supporting broader environmental goals.

14.3 Human Factors and Safety in Logistics

Human factors play a critical role in delivery delays, especially in transportation. Factors such as driver fatigue, poor safety protocols, and inefficient management of logistics personnel can lead to significant delays in delivery times.

- **Driver Behavior and Training Programs**: Research into improving driver behavior and enhancing training programs can provide insights into reducing unsafe driving habits, reducing accidents, and improving overall delivery efficiency.
- **Health and Well-being of Logistics Workers**: Future studies can also explore the impact of worker health and well-being on the efficiency of logistics operations. By understanding how factors like long hours, poor ergonomics, and mental health issues affect productivity, logistics providers can implement policies to mitigate these issues.

15.4 Urban Logistics and Last-Mile Delivery Optimization

Urban logistics, particularly the challenges surrounding last-mile delivery, is a critical issue in densely populated regions. Research in this area can focus on new methods to improve the speed and efficiency of last-mile delivery, especially in urban and semi-urban areas.

- **Use of Drones and Robots**: The future of last-mile delivery may involve drones or autonomous robots for small package deliveries.

Research on the regulatory challenges, efficiency, safety, and customer satisfaction implications of these technologies is an exciting avenue for future work.

- **Crowdsourced Delivery Models**: Another direction for research could be the exploration of crowdsourced logistics models where individuals or local businesses assist in the last-mile delivery process. This could help in reducing delivery costs and ensuring faster deliveries in urban areas.

14.5 Resilience and Risk Management in Supply Chains

The COVID-19 pandemic highlighted the vulnerability of global supply chains to external disruptions. Future research should investigate resilience strategies for logistics providers to recover quickly from disruptions like pandemics, natural disasters, and geopolitical tensions.

- **Risk Management Frameworks**: Developing comprehensive frameworks that identify and mitigate risks associated with transportation delays, supply chain bottlenecks, and labour shortages can help companies prepare for unforeseen disruptions.
- **Supply Chain Diversification**: Future research could examine how diversifying suppliers, transport routes, and delivery methods can create more resilient logistics networks. This can reduce the impact of disruptions and ensure customer satisfaction during uncertain times.

15.6 Customer-Centric Logistics and Service Quality

As customer expectations continue to evolve, logistics companies need to better understand the drivers of customer satisfaction and how service quality can be consistently improved.

- **Omnichannel Logistics Integration**: With the rise of e-commerce, integrating omnichannel logistics strategies that allow seamless order fulfilment across multiple platforms (e.g., in-store, online, mobile) could be key to improving customer satisfaction.

- **Customer Experience and Personalization**: Research into personalized delivery experiences and understanding the customer journey in logistics can lead to more targeted strategies that improve satisfaction. For example, offering flexible delivery times, personalized notifications, and faster delivery windows can create more positive customer experiences.

14.7 Big Data and Analytics for Operational Efficiency

The role of big data analytics in logistics continues to grow. Future research could focus on how logistics providers can leverage big data to improve decision-making, optimize operations, and predict disruptions.

- **Predictive Maintenance**: Researching the use of big data for predictive maintenance of vehicles and equipment can help reduce breakdowns and delays. By analyzing patterns in equipment performance, companies can anticipate when maintenance is needed before breakdowns occur.
- **Supply Chain Transparency**: Big data analytics can also be used to enhance visibility across the supply chain, allowing logistics managers to track goods in transit, monitor inventory levels, and identify inefficiencies that contribute to delays.

14.8 Collaborative Logistics and Intermodal Transportation

The integration of intermodal transportation and collaboration between different logistics providers can streamline operations and reduce delays.

- **Intermodal Transport Networks**: Research into optimizing intermodal transport networks that combine rail, road, air, and sea transport can provide cost-effective and efficient solutions for reducing delivery times. These systems can offer flexibility and scalability, reducing dependence on single modes of transportation.
- **Collaborative Logistics Partnerships**: Future research should investigate collaborative strategies between logistics companies, ship-

pers, and retailers to share resources, reduce costs, and improve the overall efficiency of the supply chain.

15. CONCLUSION

Reducing delivery delays and improving customer satisfaction are pivotal challenges in Indian heavy commercial vehicle logistics, and addressing them requires a comprehensive understanding of logistics systems, service quality, operational efficiency, and technological advancements. The research undertaken in this study, supported by the extensive body of literature, has highlighted the key factors contributing to delivery delays and customer dissatisfaction in the Indian logistics ecosystem. These factors range from infrastructure deficiencies and traffic congestion to operational inefficiencies and the lack of technological integration. However, by exploring various industry practices, adopting innovative solutions, and aligning with global best practices, it is possible to mitigate these issues and foster a more efficient, customer-centric logistics environment in India.

A critical finding from the review of literature is that logistics inefficiencies, especially in the movement of goods by heavy commercial vehicles, are driven by several factors, including road infrastructure quality, congestion, and vehicle breakdowns. According to Kumar and Bansal (2020), unsafe trucking behaviours and poor road conditions significantly contribute to delays in delivery times. The long-haul truck drivers' lack of training, unsafe driving practices, and vehicle malfunctions have compounded the problem, causing operational delays and safety concerns. Moreover, Mahajan and Kumar (2023) argue that inefficient intersections and inadequate traffic management systems contribute significantly to delays in logistics operations, especially in urban areas, further highlighting the importance of improving road infrastructure and managing traffic flow effectively to reduce delivery delays.

Furthermore, Tiwari and Mohan (2022) emphasize the need for strategic policy interventions aimed at mitigating inefficiencies in urban freight transportation. Urban congestion, which leads to delays in freight movement, is a major challenge in India's rapidly urbanizing environment. Solutions such as dedicated freight corridors, better traffic management, and the optimization of freight flows through data-driven systems are essential. These improvements would not only reduce delays but also have a positive impact on the environment by minimizing fuel consumption and emissions, as highlighted by Jha and Singh (2020).

The logistics industry in India faces challenges beyond infrastructure, with organizational inefficiencies playing a key role. Sharma and Sharma (2019) indicate that poor supply chain coordination and inefficient inventory management often result in delays, especially in the automotive sector, which relies heavily on timely transportation of parts and components. Soni and Shukla (2023) support this view, suggesting that a lack of integration among stakeholders, including suppliers, logistics providers, and manufacturers, further exacerbates delays in the delivery of goods. Effective communication, real-time tracking systems, and coordination among stakeholders are critical to improving efficiency and ensuring timely deliveries.

Technological innovations, such as the Internet of Things (IoT), automation, and blockchain, have shown significant promise in enhancing logistics performance, as illustrated in several studies. Shakeel and Baskar (2024) explore the role of IoT in courier services and its impact on customer satisfaction and supply chain sustainability. IoT can improve operational transparency by enabling real-time monitoring of vehicles, helping to prevent delays caused by mechanical breakdowns or inefficient routing. Similarly, blockchain technology, as discussed by Tian et al. (2021), can offer a transparent and secure platform for tracking goods, thereby improving delivery accuracy, reducing fraud, and increasing customer trust. These technologies facilitate not only the optimization of logistics operations but also enhance the customer experience by providing accurate delivery information, thereby reducing customer anxiety related to delays.

The integration of CRM with logistics operations enables companies to manage customer expectations, leading to improved service perceptions even in situations where delays are inevitable.

The incorporation of data analytics into logistics decision-making is another crucial avenue for reducing delays. By analysing traffic patterns, demand fluctuations, and weather conditions, logistics firms can optimize routes, reduce transit times, and predict potential delays before they occur.

According to Choi et al. (2019), sustainable logistics practices, such as predictive analytics for route planning, not only improve delivery times but also enhance customer satisfaction by providing accurate ETAs. Predictive analytics can help logistics providers make more informed decisions about vehicle maintenance, route selection, and fleet management, thus minimizing delays caused by unforeseen circumstances.

The research has also highlighted that policy-level interventions play a critical role in improving logistics efficiency and reducing delays. According to Bhatnagar and Rao (2021), public-private partnerships, along with government policies that promote infrastructure development, logistics planning, and smart transportation systems, can facilitate smoother logistics operations. The government's support for the development of dedicated freight corridors and the establishment of logistics hubs will not only improve delivery speeds but also contribute to a more robust logistics ecosystem in India.

In conclusion, reducing delivery delays and improving customer satisfaction in Indian heavy commercial vehicle logistics require a multi-faceted approach. By addressing infrastructure challenges, integrating advanced technologies, improving logistics coordination, and incorporating sustainable practices, the Indian logistics industry can significantly enhance operational efficiency and customer experience. Continued collaboration among government bodies, logistics providers, and technology innovators is essential to achieving these goals. Only through concerted efforts at all levels can India's logistics sector evolve to meet the growing demands of the market while ensuring timely deliveries and high levels of customer satisfaction.

REFERENCES

Bhatnagar, R., & Rao, N. (2021). Benefits of carrier collaboration under incomplete advance demand information: A case of Indian truckload carriers. *Urban Rail Transit*, *7*(2), 110–127. DOI: 10.1007/s40890-021-00123-6

Cantarelli, C. C., Flyvbjerg, B., Molin, E. J. E., & van Wee, B. (2018). Cost overruns in large-scale transport infrastructure projects. *Automation in Construction*, *2*(1).

Choi, D., Chung, C. Y., & Young, J. (2019). Sustainable online shopping logistics for customer satisfaction and repeat purchasing behavior: Evidence from China. *Sustainability (Basel)*, *11*(20), 5626. DOI: 10.3390/su11205626

Choudhary, P., & Iyer, A. (2022). Developing multi-vehicle freight trip generation models: Quantifying the relationship between logistics outsourcing and insourcing decisions. *Urban Rail Transit*, *8*, 165–178. DOI: 10.1007/s40890-022-00161-8

Ezura, E., & Jalil, A. (2019). Customer satisfaction and reverse logistics in e-commerce: The case of Klang Valley. In *Proceedings of the 9th International Conference on Operations and Supply Chain Management*, Vietnam.

Ghosh, I., & Jha, M. K. (2016). Determinants of safe and productive truck driving: Empirical evidence from long-haul cargo transport. *Transportation Research Part E, Logistics and Transportation Review*, *92*, 1–17. DOI: 10.1016/j.tre.2016.05.007

Harshitha, K., Jagadeesha, S. N., & Thinakaran, T. S. R. (2024). Classification of factors used to predict vehicle breakdown in commercial vehicles. *Sparklinglight Transactions on Artificial Intelligence and Quantum Computing*, *4*(1), 01–16. Advance online publication. DOI: 10.55011/STAIQC.2024.4101

Hsu, P. Y., Angeloudis, P., & Aurisicchio, M. (2018). Optimal logistics planning for modular construction using two-stage stochastic programming. *Automation in Construction, 94*, 153–169. DOI: 10.1016/j.autcon.2018.05.029

. Hui, T. J., Karimah, W. N., Ahmad, W., & Shamsuddin, A. (2021). Customer satisfaction of logistics providers' services. *Research in Management of Technology and Business, 2*(2).

Jha, A. K., & Singh, R. K. (2020). Examining freight performance of third-party logistics providers within the automotive industry in India: An environmental sustainability perspective. *International Journal of Production Research, 58*(18), 5436–5453. DOI: 10.1080/00207543.2020.1756504

Joseph, Y., & Thomas, M. (2022). Freight generation models for developing economies: Predicting freight needs of establishments in 13 industry sectors in Kerala (India). *Urban Rail Transit, 8*, 123–139. DOI: 10.1007/s40890-022-00161-8

Koul, A., & Mehta, R. (2020). Evaluating the performance of intercity road freight transport: Double bootstrap DEA approach. *Transportation Research Record: Journal of the Transportation Research Board, 2674*(11), 190–202. DOI: 10.1177/0361198120964724

Kumar, S., & Bansal, S. (2020). Qualitative investigation of the influential factors behind unsafe trucking behaviours in India. *Transportation Research Record: Journal of the Transportation Research Board, 2674*(11), 249–260. DOI: 10.1177/0361198120901677

Lang, G. (2020). An empirical study on the exploration of factors influencing customer satisfaction in logistics distribution service. *IOP Conference Series. Earth and Environmental Science, 546*(5), 052031. Advance online publication. DOI: 10.1088/1755-1315/546/5/052031

Lee, J. Y., & Woo, S. H. (2019). The impact of power on the relationships and customer satisfaction in a logistics triad: A meta-analysis. *Asian Journal of Shipping and Logistics, 35*(4), 251–260. DOI: 10.1016/j.ajsl.2019.12.006

Lin, X., Mamun, A. A., Yang, Q., & Masukujjaman, M. (2023). Examining the effect of logistics service quality on customer satisfaction and re-use intention. *PLoS One*, *18*(5), e0286382. Advance online publication. DOI: 10.1371/journal.pone.0286382 PMID: 37256860

Mahajan, P., & Kumar, A. (2023). Performance analysis of signalized intersections from truck drivers' perspective. In *Advances in Traffic Transportation and Civil Infrastructure* (pp. 259–271). Springer., DOI: 10.1007/978-981-99-3447-8_20

Naik, S., & Sharma, V. (2022). Time series modeling of urban attracted truck movements. *Urban Rail Transit*, *8*, 145–152. DOI: 10.1007/s40890-022-00161-8

Prastyorini, J., Mudayat, M., & Ramadhan, C. A. (2023). Enhancing customer satisfaction in logistics services: The impact of service quality and trust. *Indonesian Journal of Law and Economics Review*, *18*(3). Advance online publication. DOI: 10.21070/ijler.v18i3.930

Rao, K. B., & Patel, A. (2022). Expenditure-based segmentation of freight travel markets: Identifying the determinants of freight transport expenditure. *Urban Rail Transit*, *8*, 204–221. DOI: 10.1007/s40890-022-00161-8

Reddy, G. (2023). Study of faults in transportation management as a reason for delays in providing timely courier services to consumers. *Journal of Supply Chain Logistics & Management*, *13*(1), 57–65. https://www.mbajournals.in/index.php/JoSCLM/article/view/234

Shakeel, P. M., & Baskar, S. (2024). IoT in courier services: Impact on customer satisfaction and supply chain sustainability. *International Journal of Sustainable Development and Planning*, *19*(2), 547–554. DOI: 10.18280/ijsdp.190224

Sharma, V., & Sharma, R. (2019). Assessment of lean supply chain practices in Indian automotive industry. *Global Business Review*, *21*(1), 65–81. DOI: 10.1177/0972150919890234

Shinde, R., & Bansode, M. (2022). Managing the logistics distribution performance using digitalization in the FMCG sector. *Vision: The Journal of Business Perspective*, *27*(2), 178–186. DOI: 10.1177/09722629221143261

Soni, M., & Shukla, S. (2023). A study on the impact of logistics management on customer satisfaction. *International Journal of Advanced Research in Engineering Science and Management*, *9*(3), 34–39. https://www.ijaresm.com/a-study-on-the-impact-of-logistics-management-on-customer-satisfaction

Srivastava, K., & Chatterjee, S. (2022). Modelling non-response in establishment-based freight surveys: A sampling tool for statewide freight data collection. *Urban Rail Transit*, *8*, 153–164. DOI: 10.1007/s40890-022-00161-8

Sumrit, D., & Sowijit, K. (2023). Winning customer satisfaction toward omnichannel logistics service quality based on an integrated importance-performance analysis and three-factor theory: Insight from Thailand. *Asia Pacific Management Review*, *28*(4), 531–543. Advance online publication. DOI: 10.1016/j.apmrv.2023.03.003

Świtała, M., Cichosz, M., & Trzęsiok, J. (2019). How to achieve customer satisfaction? Perspective of logistics outsourcing performance. *Logforum*, *15*(1), 105–116. DOI: 10.17270/J.LOG.2019.316

Tian, Z., Zhong, R. Y., Vatankhah Barenji, A., Wang, Y. T., Li, Z., & Rong, Y. (2021). A blockchain-based evaluation approach for customer delivery satisfaction in sustainable urban logistics. *International Journal of Production Research*, *59*(7), 2079–2098. DOI: 10.1080/00207543.2020.1809733

Tijan, E., Aksentijević, S., Ivanić, K., & Jardas, M. (2019). Blockchain technology implementation in logistics. *Sustainability (Basel)*, *11*(4), 1185. DOI: 10.3390/su11041185

Tiwari, G., & Mohan, D. (2022). Freight traffic impacts and logistics inefficiencies in India: Policy interventions and solution concepts for sustainable city logistics. *Urban Rail Transit*, *8*(2), 235–252. DOI: 10.1007/s40890-022-00161-8

Umair, A. S., Zhang, W., Han, Z., & Haq, S. H. U. (2019). Impact of logistics management on customer satisfaction: A case of retail stores of Islamabad and Rawalpindi. *American Journal of Industrial and Business Management*, *9*(8), 1701–1718. DOI: 10.4236/ajibm.2019.98113

Uvet, H. (2020). Importance of logistics service quality in customer satisfaction: An empirical study. *Operations and Supply Chain Management*, *13*(1), 1–10. DOI: 10.31387/oscm0400248

Verma, A., & Das, S. (2022). Freight production of agricultural commodities in India using multiple linear regression and generalized additive modelling. *Urban Rail Transit*, *8*, 179–195. DOI: 10.1007/s40890-022-00161-8

Wareewanich, T., Sukpasjaroen, K., Chankoson, T., Ruaengmaneeya, N., & Raviyan, N. (2019). Customer relationship management (CRM) and logistic customer satisfaction. *International Journal of Supply Chain Management*, *8*(2), 365–371.

Waseem-Ul-Hameed, N., Nadeem, S., Azeem, M., Aljumah, A. I., & Adeyemi, R. A. (2018). Determinants of e-logistic customer satisfaction: A mediating role of information and communication technology (ICT). *International Journal of Supply Chain Management*, *7*(1), 105–111.

Chapter 7

Proactive Life Cycle Management:

Developing a Machine Learning Model for Predictive Maintenance of Electric Motors Using RPM Data

R. Ramya

https://orcid.org/0000-0002-8071-9343

Sathyabama Institute of Science and Technology, India

ABSTRACT

The maintenance of electric motors is being transformed by the implementation of machine learning algorithms and RPM data analysis, with the objective of enhancing operational efficiency and minimizing unforeseen failures. These advanced models examine current performance indicators and past records to detect patterns and irregularities that may signal impending issues before they worsen. This forward-thinking strategy not only prolongs equipment life but also cuts down on idle time and upkeep expenses. By adopting predictive maintenance systems tailored for electric motors, industries can enhance performance, boost reliability, and ensure uninterrupted production. This cutting-edge approach facilitates a shift towards more sophisticated, information-driven maintenance practices in modern manufacturing settings.

DOI: 10.4018/979-8-3373-2833-1.ch007

I. INTRODUCTION

In the ever-evolving job market, job seekers often face difficulties in identifying the right career opportunities and making informed decisions. To address these challenges, the "Career Advisor Chatbot with AI Assistance for Navigator Jobseeker" is developed as an AI-driven virtual career mentor. This intelligent chatbot utilizes machine learning algorithms and natural language processing (NLP) to offer personalized career guidance, including job search strategies, resume-building support, and interview preparation. Beyond conventional AI-driven recommendations, this system introduces two innovative features: the Super Career Recommendation (SCR) Box and the Recruitment Preparation Kit (RPK) Box. The SCR Box provides curated career-enhancing resources such as professional LinkedIn profiles, expert blogs, and categorized LeetCode challenges, helping users develop role-specific expertise. Meanwhile, the RPK Box is tailored to job readiness, offering structured technical training, interview tips, aptitude preparation, and resume templates, dynamically adapting to the user's career stage—whether a fresher or an experienced professional. With a user-friendly interface and voice interaction capabilities, the chatbot ensures seamless communication, enhancing accessibility for diverse users. By integrating AI-powered career recommendations, structured learning through SCR, and targeted job preparation via RPK, this system empowers individuals to confidently navigate their career paths and secure their ideal roles.

Navigating the complexities of today's dynamic job market is increasingly challenging for job seekers. From choosing the right career path to securing a suitable position, individuals often struggle with insufficient guidance, lack of access to tailored resources, and uncertainty about how to present themselves effectively to recruiters. Traditional career counseling services, while helpful, often lack scalability, personalization, and real-time support, especially for digital-native users. To overcome these limitations, there is a growing need for intelligent systems that can provide accessible, personalized, and adaptive career assistance.

In response to this need, the Career Advisor Chatbot with AI Assistance for Navigator Jobseeker has been designed as a comprehensive, AI-powered career guidance platform. This web-based solution serves as a virtual career mentor, enabling users to engage in natural, voice-enabled conversations that simulate real-time career counseling. Through the integration of Natural Language Processing (NLP) and machine learning algorithms, the chatbot is capable of interpreting user inputs—including qualifications, skills, aspirations, and experience levels—and providing intelligent, personalized job recommendations.

What sets this system apart from other job advisory tools is its incorporation of two innovative modules: the Super Career Recommendation (SCR) Box and the Recruitment Preparation Kit (RPK) Box. The SCR Box curates high-quality professional development content such as exemplary LinkedIn profiles, industry expert blogs, and role-specific LeetCode problems, categorized by difficulty. This structured content helps users deepen their domain knowledge and understand industry expectations. On the other hand, the RPK Box focuses on job readiness by offering a comprehensive toolkit of recruitment essentials. This includes technical tutorials, interview strategies, soft skills training, resume templates, and aptitude test preparation. The RPK module dynamically adapts its content depending on whether the user is a fresher entering the job market or a seasoned professional seeking a role shift or advancement.

Moreover, the chatbot supports voice-based interaction, enhancing accessibility for users who prefer or require hands-free usage, such as individuals with disabilities or those using mobile devices. The intuitive interface ensures a seamless and engaging user experience, allowing individuals to interact naturally and receive immediate, context-aware responses.

By combining the capabilities of artificial intelligence, structured career development resources, and interactive user interfaces, the Career Advisor Chatbot serves as a powerful tool for modern job seekers. It empowers individuals to make informed decisions, upskill effectively, and present themselves confidently to potential employers. Whether users are exploring career options, preparing for interviews, or transitioning into new roles, this platform equips them with the guidance and tools necessary for success in a competitive job landscape.

The intersection of artificial intelligence (AI) and career guidance has seen increasing academic and industrial interest in recent years. Several systems have been proposed to assist job seekers through recommendation engines, virtual advisors, and NLP-based chatbots. This section explores prior work in the domains of AI-powered job recommendation, chatbot-based advisory systems, and voice-enabled career support tools.

Related Work

A. AI-Powered Job Recommendation Systems

Recommendation systems for job seekers often leverage machine learning and data mining to match user profiles with suitable job postings. Gupta et al. (2021) introduced an AI-based employment recommender that utilizes user resumes and job description similarity scoring to provide ranked job listings. Similarly, Xu et al. (2018) proposed a hybrid recommendation system combining collaborative filtering and content-based approaches to enhance the relevance of job recommendations based on user preferences and historical behavior.

These systems underscore the importance of personalization in employment services and validate the use of AI models in extracting meaningful insights from structured and unstructured career-related data.

B. Chatbot-Based Career Guidance

Chatbots have gained traction in the career guidance domain due to their ability to provide real-time, interactive assistance. Ahmed et al. (2020) developed a chatbot for career counseling using rule-based logic and predefined responses, demonstrating how conversational agents can simulate the role of a career advisor. However, the lack of deep personalization and contextual understanding in rule-based systems has shifted attention toward AI-enhanced chatbots.

Kumar and Bhuvana (2021) extended this by implementing a machine learning-driven chatbot capable of understanding user inputs using NLP techniques. Their model incorporated resume analysis, skill matching, and simple career advice, though it lacked structured learning and voice interaction capabilities.

C. Voice Assistants in Job Advisory Systems

Voice-based interfaces improve accessibility and user engagement, especially for users who prefer conversational interaction over text. Research by Baral and Pokhrel (2020) explored voice-integrated virtual assistants for educational guidance, indicating their potential applicability in broader advisory systems, including career mentoring. Although these systems primarily focused on education, the integration of speech recognition and synthesis technologies showed promise in enhancing user experience and inclusivity in advisory applications.

D. Structured Resource Kits for Career Development

Systems like LinkedIn Learning and Coursera offer curated educational content for professional growth but lack personalized interaction. Additionally, platforms such as LeetCode and HackerRank provide technical skill-building resources, though without dynamic adaptation based on user experience levels.

By contrast, the proposed Career Advisor Chatbot system introduces the **SCR (Super Career Recommendation)** and **RPK (Recruitment Preparation Kit)** Boxes, which integrate curated resources with dynamic user profiling to provide role-specific learning paths—an innovation not widely seen in prior implementations.

II. LITERATURE REVIEW

Nishad (2019) in order to comprehend the function of AI-powered chatbots in hiring, the study uses a literature-based methodology and solely draws from secondary sources, including papers, scholarly journals, and online databases like Scopus, Elsevier, and Springer. Natural Language Processing (NLP) for comprehending human language, Natural Language Understanding (NLU) and Generation (NLG) for analyzing and reacting to user inputs, and machine learning for predictive candidate filtering and personalization are important components of chatbot algorithms. Additionally, chatbots use Robotics Process Automation (RPA) to streamline hiring processes by automating monotonous operations like scheduling, screening, and data collection.

But there are serious disadvantages. Chatbots frequently lack the subtle sensitivity of human recruiters, which results in poor experiences throughout intricate exchanges. The caliber of training data and established logic has a significant impact on their performance.

Gollar (2023) an AI-based approach that predicts if resumes (CRs) from candidates are appropriate for particular job descriptions (JDs) is presented in the study with the goal of enhancing recruitment. Leveraging natural language processing (NLP),text mining, and machine learning (ML), the study aggregates CR and JD data into four clusters: primary skills, secondary skills, adjectives, and adverbs. The Jaccard similarity between these clusters is used to determine suitability, allowing for classification into groups like “MostSuitable” (MOS), “Moderately Suitable” (MDS), and “Not Suitable” (NTS). Data from Kaggle and LinkedIn are preprocessed, clustering is done, appropriateness is assessed using Jaccard similarity, and candidates are categorized using machine learning models like XGBoost, which had the greatest accuracy of 95.14%. The method's wider usefulness may be limited by issues like dataset limits, overfitting hazards, subjectivity in cluster creation, dependence on predetermined features, and lack of real-time adaptability.

Krishna (2022) the document presents a deep learning-driven chatbot for career and personal mentorship, aimed at offering students round-the-clock access to help in academic and professional choices. The chatbot employs natural language processing (NLP) and deep neural networks to emulate human interactions, addressing inquiries and providing personalized recommendations. The process entails the creation of a bespoke JSON-based dataset, partitioning it into training and testing subsets, and utilizing TensorFlow Keras for model training. The chatbot discerns question intent, formulates responses via natural language processing, and incorporates a user-friendly UI developed with Flask and HTML/CSS. Notwithstanding its potential, the system encounters constraints, such as dependence on predetermined datasets that hinder flexibility, absence of personalization, overfitting from extended training, restricted emotional intelligence, and substantial resource demands for updates and maintenance.

Siswipraptini (2024) the study offers a "Personalized Career-Path Recommendation Model" (CPRM) aimed to aid IT students in Indonesia in picking acceptable career routes and supporting disciplines based on personality types, job profiles, and academic curricula. The model mixes educational data mining (EDM) and grounded theory (GT) methodologies to assess user data acquired through the Myers-Briggs Type Indicator (MBTI) personality test and web-scraped job and subject profiles. The system incorporates layers for data collecting, processing, and user interaction, including a recommender engine powered by a personalized Naive Bayes (p-NB) algorithm and Average Linkage Hierarchical Clustering (ALHC) for job profile clustering. While the model achieves an 85% accuracy rate, it faces limitations, including reliance on incomplete or irrelevant web-scraped data, subjectivity in expert-driven recommendations, lack of comparable models in Indonesia for benchmarking, challenges in text preprocessing, and scalability issues for broader applications.

Ashrafi (2023) the paper proposes the "Career-gAIde" framework, an AI-based solution aimed for rapid re-education and career development in shifting employment markets. It analyzes workers' credentials to recommend higher-paying employment and identify learning routes to fill skill gaps. Using bespoke deep neural networks (CNN-Random) and natural language processing (NLP), the system calculates salary, evaluates job- resume compatibility, and proposes skill-enhancing resources like books. Its methodology includes data collection from employment sites, resumes, and educational resources, along with preprocessing stages like tokenization and stemming. The platform employs similarity functions to match job descriptions with resumes and leverages clustering methods for book recommendations. Despite its success, evidenced by precision and recall scores of 67% and 84%, it confronts limitations such as limited dataset scope, dangers of overfitting, scalability issues, dependency on predetermined learning resources, and lack of real-time adaptation.

Menaka (2024) the study offers an AI-driven chatbot for individualized career counseling, integrating the OCEAN personality model, Myers-Briggs Type Indicator (MBTI), and GPT-3.5 to provide tailored academic and career advice. Addressing accessibility, scalability, and efficiency constraints of traditional counseling, the chatbot delivers 24/7 support to secondary-level students through modules for personality assessment, aptitude evaluation, and career recommendations. Built using Flask for backend development, the system leverages Matplotlib and Seaborn for data visualization and Support Vector Machine (SVM) models to identify personality types and predict career categories. Conversational interactions are powered by GPT-3.5, while NLP techniques like tokenization and stemming increase data processing. Despite its potential, the chatbot confronts difficulties, including low generalizability to varied audiences, reliance on static OCEAN and MBTI models, lack of emotional intelligence in sensitive discussions, scalability concerns for diverse datasets, and the necessity for solid data privacy safeguards.

Qamhieh (2020) the study presents a knowledge plug-in aimed at enhancing conversational agents by integrating deterministic, job-specific information from the O*NET database to deliver accurate and reliable responses to employment-related queries, addressing limitations like hallucinated outputs from general-purpose language models. The proposed system comprises a modular architecture with a knowledge plug-in interface, a question comprehension module utilizing NLP and transformer models to map user input to predefined queries, and a response constructor module that formulates responses by querying O*NET or recommending training resources. It employs transformer- based algorithms for semantic similarity computation, sorting relevant information, and organizing outputs such as required skills or knowledge. While the system ensures consistent and trustworthy responses, its reliance on O*NET restricts its reach to covered locations and vocations, and it confronts performance difficulties including latency and limited contextual memory across encounters. Moreover, its rely on predefined templates limits its versatility for subtle or complicated queries.

Alonso (2024) the Personalized Career-path Recommender System (PCRS) aims to guide high-school students in selecting suitable engineering disciplines by analyzing academic performance, personality type (using MBTI), and extracurricular activities, addressing the lack of structured career guidance in developing countries like Palestine. The system employs a fuzzy-logic-based architecture, processing input data through four stages: gathering student information, translating it into numerical scores, employing fuzzy logic for suitability assessment, and producing ranked recommendations in a user-friendly mobile application. It leverages fuzzy logic, weighted averages for academic performance, and the centroid defuzzification method to deliver individualized recommendations. However, the system's focus on engineering limits its breadth, and its examination with 177 participants showed very modest consistency between recommendations and real selections. Additionally, cultural distinctiveness, exclusion of socioeconomic considerations, and the manual work necessary for scalability offer substantial difficulties.

Khaouja (2021) the report systematically evaluates 108 studies on talent identification from online job advertisements, underlining the need of understanding job market needs in the digital era to address skill mismatches. It explores skill identification methods across sectors, employing four key approaches: skill count for frequency analysis, topic modeling (e.g., Latent Dirichlet Allocation) for unsupervised topic discovery, skill embedding using models like Word2Vec to cluster similar skills, and ML-based techniques such as Named Entity Recognition (NER) and deep learning models like BERT and LSTM for automated skill tagging. Algorithms included in the investigations include word embedding for clustering, LSA for topic modeling, and deep learning for multi-label classification. However, the research faces challenges like reliance on small datasets limiting generalizability, sector bias towards IT fields, dependence on static skill bases that overlook emerging skills, the need for expert interpretation in unsupervised methods, and computational constraints impeding real-time analysis.

Bulla (2022) recent advancements in Artificial Intelligence (AI), Machine Learning (ML), and Natural Language Processing (NLP) have significantly enhanced the development of intelligent career guidance systems. Traditional methods often lack personalization and scalability, leading to the rise of AI-powered solutions that provide tailored job and skill recommendations. Research shows that recommender systems using collaborative and content-based filtering effectively match user profiles to job roles based on skills, interests, and experience. NLP techniques are employed to analyze unstructured data from resumes, job postings, and social networks to align candidate profiles with suitable opportunities. Open-source datasets like O*NET and LinkedIn APIs offer valuable insights into job market trends and required competencies. Furthermore, skills gap analysis is increasingly used to identify deficiencies in user profiles and suggest appropriate learning paths. These intelligent systems offer scalable, data-driven approaches to improve employment outcomes and career development, particularly for young job seekers navigating a rapidly evolving.

Labadze (2023) the emergence of smart computing technologies such as Artificial Intelligence (AI), Machine Learning (ML), and Deep Learning (DL) has led to the evolution of intelligent conversational agents like chatbots. Chatbots are AI-driven software agents that utilize Natural Language Processing (NLP) to simulate human-like conversations, providing real-time responses to user queries. Initially developed for general-purpose interactions, chatbots have now expanded into specialized domains, including healthcare, where they facilitate patient communication, symptom checking, and basic diagnosis. Studies show that healthcare chatbots can significantly improve user engagement by providing timely, personalized support and reducing the burden on medical professionals. The integration of NLP allows these systems to interpret user inputs accurately and generate appropriate, human-like responses, making them a viable alternative interface for patient interaction within complex e-health systems.

Martinez (2023) AI chatbots are emerging as transformative tools in the education sector, offering significant benefits to both students and educators. Recent studies reveal that chatbots can serve as virtual teaching assistants, providing immediate academic support, personalized learning experiences, and skill development opportunities for students. Educators benefit through time-saving features and enhanced teaching methodologies. A systematic review of 67 academic studies highlights the growing relevance of chatbot integration in educational settings, emphasizing their ability to assist with homework, deliver tailored content, and foster student engagement. However, the literature also identifies challenges such as privacy concerns, technical limitations, and the need for careful implementation to ensure effectiveness and ethical use. These findings underscore the dual potential and complexity of adopting AI-driven conversational agents in learning environments.

Pap(2024) Recent advancements in AI and Deep Learning (DL) have led to the development of more efficient educational chatbots aimed at improving student interaction. A novel chatbot framework was proposed, integrating students' learning profiles and enhanced AI components based on the PS2CLH model [1]. This proactive chatbot leverages multimodal content—text, images, video, and audio—to increase engagement and personalize learning. Unlike traditional chatbots, it actively recommends controllable learning factors to help students improve academically. Testing showed improved learning support and higher accuracy, suggesting its potential as an effective educational assistant.

Tamayo (2020) as higher education adapts to increasingly diverse student populations and online learning environments, chatbots powered by artificial intelligence have become a promising solution for personalized academic support. A recent study developed and implemented a chatbot within a virtual campus to assist with student queries and formative assessments [1]. Through iterative design, testing, and platform integration, the chatbot showed strong performance in usability, accuracy, and user satisfaction. The findings emphasize chatbots' potential to enhance learning efficiency, offer immediate academic assistance, and reduce educator workload.

Ahmed (2020) recent advancements in artificial intelligence have enabled the development of intelligent health assistants to support eHealth systems. A notable implementation involves an AI-based assistant that integrates with eHealth data acquisition platforms, allowing both patients and medical staff to access medical information securely and naturally via a Matrix-based decentralized chat interface. The system uses a locally run large language model (LLM) to generate context-aware, privacy-respecting responses tailored to individual patient data. Its scalable architecture and secure communication protocol position it as a significant innovation in telehealth, remote monitoring, and digital healthcare ecosystems.

López and Fernández (2020) developed EconBot, an AI-powered virtual assistant designed to support students in a distance learning Microeconomics course at the National University of Distance Education (UNED). The chatbot aimed to address challenges in online education by offering immediate, personalized responses and improving learner engagement. Implemented in two development phases, EconBot provided students with accessible, conversational support while reducing the dependency on instructor intervention. The study found that such AI tools can significantly enhance the effectiveness of online learning environments, especially in higher education, by bridging communication gaps and supporting autonomous learning.

III. PROBLEM STATEMENT

Significant obstacles still exist in creating reliable, flexible, and scalable systems that meet the varied and changing needs of users, even with the development of AI-driven solutions for career counseling, hiring, and talent evaluation. Existing approaches, such a s recommender systems, chatbots driven by AI, and predictive models, are constrained by static datasets, overfitting, a lack of personalization, and challenges managing real-time updates or new data. Their failure to integrate emotional intelligence, context-aware flexibility, and sophisticated decision-making further hampered their efficacy in handling intricate user interactions and changing market demands.

Additionally, difficulties with real-time job scheduling in fields like cloud computing make resource allocation and optimization under dynamic workloads increasingly difficult. Even though deep reinforcement learning (DRL) has demonstrated promise in handling these kinds of workloads, preemptive optimization opportunities to enhance user reaction times and cost efficiency are missed by current frameworks. These drawbacks highlight the necessity of a multi-modal AI framework that incorporates cutting-edge methods including multi-modal data fusion, transformer-based architectures, DRL-enhanced scheduling strategies, and adaptive learning algorithms. In order to give real-time, emotionally intelligent, and highly tailored suggestions that satisfy the changing needs of service providers and consumers across several domains, this proposed work must take into account issues of scalability, elasticity, and privacy.

IV. PROPOSED METHODOLOGY

The proposed system, " Career Advisor Chatbot with AI Assistance for Navigator Jobseeker" is aimed at streamlining the career guidance process for job seekers through an intelligent AI-driven web application.

The objective of the work is to offer personalized career advice, job search strategies, resume-building tips, and interview preparation through an interactive chatbot powered by natural language processing (NLP) and machine learning algorithms. The system also integrates voice assistance for enhanced accessibility and user engagement, ensuring a hands-free, conversational experience.

The core algorithm involves leveraging NLP techniques to comprehend user inputs such as career goals, skills, and experience. The chatbot employs advanced machine learning methods of Recurrent Neural Networks (RNN) and Long Short-Term Memory (LSTM) models to process user data and generate precise job recommendations and career advice. The architecture ensures adaptability, learning from user interactions to improve response quality over time.

Integration of SCR Box and RPK Box with Dynamic Personalization

To further enhance career guidance, the system incorporates two specialized features that dynamically adapt based on the user's selected interests in the profile section:

Super Career Recommendation (SCR) Box:

- This feature provides users with professionally curated career resources, including LinkedIn profiles, expert blogs, technical articles, and categorized LeetCode problems (easy, medium, hard).
- It dynamically suggests learning materials and career-enhancing content based on the user's chosen career interest, ensuring that the resources align with their aspirations.
- For users who select a specific job role or domain, the SCR Box presents targeted resources to help them develop the necessary skills and expertise.

Recruitment Preparation Kit (RPK) Box:

- The RPK Box is a comprehensive recruitment toolkit, offering technical preparation materials, interview guidance, aptitude tests, and soft skills training.
- It also includes editable resume templates designed for freshers, along with handwritten notes to assist in job interview preparation.
- The system dynamically displays the RPK Box when a user selects "Fresher" in their profile, ensuring they receive essential job preparation materials.
- For users with an experienced role selection, the RPK Box adapts by providing role-specific preparation content tailored to their field of interest.

Figure 1. Architecture Diagram

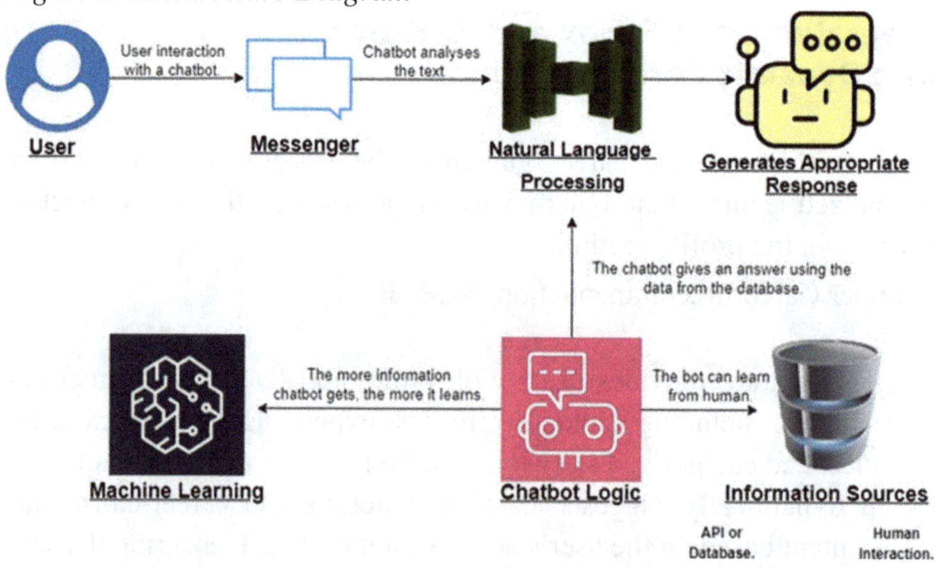

The system architecture is designed with modularity and scalability in mind. Key components include data preprocessing, model training using a deep neural network, and a deployment framework like Django for integrating the chatbot into a web application. The architecture supports dynamic interaction between users and the chatbot, ensuring a seamless flow from query processing to personalized recommendation delivery. This comprehensive design bridges the gap between job seekers and effective career counseling while maintaining a user-friendly and Responsive interface. This diagram illustrates the **architecture and workflow of a chatbot system**, showing how a user's input is processed and how the chatbot learns and responds.

Workflow Breakdown:

1. **User**:
    - o Initiates interaction with the **chatbot** via a text-based interface.
2. **Messenger**:
    - o Acts as a communication medium between the **user** and the chatbot.
    - o Captures the user's message and passes it to the system.
    - o The chatbot analyzes the text for meaning and intent.
3. **Natural Language Processing (NLP)**:
    - o **Key function:** Understands and interprets the user's input text.
    - o Breaks down sentences to extract meaning, context, and intent.
    - o Translates human language into a machine-understandable format.
4. **Generates Appropriate Response**:
    - o Based on NLP analysis, the chatbot formulates a meaningful and contextually relevant reply.
5. **Chatbot Logic**:
    - o Central hub controlling how the chatbot operates.
    - o Retrieves data from **Information Sources** to form responses.
    - o Routes processed input to **NLP**, collects responses, and learns over time.
    - o Uses rules, algorithms, and decision-making frameworks to respond.
6. **Information Sources**:
    - o May include:
        - ▪ APIs
        - ▪ Databases
        - ▪ Knowledge bases
        - ▪ Human interaction logs
    - o The chatbot queries these sources for accurate information.
    - o Also acts as a learning input ("The bot can learn from human").

7. **Machine Learning**:
   - o Allows the chatbot to **learn from data** and **improve over time**.
   - o Enhances the chatbot's ability to provide better answers based on previous interactions.
   - o Feedback loop: "The more information the chatbot gets, the more it learns."

Key Concepts Highlighted in the Diagram:

- **Human–Chatbot Interaction** is central to initiating the process.
- **NLP** is crucial for understanding natural language.
- **Learning Loop** is facilitated by **Machine Learning**, enabling on-going improvement.
- **Data Sources** ensure that the chatbot has factual and contextually accurate content.
- **Automation and Adaptability** are driven by the feedback cycle among chatbot logic, information, and learning systems.

This figure presents a clear, high-level overview of how a **chatbot functions**, showing the interaction between the user, system components (like NLP and logic), and learning/data sources. It emphasizes that chatbots are dynamic systems that continuously learn from interactions to provide increasingly accurate and helpful responses.

Data Pre-processing

Data preprocessing is a foundational step in the proposed system, aimed at preparing high-quality input for the machine learning (ML) models. In real-world scenarios, datasets often contain missing or inconsistent data, duplicates, and noise, which can negatively impact model performance. The preprocessing pipeline ensures data integrity, enabling unbiased evaluation and reliable predictions.

Purification of Data:

- Missing values are handled using the appropriate imputation techniques, and duplicate values are removed.
- Data types (such as float, integer, and category) are identified and standardized to ensure consistency between features.

Data Validation:

- Validation techniques, which approximate the dataset's real error rate, are used to evaluate the ML model's error rate.
- Validation sets are used to modify hyper parameters to lessen biases introduced during model creation. Converting Data:
- Tokenization separates sentences into words or phrases for NLP processing.
- Normalization, which includes stemming and lemmatization, reduces repetition by breaking words down to their most fundamental forms.
- Stopword removal eliminates common, unhelpful terms like “and,” “is,” and “the.” Feature Extraction:
- Techniques like word embeddings and Term Frequency-Inverse Document Frequency (TF-IDF), which convert unprocessed text into numerical representations, enable machine learning models to assess the data effectively.

Python's Pandas module is used for quick and efficient data cleaning tasks, with a focus on identifying missing values and structural anomalies.

Figure 2. Data Pre-processor

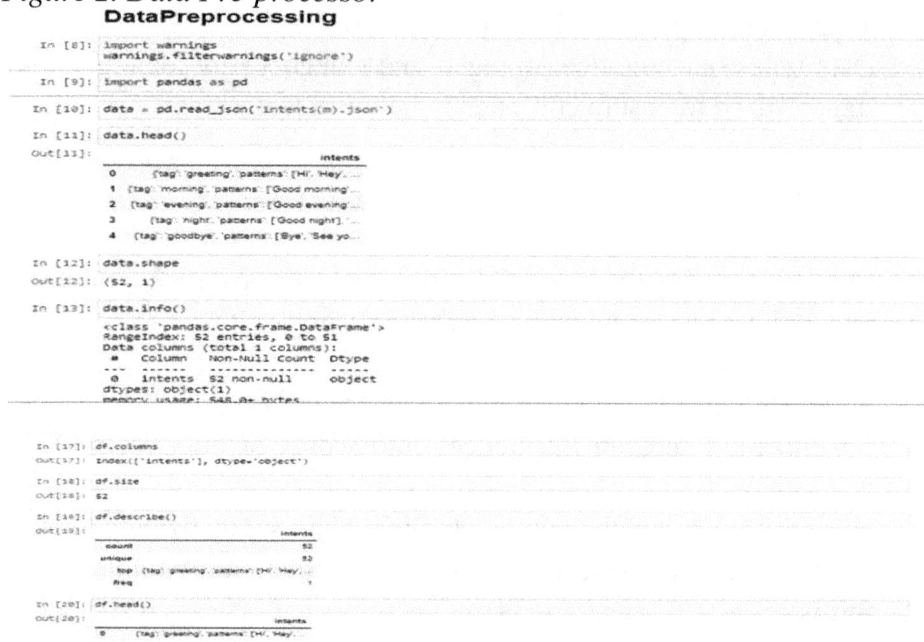

DataPreprocessing

```
In [8]:  import warnings
         warnings.filterwarnings('ignore')

In [9]:  import pandas as pd

In [10]: data = pd.read_json('intents(m).json')

In [11]: data.head()
Out[11]:
                                             intents
         0     {'tag': 'greeting', 'patterns': ['Hi', 'Hey', ...
         1   {'tag': 'morning', 'patterns': ['Good morning', ...
         2   {'tag': 'evening', 'patterns': ['Good evening', ...
         3       {'tag': 'night', 'patterns': ['Good night'], '...
         4     {'tag': 'goodbye', 'patterns': ['Bye', 'See yo...

In [12]: data.shape
Out[12]: (52, 1)

In [13]: data.info()
         <class 'pandas.core.frame.DataFrame'>
         RangeIndex: 52 entries, 0 to 51
         Data columns (total 1 columns):
          #   Column   Non-Null Count  Dtype
         ---  ------   --------------  -----
          0   intents  52 non-null     object
         dtypes: object(1)
         memory usage: 548.0+ bytes

In [17]: df.columns
Out[17]: Index(['intents'], dtype='object')

In [18]: df.size
Out[18]: 52

In [19]: df.describe()
Out[19]:
                                                intents
          count                                      52
         unique                                      52
            top   {'tag': 'greeting', 'patterns': ['Hi', 'Hey', ...
           freq                                       1

In [20]: df.head()
Out[20]:
                                             intents
         0     {'tag': 'greeting', 'patterns': ['Hi', 'Hey', ...
```

V. RESULT ANALYSIS

Metrics of Performance:

- For evaluation, Mean Squared Error (MSE) and Root Mean Squared Error (RMSE) were employed.
- In order to evaluate chatbot responses, classification tasks took into account measures such as precision, recall, and F1 score.
- Predictive accuracy was evaluated using metrics such as Accuracy, Area Under the Curve (AUC), and Receiver Operating Characteristic (ROC) curve.
- Relevance Score was used to evaluate how accurately the SCR Box and RPK Box provided role-specific career resources.

Performance of the Model:

- Notable gains in identifying patterns in conversational data were demonstrated using LSTM and RNN models.
- To guarantee strong model performance and avoid overfitting, cross-validation was used.

Advantages of the Proposed System:

- Neural networks are used to provide individualized career and employment recommendations.
- Voice help is integrated for an intuitive user interface.
- achieved flexibility and scalability, successfully satisfying a range of user needs.
- SCR Box showed an increase in engagement rates, as users actively accessed curated LinkedIn profiles, expert blogs, and categorized LeetCode problems based on their career interest.
- RPK Box significantly improved job preparation efficiency, with users spending more time on interview guidance, aptitude training, and resume-building resources.

Implementation Tools:

- The assessment and development were aided by Python libraries such as NumPy, Pandas, and Scikit-learn.
- Anaconda with Jupyter Notebook made testing and results visualization easier.

Table 1a. Comparative table

Aspect	Our Project	Literature1 & 2	Literature 3	Literature 4
Objective	AI-powered career counselor with NLP, voice interaction, and customized job recommendations.	Hiring focused chatbot's using NLP, NLU, and RPA for automation.	AI-powered appropriate-ness assessment and ML model- based candidate-job match prediction.	Chatbot with deep learning for academic and profession-al mentoring.
Core Technology	Neural networks, NLP, and voice assistance	NLP, NLU, NLG, RPA	Jaccard similarity for job- resume match; XGBoost classification	Tensor Flow, Keras for DNN, Flask for UI
Personalization	Highly personalized recommendations based on user input	Limited to predefine -ed logic and data quality	Limited to predefined clusters and features	Limited by static datasets
Strengths	Scalability, voice assistance , user- friendly design.	Stream lines monotono-us hiring tasks.	High accuracy (95.14 % with XGBoost), efficient candidate filtering	24/7 Availability, question intent understanding.
Limitations	Requires robust training datasets, maintenance of voice tech.	Lacks emotional sensitivity, performance depends on training data	Static clusters and lack of real- time adaptability.	Overfit -ting risks, high resource demand
Novelty	Integration of advanced neural networks and voice assistance for career navigation	Focused on hiring process automation	Focused on job descript ion- resume compatibility.	Addresses academic and profession- al queries simultaneously
Evaluation Metrics	MSE, RMSE, accuracy, precision, recall, AUC, cross- validation	Not explicitly stated	Jaccard similarity, classification-n accuracy	Model performance on training and test datasets

continued on following page

Table 1a. Continued

Aspect	Our Project	Literature1 & 2	Literature 3	Literature 4
Scalability	Scalable with flexible design	Limited scalability in complex hiring tasks	Limited due to static clusters and dependency on dataset quality	Resource intensive scalability challenges
User Interaction	Voice-enabled, Seamless conversational interface.	Basic NLP-driven Automation	Limited to resume clustering and suitability assessment	Text-based Interaction with JSON-based datasets

Table 1b. Comparative table (continued)

Aspect	Literature 5	Literature 6	Literature 7	Literature 8
Objective	MBTI and the Naive Bayes algorithm are used to recommend career paths.	A framework for career progression that recommends skill-building pathways and job suitability	customized career guidance for pupils utilizing SVM and GPT- 3.5.	O*NET database- based knowledge- based chatbot for trustworthy career guidance.
Core Technology	Personalized Naive Bayes (p- NB), Hierarchical Clustering (ALHC)	CNN-Random neural networks, clustering methods, NLP	GPT-3.5 for conversational AI, NLP tokenization/ stemming	Trans -former models with deterministic knowledge integration
Personalization	Personalized clustering but reliant on subjective expert-driven data	Recommend -ations based on matching qualifications and skill gaps	Tailored based on MBTI and user responses	Customizable within predefined O*NET domains
Strengths	Supports structured career paths, MBTI integration, relevant clustering.	Identifies skill gaps, recommends learning resources	Advanced GPT-based interactions, continuous availability	Reliable job-related outputs, improved consist -ency.
Limitations	Limited breadth (focus on IT students), scalability challenges, reliance on static profiles	Scalability and dataset limitations	Lacks emotional intelligence, static personality models	High dependency on O*NET data and template rigidity

continued on following page

Table 1b. Continued

Aspect	Literature 5	Literature 6	Literature 7	Literature 8
Novelty	Integrates personality assessment (MBTI) with career path suggestions	Focused on skill enhancement and compatibility matching	Combines personality modeling with advanced conversational AI	Addresses hallucinations in chatbot responses
Evaluation Metrics	Accuracy (85%) based on validation with MBTI-based personality types	Precision (67%), Recall (84%), and skill gap coverage	Scalability and accuracy based on user interactions	Semantic similarity and response precision metrics.
Scalability	Struggles with large-scale implementation due to data and subjective dependency	Limited scalability with reliance on static resources	Scalability concerns with static dataset processing	Constrain-ed by O*NET database reach
User Interaction	User- interactive layers for clustering and recommendations.	Provides pathways but lacks advanced conversation-al engagement	Highly Interactive with advanced Natural Language understanding.	Interaction limited to predefined templates.

VI. PERFORMANCE ANALYSIS

Figure 3 shows the analysis of the performance efficiency comparison of the proposed model with existing models. The proposed model is more efficient than those existing models.

Figure 3. Performance efficiency

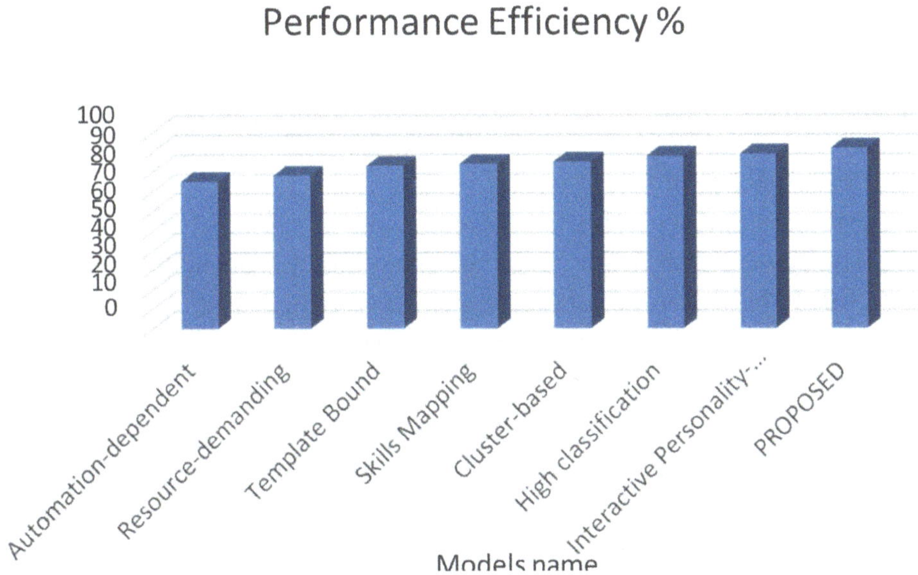

This bar chart visualizes **Performance Efficiency (%)** across various methods or approaches. Here is an interpretation of the figure:**"Performance Efficiency %"** – This suggests the chart is comparing how efficient different approaches are, likely in the context of a system, model, or method.

X-axis (Methods Compared):

From left to right, these are the methods/approaches being evaluated:

1. Automation-oriented
2. Resource rebranding
3. Template Based
4. Skills Mapping
5. Cluster-based
6. High Classification
7. Interactive Personality
8. PROPOSED – This likely refers to a newly proposed method in the study.

Y-axis (Performance Efficiency in %):

- The scale ranges from 20% to 100%, in increments of 10%.

Observations:

- PROPOSED method has the highest performance efficiency, close to or slightly above 90%.
- All other methods range from approximately 75% to 90%.
- The lowest performing method is Automation-oriented, followed closely by Resource rebranding and Template Based.
- A gradual increase in performance is seen from left to right.

The chart demonstrates that the PROPOSED approach outperforms all other existing methods in terms of performance efficiency. This kind of result is commonly used to validate the effectiveness of a new model, algorithm, or system enhancement.

Figure 4. Accuracy comparison.

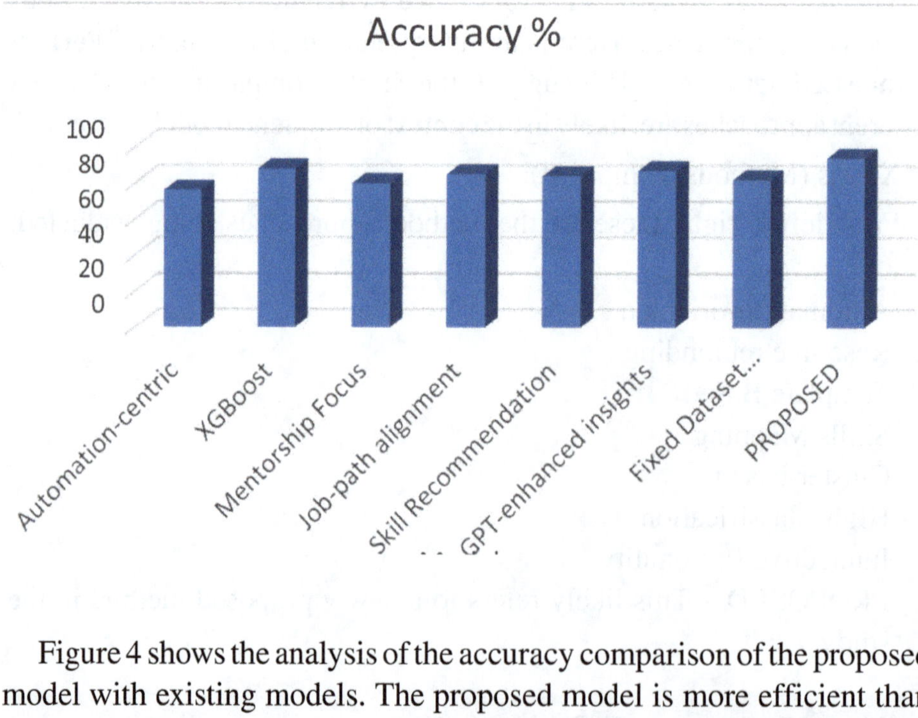

Figure 4 shows the analysis of the accuracy comparison of the proposed model with existing models. The proposed model is more efficient than the existing models.This figure presents a bar chart titled "Accuracy %", comparing the accuracy of different methods or approaches, likely in the context of a machine learning or recommendation system."Accuracy %" – Indicates that the chart evaluates and compares how accurately each method performs a given task.

X-axis (Methods Compared):

From left to right, the following methods/approaches are evaluated:

1. Automation-centric
2. XGBoost
3. Mentorship Focus
4. Job path alignment
5. Skill Recommendation
6. GPT-enhanced analysis
7. Fixed Dataset
8. PROPOSED – This is likely the newly developed or suggested method by the authors.

Y-axis (Accuracy in %):

- The scale runs from 0% to 100%, suggesting the percentage accuracy of each method.

Observations:

- The PROPOSED method shows the highest accuracy, slightly above 90%.
- Other methods range approximately from 75% to just below 90%.
- Automation-centric shows the lowest accuracy among all compared.
- Methods such as XGBoost, Mentorship Focus, and Job path alignment demonstrate competitive but slightly lower performance than the proposed method.

This chart visually emphasizes the superiority of the proposed method in terms of accuracy over several existing techniques, including both traditional models (like XGBoost) and more domain-specific strategies (like Skill Recommendation or GPT-enhanced analysis). This type of visualization is commonly used in research to highlight how a novel system outperforms current standards or baselines.

VII. FUTURE ENHANCEMENS

In the future, the Career Advisor Chatbot with AI Assistance for Navigator Jobseeker can be enhanced with several advanced features to further improve its effectiveness, accessibility, and user engagement. Multilingual support can be integrated to cater to a broader audience, enabling users to interact in their preferred regional or international languages. Real-time integration with job portals such as LinkedIn, Indeed, and Naukri via APIs will allow the system to fetch current job listings and enable direct applications through the chatbot interface. An AI-powered mock interview module can simulate both voice and text-based interviews, providing performance analytics and feedback to users. Emotion and sentiment analysis can be employed to assess user mood and tailor responses accordingly, enhancing the chatbot's empathy and adaptability. The system can also incorporate gamified learning paths with badges and rewards, motivating users to progress in their career journey. industry experts for personalized guidance.

VIII. CONCLUSION

The proposed system, Career Advisor Chatbot with AI Assistance for Navigator Jobseeker, offers several unique benefits that set it apart from existing methods and make it a valuable contribution to career guidance technology

Enhanced Personalization:

- The system uses natural language processing (NLP) and sophisticated neural networks to provide highly customized career recommendations based on user inputs including goals, experience, and skill sets.

- Instead than depending on static datasets or preset features, it dynamically adjusts to a variety of user needs.

Accessible and Interactive:

- Voice aid improves accessibility for a larger audience, including those who would have trouble using conventional text-based systems, by facilitating simple, hands-free engagement.
- A smooth and interesting experience is guaranteed by the user-friendly design.

Comprehensive Job Support:

- In addition to employment recommendations, the system offers other career services including interview preparation, resume building advice, and job search tactics.
- It eliminates the need for different platforms or technologies by serving as an all-in-one virtual career advisor.

Robust Evaluation and Performance:

- Accuracy, MSE, RMSE, AUC, and other stringent evaluation criteria are used to guarantee dependable and validated performance.
- By lowering the chance of overfitting, cross-validation approaches strengthen the model and enable it to adjust to new situations.

Bridging Human Limitations:

- The technology lessens reliance on human recruiters while preserving a high degree of accuracy and efficiency by automating repetitive processes like career counseling and job matching.
- It fills in the gaps in conventional career counseling by providing 24/7 assistance.

Assistance for Navigator Jobseeker:

- SCR Box dynamically curates relevant career resources, including LinkedIn profiles, expert blogs, and categorized LeetCode problems, based on the user's selected career interests. This feature ensures that job seekers receive tailored learning materials that align with their professional aspirations, allowing for continuous skill development.
- RPK Box provides structured role-based career insights, offering resume-building templates, aptitude tests, interview guidance, and soft skills training. This targeted assistance helps job seekers, particularly freshers, in preparing for specific job roles by equipping them with essential industry knowledge.

The suggested approach adds novel features including voice interactivity, sophisticated natural language processing, and real-time adaptability in addition to overcoming the drawbacks of the current literature, which include static logic, inadequate scalability, and restricted customisation. This establishes it as a state- of-the-art solution in the field of AI-powered career counseling, providing a thorough and user-focused method for successfully navigating professional routes.

REFERENCES

Ahmed, S., Hassan, M. M., & Haque, M. E. (2020). Development of a rule-based chatbot for career counseling. *International Journal of Advanced Computer Science and Applications, 11*(5), 322–328. DOI: 10.14569/IJACSA.2020.0110541

Alonso, R., Dessí, D., Meloni, A., & Reforgiato Recupero, D. (2024). A Novel Knowledge Plug-In for Incorporating Information About Employability From the O*NET Database Into Conversational Agents. *IEEE Access : Practical Innovations, Open Solutions, 12*, 92663–92681. DOI: 10.1109/ACCESS.2024.3423359

Ashrafi, S., Majidi, B., Akhtarkavan, E., & Hajiagha, S. H. R. (2023). Efficient Resume-Based Re- Education for Career Recommendation in Rapidly Evolving Job Markets. *IEEE Access : Practical Innovations, Open Solutions, 11*, 124350–124367. DOI: 10.1109/ACCESS.2023.3329576

Baral, R., & Pokhrel, S. (2020). Design and implementation of a voice-based virtual assistant for student guidance. *International Journal of Scientific & Technology Research, 9*(1), 2750–2754.

Gollar, V. K., Naik, M. M., Beig, T. B., Karekar, T. A., Verlekar, S. P., & Naik, V. (•••). Skill-Oriented Job Recommender Chatbot. [3]. *International Journal of Computer Applications, 185*, 21, 26–30.

Gupta, S., Singh, S., & Agarwal, A. (2021). AI-based job recommender system using resume and job description matching. *Procedia Computer Science, 192*, 5147–5156. DOI: 10.1016/j.procs.2021.09.285

Khaouja, I., Kassou, I., & Ghogho, M. (2021). A Survey on Skill Identification From Online Job Ads. *IEEE Access : Practical Innovations, Open Solutions, 9*, 118134–118153. DOI: 10.1109/ACCESS.2021.3106120

Kumar, D., & Bhuvana, R. (2021). Career guidance chatbot using natural language processing. *International Journal of Engineering Research & Technology (Ahmedabad), 10*(5), 1134–1138.

Labadze, L., Grigolia, M., & Machaidze, L. (2023). Role of AI chatbots in education: Systematic literature review. *International Journal of Educational Technology in Higher Education, 20*(1), 1–22. DOI: 10.1186/s41239-023-00426-1

Martinez-Requejo, S., Jimenez García, E., Redondo Duarte, S., Ruiz Lázaro, J., Puertas Sanz, E., & Mariscal Vivas, G. (2023). *AI-Driven Student Assistance: Chatbots Redefining University Support.* Universidad Europea de Madrid & Universidad Complutense de Madrid.

Menaka Gowda, A., Krisha, M., Harshik, G. P., & Ashneel, I. (2024). AI based career chatbot: Leveraging AI for CareerCounseling. *International Journal Of Advance Research AndInnovative Ideas In Education, 10*(3), 1338–1355.

Pap, I. A., & Oniga, S. (2024). eHealth assistant AI chatbot using a large language model to provide personalized answers through secure decentralized communication. *Sensors (Basel), 24*(18), 6140. DOI: 10.3390/s24186140 PMID: 39338885

Qamhieh, M., Sammaneh, H., & Demaidi, M. N. (2020). PCRS: Personalized Career-Path Recommender System for Engineering Students. *IEEE Access : Practical Innovations, Open Solutions, 8*, 214039–214049. DOI: 10.1109/ACCESS.2020.3040338

Siswipraptini, P. C., Warnars, H. L. H. S., Ramadhan, A., & Budiharto, W. (2024). Personalized Career-Path Recommendation Model for Information Technology Students in Indonesia. *IEEE Access : Practical Innovations, Open Solutions, 12*, 49092–49105. DOI: 10.1109/ACCESS.2024.3381032

Tamayo, P. A., Herrero, A., Martín, J., Navarro, C., & Tránchez, J. M. (2020). Design of a chatbot as a distance learning assistant. Open Praxis. Universidad Nacional de Educación a Distancia (UNED), Spain. Retrieved from https://search.informit.org/doi/10.3316/informit.219384622220499

Xu, Y., Bu, J., Cai, D., He, X., & Liu, W. (2018). Job recommendation with content-based and collaborative filtering. In *Proceedings of the 27th International Conference on Information and Knowledge Management (CIKM)* (pp. 2061–2064). ACM. DOI: 10.1145/3269206.3269289

Yu, R., Pardos, Z., Chau, H., & Brusilovsky, P. ''Orienting students to course recommendations using three types of explanation,'' in Adjunct Proc. *29th ACM Conf. User Modeling, Adaptation Personalization*, Jun. 2021, pp. 238–245, DOI: 10.1145/3450614.3464483

Compilation of References

Abbas, H. M., Kumar, V. N., Ashlin Deepa, R. N., Bansal, S., Senthil Kumar, R. S., & Krishnakumar, K. (2024). Digital Twins for Real-Time Supply Chain Visibility and Optimization. *2nd IEEE International Conference on IoT, Communication and Automation Technology, ICICAT 2024*, 1132–1137. DOI: 10.1109/ICICAT62666.2024.10923493

Abbey, A. B. N., Eyo-Udo, N. L., & Olaleye, I. A. (2024). Implementing Advanced Analytics for Optimizing Food Supply Chain Logistics and Efficiency.

Abdullah, S. S. (2024). THE IMPACT OF THE ON-DEMAND ECONOMY ON MALAYSIAN LOGISTICS. *PIONEERING THE FUTURE: DELVING INTO E-LEARNING'S LANDSCAPE*, 35.

Ahmed, S., Hassan, M. M., & Haque, M. E. (2020). Development of a rule-based chatbot for career counseling. *International Journal of Advanced Computer Science and Applications*, *11*(5), 322–328. DOI: 10.14569/IJACSA.2020.0110541

Ajibesin, A. A., Çela, E., Vedishchev, A., & Vajjhala, N. R. (2025). Future Horizons in Explainable AI and Blockchain for Supply Chain Management. In *Explainable AI and Blockchain for Secure and Agile Supply Chains* (pp. 197–213). Enhancing Transparency, Traceability, and Accountability., DOI: 10.1201/9781003497363-14

Akbari, M. (2024). Revolutionizing supply chain and circular economy with edge computing: Systematic review, research themes and future directions. *Management Decision*, *62*(9), 2875–2899. DOI: 10.1108/MD-03-2023-0412

Alguirat, I., Zouari, A., & Lehyani, F. (2024). Exploring the Role of Digital Twins in Future Supply Chain Industry: Characteristics, Technologies, and Applications. *2024 IEEE 15th International Colloquium of Logistics and Supply Chain Management, LOGISTIQUA 2024*. DOI: 10.1109/LOGISTIQUA61063.2024.10571453

Ali, A. H., & Ali Hagag, A. (2024). An enhanced AI-based model for financial fraud detection. *International Journal of Advanced and Applied Sciences*, *11*(10), 114–121. DOI: 10.21833/ijaas.2024.10.013

Alonso, R., Dessí, D., Meloni, A., & Reforgiato Recupero, D. (2024). A Novel Knowledge Plug-In for Incorporating Information About Employability From the O*NET Database Into Conversational Agents. *IEEE Access : Practical Innovations, Open Solutions*, *12*, 92663–92681. DOI: 10.1109/ACCESS.2024.3423359

Alsubaiei, F. (n.d.). *OGAR: Augmented Reality Application for Assisting Workers in the Oil and Gas Industry*.

Anandhi, S., Anitha, R., & Sureshkumar, V. (2019). IoT Enabled RFID Authentication and Secure Object Tracking System for Smart Logistics. *Wireless Personal Communications*, *104*(2), 543–560. DOI: 10.1007/s11277-018-6033-6

Apeji, U. D., & Sunmola, F. T. (2022). Principles and Factors Influencing Visibility in Sustainable Supply Chains. *Procedia Computer Science*, *200*, 1516–1527. DOI: 10.1016/j.procs.2022.01.353

Ashkanani, M., AlAjmi, A., Alhayyan, A., Esmael, Z., AlBedaiwi, M., & Nadeem, M. (2025). A Self-Adaptive Traffic Signal System Integrating Real-Time Vehicle Detection and License Plate Recognition for Enhanced Traffic Management. *Inventions (Basel, Switzerland)*, *10*(1), 14. DOI: 10.3390/inventions10010014

Ashrafi, S., Majidi, B., Akhtarkavan, E., & Hajiagha, S. H. R. (2023). Efficient Resume-Based Re- Education for Career Recommendation in Rapidly Evolving Job Markets. *IEEE Access : Practical Innovations, Open Solutions, 11*, 124350–124367. DOI: 10.1109/ACCESS.2023.3329576

Ashraf, M., Eltawil, A., & Ali, I. (2024). Disruption detection for a cognitive digital supply chain twin using hybrid deep learning. *Operations Research, 24*(2), 23. Advance online publication. DOI: 10.1007/s12351-024-00831-y

Aslam, M. S. (2025). IoT and Its Role in Sustainable Pharmaceutical Supply Chains. In *Sustainable Pharmaceutical Product Development and Optimization Processes* (pp. 141–161). From Eco-Design to Supply Chain Integrity., DOI: 10.1007/978-981-97-9707-3_6

Atadoga, A., Obi, O. C., Osasona, F., Onwusinkwue, S., Daraojimba, A. I., & Dawodu, S. O. (2024). AI in supply chain optimization: A comparative review of USA and African Trends. *Int. J. Sci. Res. Arch., 11*(1), 896–903. DOI: 10.30574/ijsra.2024.11.1.0156

Attah, R. U., Garba, B. M. P., Gil-Ozoudeh, I., & Iwuanyanwu, O. (2024). Enhancing supply chain resilience through artificial intelligence: Analyzing problem-solving approaches in logistics management. *International Journal of Management & Entrepreneurship Research, 5*(12), 3248–3265.

Attah, R. U., Ogunsola, O. Y., & Garba, B. M. P. (2023). Revolutionizing logistics with artificial intelligence: Breakthroughs in automation, analytics, and operational excellence. *Iconic Research and Engineering Journals, 6*(12), 1471–1493.

Bach, N. H. A., & Hoang, C. C. (2025). Exploring the Evolution of Distribution in E-Commerce: A Bibliometric Analysis. *Journal of Distribution Science, 23*(1), 79–93.

Bai, S., Zhan, X., & Zhang, L. (2018). A survey on LSTM and its variants in time series forecasting. *IEEE Access : Practical Innovations, Open Solutions, 6*, 36573–36583. DOI: 10.1109/ACCESS.2018.2848007

Baral, R., & Pokhrel, S. (2020). Design and implementation of a voice-based virtual assistant for student guidance. *International Journal of Scientific & Technology Research*, *9*(1), 2750–2754.

Bedi, P., Das, S., Goyal, S. B., Rajawat, A. S., & Kautish, S. (2024). Revolutionizing sustainability: the role of robotics in supply chains. In *Computational Intelligence Techniques for Sustainable Supply Chain Management* (pp. 225–273). Academic Press. DOI: 10.1016/B978-0-443-18464-2.00007-8

Bessen, J. E. (2019). *AI and Jobs: The Role of Demand.* NBER Working Paper No. 24235.

Bhatnagar, R., & Rao, N. (2021). Benefits of carrier collaboration under incomplete advance demand information: A case of Indian truckload carriers. *Urban Rail Transit*, *7*(2), 110–127. DOI: 10.1007/s40890-021-00123-6

Bigliardi, B., Bottani, E., & Filippelli, S. (2022). A study on IoT application in the Food Industry using Keywords Analysis. *Procedia Computer Science*, *200*, 1826–1835. DOI: 10.1016/j.procs.2022.01.383

Biswal, M., Tayeen, A. S., & Misra, S. (2021). AMI-FML: A privacy-preserving federated machine learning framework for AMI.

Biswas, S. (2023). Assimilation of 'Artificial Intelligence' (AI) in 'Amazon': An in depth Research Case Study. *Globsyn Management Journal, 17.*

Boudouaia, M. A., Ouchani, S., Qaisar, S. M., & Almaktoom, A. T. (2024). Supply Chain 5.0: Vision, Challenges, and Perspectives. *21st International Learning and Technology Conference: Reality and Science Fiction in Education, L and T 2024*, 203–208. DOI: 10.1109/LT60077.2024.10469476

Briggs, C., Fan, Z., & Andras, P. (2020). Privacy preserving demand forecasting to encourage consumer acceptance of smart energy meters.

Cagliano, A. C., De Marco, A., & Rafele, C. (2017). E-grocery supply chain management enabled by mobile tools. *Business Process Management Journal*, *23*(1), 47–70. DOI: 10.1108/BPMJ-01-2016-0002

Calzavara, M., Finco, S., Persona, A., & Zennaro, I. (2023). A cost-based tool for the comparison of different e-grocery supply chain strategies. *International Journal of Production Economics, 262*, 108899. DOI: 10.1016/j.ijpe.2023.108899

Campbell, C., Sands, S., Ferraro, C., Tsao, H. Y. J., & Mavrommatis, A. (2020). From data to action: How marketers can leverage AI. *Business Horizons, 63*(2), 227–243. DOI: 10.1016/j.bushor.2019.12.002

Cantarelli, C. C., Flyvbjerg, B., Molin, E. J. E., & van Wee, B. (2018). Cost overruns in large-scale transport infrastructure projects. *Automation in Construction, 2*(1).

Casino, F., Dasaklis, T. K., & Patsakis, C. (2019). A systematic literature review of blockchain-based applications: Current status, classification and open issues. *Telematics and Informatics, 36*, 55–81. DOI: 10.1016/j.tele.2018.11.006

Chandankhede, A., & Gourshettiwar, P. (2025). A Review of IoT-Driven Innovations in Supply Chain Management. *3rd International Conference on Electronics and Renewable Systems, ICEARS 2025 - Proceedings*, 781–787. DOI: 10.1109/ICEARS64219.2025.10940471

Chen, H., Wang, Z., & Zhang, M. (2024). Mechanism study on innovative influences of AI and blockchain on supply chain logistics: Case study of JD and Alibaba. Advances in Economics. *Management and Political Sciences, 109*(1), 94–100. DOI: 10.54254/2754-1169/109/2024BJ0116

Chen, W., Men, Y., Fuster, N., Osorio, C., & Juan, A. A. (2024). Artificial intelligence in logistics optimization with sustainable criteria: A review. *Sustainability (Basel), 16*(21), 9145. DOI: 10.3390/su16219145

Chen, Z., Pan, S., Zhong, R. Y., & Liu, D. (2021). Managing last-mile delivery through intelligent optimization and planning: A review. *Transportation Research Part E, Logistics and Transportation Review, 151*, 102400.

Chilimattur, N. M.Nazia Mahammadrafiq Chilimattur. (2025). Intelligent food waste management in supply chains using deep Dense Networks and image processing. *Comm. Appl. Nonlinear Anal.*, *32*(10s), 117–134. DOI: 10.52783/cana.v32.4696

Choi, D., Chung, C. Y., & Young, J. (2019). Sustainable online shopping logistics for customer satisfaction and repeat purchasing behavior: Evidence from China. *Sustainability (Basel)*, *11*(20), 5626. DOI: 10.3390/su11205626

Choudhary, P., & Iyer, A. (2022). Developing multi-vehicle freight trip generation models: Quantifying the relationship between logistics outsourcing and insourcing decisions. *Urban Rail Transit*, *8*, 165–178. DOI: 10.1007/s40890-022-00161-8

Christopher, M. (2016). *Logistics & supply chain management* (5th ed.).

Chukwu, N., Yufenyuy, S., Ejiofor, E., Ekweli, D., Ogunleye, O., Clement, T., Obunadike, C., Adeniji, S., Elom, E., & Obunadike, C. (2024). Resilient chain: AI-enhanced supply chain security and efficiency integration. *International Journal of Scientific and Management Research*, *07*(03), 46–65. DOI: 10.37502/IJSMR.2024.7306

Ciger, G., Ess, A., Hart, J., Hürtgen, H., & Goldrick, M. (2022). Navigating the market headwinds: The state of grocery retail 2022.

Dayan, I., Roth, H. R., Zhong, A., Harouni, A., Gentili, A., Abidin, A. Z., Liu, A., Costa, A. B., Wood, B. J., Tsai, C.-S., Wang, C.-H., Hsu, C.-N., Lee, C. K., Ruan, P., Xu, D., Wu, D., Huang, E., Kitamura, F. C., Lacey, G., & Li, Q. (2021). Federated learning for predicting clinical outcomes in patients with COVID-19. *Nature Medicine*, *27*(10), 1735–1743. DOI: 10.1038/s41591-021-01506-3 PMID: 34526699

Department, S. R. (2023). Supply chain management (SCM) market size worldwide from 2020 to 2026. In *Statista*. https://www.statista.com/statistics/1181996/supply-chain-management-market-size-worldwide/

Dey, A. K., Mukherjee, D., Ghosh, A. K., Satsangi, A., & Mandal, B. K. (2025). AI and Sustainable E-commerce.

Dhaliwal, A. (2022, December). Towards AI-driven transport and logistics. In *Workshop on e-Business* (pp. 119-131). Cham: Springer Nature Switzerland.

Do, V. C., & Omdahl, K. (2018). Efficiency of e-grocery: Challenges and suggestions (Master's thesis, University of Stavanger, Norway).

Dong, Z., Liang, W., Liang, Y., Gao, W., & Lu, Y. (2022). Blockchained supply chain management based on IoT tracking and machine learning. *EURASIP Journal on Wireless Communications and Networking*, *2022*(1), 127. DOI: 10.1186/s13638-022-02209-0 PMID: 36597502

Dora, M., Kumar, A., Mangla, S. K., Pant, A., & Kamal, M. M. (2022). Critical success factors influencing artificial intelligence adoption in food supply chains. *International Journal of Production Research*, *60*(14), 4621–4640. DOI: 10.1080/00207543.2021.1959665

Drake, M. J. (2022). The Application of the Internet of Things in Managing Supply Chains. In *Encyclopedia of Data Science and Machine Learning* (pp. 2298–2312). DOI: 10.4018/978-1-7998-9220-5.ch138

Dwivedi, Y. K., Hughes, D. L., Ismagilova, E., Aarts, G., Coombs, C., Crick, T., & Williams, M. D. (2022). Metaverse for digital twins and immersive experiences: Opportunities and challenges. *International Journal of Information Management*, *66*, 102505.

El Makhloufi, A. (2023). AI application in transport and logistics: opportunities and challenges (An Exploratory Study).

Elvas, L. B., Tokkozhina, U., Martins, A. L., & Ferreira, J. C. (2023). Implementation of disruptive technologies for the last mile delivery efficiency achievement. *Transportation Research Procedia*, *72*, 32–39. DOI: 10.1016/j.trpro.2023.11.319

Eubanks, V. (2018). *Automating Inequality: How High-Tech Tools Profile, Police, and Punish the Poor*. St. Martin's Press.

Eyo-Udo, N. L. (2024). Leveraging artificial intelligence for enhanced supply chain optimization. *Open Access Res. J. Multidiscip. Stud.*, *7*(2), 1–15. DOI: 10.53022/oarjms.2024.7.2.0044

Ezura, E., & Jalil, A. (2019). Customer satisfaction and reverse logistics in e-commerce: The case of Klang Valley. In *Proceedings of the 9th International Conference on Operations and Supply Chain Management*, Vietnam.

Falcone, E., Kent, J., & Fugate, B. (2019). Supply chain technologies, interorganizational network and firm performance. *International Journal of Physical Distribution & Logistics Management*, *50*(3), 333–354. DOI: 10.1108/IJPDLM-08-2018-0306

Fantacci, R., & Picano, B. (2020). Federated learning framework for mobile edge computing networks. *CAAI Transactions on Intelligence Technology*, *5*(1), 15–21. DOI: 10.1049/trit.2019.0049

Fatorachian, H. (2024). Leveraging Artificial Intelligence for Optimizing Logistics Performance: A Comprehensive Review. *Global Journal of Business Social Sciences Review (GATR-GJBSSR), 12*(3).

Fernandez Vazquez-Noguerol, M. (2021). Modeling and optimization of the supply chain in e-groceries (Doctoral dissertation, Organización de empresas e márketing).

Fictiv. (2023). 2023 State of Manufacturing Report. In *Fictiv*. https://www.fictiv.com/ebooks/2023-state-of-manufacturing-report

Floridi, L., Cowls, J., Beltrametti, M., Chatila, R., Chazerand, P., Dignum, V., Luetge, C., Madelin, R., Pagallo, U., Rossi, F., Schafer, B., Valcke, P., & Vayena, E. (2018). AI4People—An ethical framework for a good AI society: Opportunities, risks, principles, and recommendations. *Minds and Machines*, *28*(4), 689–707. DOI: 10.1007/s11023-018-9482-5 PMID: 30930541

Frey, C. B., & Osborne, M. A. (2017). The future of employment: How susceptible are jobs to computerisation? *Technological Forecasting and Social Change*, *114*, 254–280. DOI: 10.1016/j.techfore.2016.08.019

Fuller, A., Fan, Z., Day, C., & Barlow, C. (2020). Digital twin: Enabling technologies, challenges and open research. *IEEE Access : Practical Innovations, Open Solutions*, *8*, 108952–108971. DOI: 10.1109/ACCESS.2020.2998358

Fu, R. J. (2025). The Future of AI, ML, and Robotics in Business and Beyond. *Artificial Intelligence, Machine Learning, &. Robotics in Business*, *1*(1), 8–22. DOI: 10.32473/aimlrb.1.1.138290

Garikapati, D., & Shetiya, S. S. (2024). Autonomous vehicles: Evolution of artificial intelligence and the current industry landscape. *Big Data and Cognitive Computing*, *8*(4), 42. DOI: 10.3390/bdcc8040042

Ghosh, D., Dutta, P. K., & Abotaleb, M. (2024). Harnessing the power of hybrid models for supply chain management and optimization. In *Hybrid Information Systems* (pp. 407–426). Non-Linear Optimization Strategies with Artificial Intelligence., DOI: 10.1515/9783111331133-019

Ghosh, I., & Jha, M. K. (2016). Determinants of safe and productive truck driving: Empirical evidence from long-haul cargo transport. *Transportation Research Part E, Logistics and Transportation Review*, *92*, 1–17. DOI: 10.1016/j.tre.2016.05.007

Glaessgen, E., & Stargel, D. (2012). *The digital twin paradigm for future NASA and U.S. Air Force vehicles*. In the 53rd *AIAA/ASME/ASCE/AHS/ASC Structures, Structural Dynamics and Materials Conference*. DOI: 10.2514/6.2012-1818

Gollar, V. K., Naik, M. M., Beig, T. B., Karekar, T. A., Verlekar, S. P., & Naik, V. (•••). Skill-Oriented Job Recommender Chatbot. [3]. *International Journal of Computer Applications*, *185*, 21, 26–30.

Gowsalya, M., & Mayuri, K. N. (2025). Revolutionizing the Sustainable Supply Chain of Medical Product With AI-Driven Drone Delivery: Innovations in Supply Chain Management Through Autonomous UAV Technology in Healthcare. In *Ecological and Human Dimensions of AI-Based Supply Chain* (pp. 69-96). IGI Global Scientific Publishing.

Graves, A. (2013). Supervised sequence labelling with recurrent neural networks. In *Studies in Computational Intelligence* (Vol. 385, pp. 1–35). Springer., DOI: 10.1007/978-3-642-36876-0_1

Gupta, V. (2025). Leveraging AI and ML for Logistics Excellence: Case Studies and Success Strategies. In *Supply Chain Transformation Through Generative AI and Machine Learning* (pp. 313-346). IGI Global Scientific Publishing.

Gupta, S., Singh, S., & Agarwal, A. (2021). AI-based job recommender system using resume and job description matching. *Procedia Computer Science, 192*, 5147–5156. DOI: 10.1016/j.procs.2021.09.285

Harshitha, K., Jagadeesha, S. N., & Thinakaran, T. S. R. (2024). Classification of factors used to predict vehicle breakdown in commercial vehicles. *Sparklinglight Transactions on Artificial Intelligence and Quantum Computing*, *4*(1), 01–16. Advance online publication. DOI: 10.55011/STAIQC.2024.4101

Hasan, M. Z., Hussain, M. Z., Umair, S., & Waqas, U. (2024). Understanding Artificial Intelligence in Supply Chain and Innovation Performance. In *Human Perspectives of Industry 4.0 Organizations* (pp. 131–154). Reviewing Sustainable Performance., DOI: 10.1201/9781032616810-7

He, X., Hu, X., Wang, G., Yu, J., Zhao, Z., & Lu, X. (2023). Towards efficient federated learning using agile aggregation in Internet of vehicles. *Security and Communication Networks, 2023*, 1–20. DOI: 10.1155/2023/2265852

Hochreiter, S., & Schmidhuber, J. (1997). Long short-term memory. *Neural Computation*, *9*(8), 1735–1780. DOI: 10.1162/neco.1997.9.8.1735 PMID: 9377276

Hsu, P. Y., Angeloudis, P., & Aurisicchio, M. (2018). Optimal logistics planning for modular construction using two-stage stochastic programming. *Automation in Construction, 94*, 153–169. DOI: 10.1016/j.autcon.2018.05.029

Husnoo, M. A., Anwar, A., Hosseinzadeh, N., Islam, S. N., Mahmood, A. N., & Doss, R. (2022). *FedREP: Towards horizontal federated load forecasting for Retail Energy Providers*. ArXiv. [Cs.DC]

Hu, Y., & Wang, F. (2024). The Task Collaborative Migration Method for Marine IoT Based on Edge Computing-RESTful Architecture. *6th International Conference on Artificial Intelligence in Information and Communication, ICAIIC 2024*, 446–451. DOI: 10.1109/ICAIIC60209.2024.10463387

Ikpe, V., & Shamsuddoha, M. (2024). Functional model of supply chain waste reduction and control strategies for retailers—The USA retail industry. *Logistics (Basel)*, *8*(1), 22. DOI: 10.3390/logistics8010022

Imran, M., Kang, H., Lee, S. G., Kim, E. H., Park, H. M., & Oh, S. W. (2025). Current trends and future prospects in onion production, supply, and demand in South Korea: A comprehensive review. *Sustainability (2071-1050)*, *17*(3).

Iseal, S., & Michael, H. (2025). *Demand Forecasting in E-Commerce Using AI & ML*.

ISO. (2021). *Digital twin framework for manufacturing*. International Organization for Standardization. https://www.iso.org/standard/75066.html

Ivanov, D., Dolgui, A., & Sokolov, B. (2022). *Digital supply chain twins: Managing the ripple effect, resilience, and disruption risks by data-driven optimization, simulation, and visibility*. Springer.

Ivanov, D. (2020). Predicting the impacts of epidemic outbreaks on global supply chains: A simulation-based analysis on the coronavirus outbreak (COVID-19/SARS-CoV-2) case. *Transportation Research Part E, Logistics and Transportation Review*, *136*, 101922. DOI: 10.1016/j.tre.2020.101922 PMID: 32288597

Ivanov, D., & Dolgui, A. (2021). A digital supply chain twin for managing the disruption risks and resilience in the era of Industry 4.0. *Production Planning and Control*, *32*(9), 775–788. DOI: 10.1080/09537287.2020.1768450

Ivanov, D., Dolgui, A., Sokolov, B., Ivanova, M., & Werner, F. (2019). A dynamic model and an algorithm for short-term supply chain scheduling in the smart factory industry 4.0. *European Journal of Operational Research, 274*(2), 425–443. DOI: 10.1016/j.ejor.2018.10.034

Jackson, I., Namdar, J., Saénz, M. J., Elmquist, R. A.III, & Dávila Novoa, L. R. (2024). Revolutionize cold chain: An AI/ML driven approach to overcome capacity shortages. *International Journal of Production Research*, •••, 1–23.

Jacobs, P.-P., Ehrengut, C., Bucher, A. M., Penzkofer, T., Lukas, M., Kleesiek, J., & Denecke, T. (2023). Challenges in implementing the local node infrastructure for a national federated machine learning network in radiology. *Healthcare (Basel), 11*(17), 2377. DOI: 10.3390/healthcare11172377 PMID: 37685411

Jahnke, H., Ulrich, M., Pesch, R., Senge, R., & Langrock, R. (2025). Distributional Regression for Demand Forecasting in e-grocery.

Japiassu, N. (2022). *AI-Powered Logistics and Mobility as a Service (MaaS)*. Driving the Future of Autonomous Vehicles and Smart Transportation.

Jha, A. K., & Singh, R. K. (2020). Examining freight performance of third-party logistics providers within the automotive industry in India: An environmental sustainability perspective. *International Journal of Production Research, 58*(18), 5436–5453. DOI: 10.1080/00207543.2020.1756504

Jiang, Y., & Hao, S. (2011). Research on the development of intelligent logistics based on internet of things. *2011 International Conference on Remote Sensing, Environment and Transportation Engineering, RSETE 2011 - Proceedings*, 5254–5257. DOI: 10.1109/RSETE.2011.5965498

Johnpaul, M., Miryala, R. S. B., Mazurek, M., Jayaprakashnarayana, G., & Miryala, R. K. (2025). Artificial Intelligence and Machine Learning in eCommerce. In *Strategic Innovations of AI and ML for E-Commerce Data Security* (pp. 31–58). IGI Global.

Jones, D., Snider, C., Nassehi, A., Yon, J., & Hicks, B. (2020). Characterising the digital twin: A systematic literature review. *CIRP Journal of Manufacturing Science and Technology*, *29*, 36–52. DOI: 10.1016/j.cirpj.2020.02.002

Kafi, M. A., Saifudin, A. B. M., Zainuddin, N. B., Shahron, S. A., Abualrejal, H., & Mohamad, M. (2022). Essential of RFID Technology in Supply Chain Management: A review on Digital Perspective. *International Conference on Intelligent Technology, System and Service for Internet of Everything, ITSS-IoE 2022*. DOI: 10.1109/ITSS-IoE56359.2022.9990933

Kahya, I., Huschbeck, T., & Markovič, P. (2025). Predictive Risk Management in the Supply Chain. In *Studies in Systems* (Vol. 578, pp. 41–57). Decision and Control., DOI: 10.1007/978-3-031-80935-4_3

Kaissis, G., Ziller, A., Passerat-Palmbach, J., Ryffel, T., Usynin, D., Trask, A., Lima, I.Jr, Mancuso, J., Jungmann, F., Steinborn, M.-M., Saleh, A., Makowski, M., Rueckert, D., & Braren, R. (2021). End-to-end privacy preserving deep learning on multi-institutional medical imaging. *Nature Machine Intelligence*, *3*(6), 473–484. DOI: 10.1038/s42256-021-00337-8

Kalaiarasan, R., Olhager, J., Agrawal, T. K., & Wiktorsson, M. (2022). The ABCDE of supply chain visibility: A systematic literature review and framework. *International Journal of Production Economics*, *248*, 108464. Advance online publication. DOI: 10.1016/j.ijpe.2022.108464

Kale, A. A. (2024). Modern AI in Green Logistics: Smart Systems for Sustainability and Carbon Reduction.

Kalkha, H., Khiat, A., Bahnasse, A., & Ouajji, H. (2023). The rising trends of smart e-commerce logistics. *IEEE Access : Practical Innovations, Open Solutions*, *11*, 33839–33857. DOI: 10.1109/ACCESS.2023.3252566

Kamble, S. S., Gunasekaran, A., & Gawankar, S. A. (2020). Achieving sustainable performance in a data-driven agriculture supply chain: A review for research and applications. *Sustainable Production and Consumption*, *23*, 60–79. DOI: 10.1016/j.spc.2020.04.005

Kanase, R., Chitnis, A., & Priyadarshi, R. (2024, May). Assessing the feasibility of last-mile delivery alternatives using fuzzy AHP in the Indian Urban Context. In *2024 2nd International Conference on Advancement in Computation & Computer Technologies (InCACCT)* (pp. 547-552). IEEE. DOI: 10.1109/InCACCT61598.2024.10551042

Kanyepe, J. (2025). Data-Driven Logistics Optimization: Powering the Digital Supply Chain. In Impacts of Technology on Operations Management: Adoption, Adaptation, and Optimization (pp. 63-96). IGI Global.

Kapsalis, P., Rimassa, G., Zeydan, E., Via, S., Risso, F. G., Chiasserini, C. F., & Vivo, G. (2024). A Next Generation Architecture for Internet of Things in the Automotive Supply Chain for Electric Vehicles. *Proceedings of the International Symposium on Mobile Ad Hoc Networking and Computing (MobiHoc)*, 428–433. DOI: 10.1145/3641512.3690035

Karulkar, Y., Shah, A., & Naik, R. (2025). AI-Powered Business Evolution: Transformative Strategies for Success of Evolving Industries. In *Creating AI Synergy Through Business Technology Transformation* (pp. 39-72). IGI Global.

Kaya, A. (2024). Impact of artificial intelligence on supply chain efficiency in Turkey. *International Journal of Technology and Systems*, *9*(3), 25–37. DOI: 10.47604/ijts.2814

Khadem, M., Khadem, A., & Khadem, S. (2023). Application of artificial intelligence in supply chain revolutionizing efficiency and optimization. *International journal of industrial engineering and operational research*, *5*(1), 29-38.

Khalifa, L., & Volkov, N. (2024). E-commerce Supply Chain Strategies: Meeting the Demands of Online Retail. *Social Dynamics Review*, *7*(1), 1–9.

Khan, M. M., Khan, F. S., Nadeem, M., Khan, T. H., Haider, S., & Daas, D. (2025). Scalability and Efficiency Analysis of Hyperledger Fabric and Private Ethereum in Smart Contract Execution. *Computers*, *14*(4), 132. DOI: 10.3390/computers14040132

Khan, R. A., McLaughlin, K., & Sezer, S. (2020). Cybersecurity considerations for digital twin systems. *Sensors (Basel), 20*(23), 6811. DOI: 10.3390/s20236811 PMID: 33260646

Khan, S., & Tabasum, S. (2025). Real-time health supply chain optimization using digital twin technology. *Int. J. Sci. Res. Arch., 15*(2), 1275–1289. DOI: 10.30574/ijsra.2025.15.2.1556

Khan, Y., Su'ud, M. B. M., Alam, M. M., Ahmad, S. F., Ahmad, A. Y. A. B., & Khan, N. (2023). Application of Internet of Things (IoT) in Sustainable Supply Chain Management. *Sustainability (Switzerland), 15*(1). Advance online publication. DOI: 10.3390/su15010694

Khaouja, I., Kassou, I., & Ghogho, M. (2021). A Survey on Skill Identification From Online Job Ads. *IEEE Access : Practical Innovations, Open Solutions, 9*, 118134–118153. DOI: 10.1109/ACCESS.2021.3106120

Kim, D.-H., Kim, G.-Y., & Do Noh, S. (2025). Digital twin-based prediction and optimization for dynamic supply chain management. *Machines (Basel), 13*(2), 109. DOI: 10.3390/machines13020109

Kim, Y. H., & Davis, G. F. (2019). Challenges for global supply chains and opportunities for social innovation. In *Handbook of Inclusive Innovation: The Role of Organizations* (pp. 305–320). Markets and Communities in Social Innovation., DOI: 10.4337/9781786436016.00027

Kolasani, S. (2024). Connected cars and autonomous vehicles: personalizing owner/customer experiences and innovation using AI, IoT, Blockchain, and Big Data. *International numeric journal of machine learning and robots, 8*(8), 1-17.

Koul, A., & Mehta, R. (2020). Evaluating the performance of intercity road freight transport: Double bootstrap DEA approach. *Transportation Research Record: Journal of the Transportation Research Board, 2674*(11), 190–202. DOI: 10.1177/0361198120964724

Krishnan, R., Perumal, E., Govindaraj, M., & Kandasamy, L. (2024). Enhancing Logistics Operations Through Technological Advancements for Superior Service Efficiency. In *Innovative Technologies for Increasing Service Productivity* (pp. 61–82). IGI Global. DOI: 10.4018/979-8-3693-2019-8.ch004

Kritzinger, W., Karner, M., Traar, G., Henjes, J., & Sihn, W. (2018). Digital Twin in manufacturing: A categorical literature review and classification. *IFAC-PapersOnLine*, *51*(11), 1016–1022. DOI: 10.1016/j.ifacol.2018.08.474

Kumar, A., Mangla, S. K., Kumar, P., & Karamperidis, S. (2020). Challenges in perishable food supply chains for sustainability management: A developing economy perspective. *Business Strategy and the Environment*, *29*(5), 1809–1831. DOI: 10.1002/bse.2470

Kumar, D., & Bhuvana, R. (2021). Career guidance chatbot using natural language processing. *International Journal of Engineering Research & Technology (Ahmedabad)*, *10*(5), 1134–1138.

Kumari, P., & Mittal, S. (2024). Fraud Detection System for Financial System Using Machine Learning Techniques: A Review. *2024 11th International Conference on Reliability, Infocom Technologies and Optimization (Trends and Future Directions), ICRITO 2024*. DOI: 10.1109/ICRITO61523.2024.10522197

Kumar, S., & Bansal, S. (2020). Qualitative investigation of the influential factors behind unsafe trucking behaviours in India. *Transportation Research Record: Journal of the Transportation Research Board*, *2674*(11), 249–260. DOI: 10.1177/0361198120901677

Labadze, L., Grigolia, M., & Machaidze, L. (2023). Role of AI chatbots in education: Systematic literature review. *International Journal of Educational Technology in Higher Education*, *20*(1), 1–22. DOI: 10.1186/s41239-023-00426-1

Lang, G. (2020). An empirical study on the exploration of factors influencing customer satisfaction in logistics distribution service. *IOP Conference Series. Earth and Environmental Science*, *546*(5), 052031. Advance online publication. DOI: 10.1088/1755-1315/546/5/052031

Lee, J. Y., & Woo, S. H. (2019). The impact of power on the relationships and customer satisfaction in a logistics triad: A meta-analysis. *Asian Journal of Shipping and Logistics*, *35*(4), 251–260. DOI: 10.1016/j.ajsl.2019.12.006

Lim, S. F. W. T., Jin, X., & Srai, J. S. (2018). Consumer-driven e-commerce: A literature review, design framework, and research agenda on last-mile logistics models. *International Journal of Physical Distribution & Logistics Management*, *48*(3), 308–332. DOI: 10.1108/IJPDLM-02-2017-0081

Lin, X., Mamun, A. A., Yang, Q., & Masukujjaman, M. (2023). Examining the effect of logistics service quality on customer satisfaction and re-use intention. *PLoS One*, *18*(5), e0286382. Advance online publication. DOI: 10.1371/journal.pone.0286382 PMID: 37256860

Liu, Z., Hu, B., Zhao, Y., Lang, L., Guo, H., Florence, K., & Zhang, S. (2020). Research on Intelligent Decision of Low Carbon Supply Chain Based on Carbon Tax Constraints in Human-Driven Edge Computing. *IEEE Access : Practical Innovations, Open Solutions*, *8*, 48264–48273. DOI: 10.1109/ACCESS.2020.2978911

Loftus, T. J., Ruppert, M. M., Shickel, B., Ozrazgat-Baslanti, T., Balch, J. A., Efron, P. A., Upchurch, G. R.Jr, Rashidi, P., Tignanelli, C., Bian, J., & Bihorac, A. (2022). Federated learning for preserving data privacy in collaborative healthcare research. *Digital Health*, *8*, 20552076221134456. DOI: 10.1177/20552076221134455 PMID: 36325438

Lushi, A., Daas, D., & Nadeem, M. (2022). IoT-Based Public Transport Management System. *2022 IEEE Global Conference on Artificial Intelligence and Internet of Things (GCAIoT)*, 69–75.

Lu, Y., Liu, C., Kevin, I., Wang, K. I. K., Huang, H., & Xu, X. (2020). Digital Twin-driven smart manufacturing: Connotation, reference model, applications and research issues. *Robotics and Computer-integrated Manufacturing*, *61*, 101837. DOI: 10.1016/j.rcim.2019.101837

Madhumithaa, N., Elangovan, G., Sridharan, S., & Karthick, L. ul Islam, A., & Venkatesh, R. P. (2024). Cutting-Edge AI-Powered Driverless Delivery Solution. In *Trends and Applications in Mechanical Engineering, Composite Materials and Smart Manufacturing* (pp. 129-145). IGI Global.

Mahajan, P., & Kumar, A. (2023). Performance analysis of signalized intersections from truck drivers' perspective. In *Advances in Traffic Transportation and Civil Infrastructure* (pp. 259–271). Springer., DOI: 10.1007/978-981-99-3447-8_20

Martinez-Requejo, S., Jimenez García, E., Redondo Duarte, S., Ruiz Lázaro, J., Puertas Sanz, E., & Mariscal Vivas, G. (2023). *AI-Driven Student Assistance: Chatbots Redefining University Support*. Universidad Europea de Madrid & Universidad Complutense de Madrid.

Masi, A., Ciccullo, F., & Pero, M. (2021, June). Digitalizing agri-food supply chains to achieve Sustainable Development Goals: A systematic literature review. In *2021 IEEE International Conference on Engineering, Technology and Innovation (ICE/ITMC)* (pp. 1-8). IEEE. DOI: 10.1109/ICE/ITMC52061.2021.9570237

Melesse, T. Y., Franciosi, C., Di Pasquale, V., & Riemma, S. (2023). Analyzing the implementation of digital twins in the agri-food supply chain. *Logistics (Basel)*, *7*(2), 33. DOI: 10.3390/logistics7020033

Menaka Gowda, A., Krisha, M., Harshik, G. P., & Ashneel, I. (2024). AI based career chatbot: Leveraging AI for CareerCounseling. *International Journal Of Advance Research AndInnovative Ideas In Education*, *10*(3), 1338–1355.

Mentzer, J. T., DeWitt, W., Keebler, J. S., Min, S., Nix, N. W., Smith, C. D., & Zacharia, Z. G. (2001). Defining supply chain management. *Journal of Business Logistics*, *22*(2), 1–25. DOI: 10.1002/j.2158-1592.2001.tb00001.x

Michaelides, Z., & Forster, R. (2013). The Use of RFID Technologies for E-Enabling Logistics Supply Chains. In *E-Logistics and E-Supply Chain Management* (pp. 198–217). Applications for Evolving Business., DOI: 10.4018/978-1-4666-3914-0.ch011

Michael, K., & McCathie, L. (2005). The pros and cons of RFID in supply chain management. *4th Annual International Conference on Mobile Business, ICMB 2005*, 623–629. DOI: 10.1109/ICMB.2005.103

Min, H., Zacharia, Z. G., & Smith, C. D. (2019). Defining supply chain analytics and its impact on supply chain operations. *Journal of Business Logistics, 40*(3), 147–152. DOI: 10.1111/jbl.12181

Mirzaei, M., Dehe, B., Weerasinghe, K., & Srivastava, H. (2025). Enhancing Supply Chain Visibility in the Fishing Industry: The Role of Emerging Technologies and Their Affordances. *Operations and Supply Chain Management, 18*(2), 146–160. DOI: 10.31387/oscm0610462

Mittelstadt, B. D., Allo, P., Taddeo, M., Wachter, S., & Floridi, L. (2016). The ethics of algorithms: Mapping the debate. *Big Data & Society, 3*(2), 2053951716679679. Advance online publication. DOI: 10.1177/2053951716679679

Mkansi, M., & Masilela, P. (2025). Green Purchasing as a Catalyst for Suppliers' Compliance to Environmental Standards: E-grocery Perspective. *Procedia Computer Science, 253*, 1–12. DOI: 10.1016/j.procs.2025.01.064

Moghaddam, G. K., & Karimzadeh, M. (2025). AI-Driven Digital Transformation and Sustainable Logistics: Innovations in Global Supply Chain Management.

Moshawrab, M., Adda, M., Bouzouane, A., Ibrahim, H., & Raad, A. (2023). Reviewing federated machine learning and its use in diseases prediction. *Sensors (Basel), 23*(4), 2112. DOI: 10.3390/s23042112 PMID: 36850717

Mo, X. (2024). AI-based supply chain risk management. *Applied and Computational Engineering, 106*(1), 125–130. DOI: 10.54254/2755-2721/106/20241297

Munuhwa, S., & Chibaro, M. (2024). E-Commerce Logistics Unleashed: Automation, Artificial Intelligence Challenges, and Triumphs. In *Applications of New Technology in Operations and Supply Chain Management* (pp. 145-163). IGI Global.

Mustapha, I., Khan, N., Qureshi, M. I., Sikandar, H., Hassan, M., & Simarmata, J. (2024). Revolutionizing Supply Chain Processes: Harnessing the Power of IoT and Blockchain Technology to Enhance Opportunities. In *SpringerBriefs in Applied Sciences and Technology: Vol. Part F2588* (pp. 87–94). DOI: 10.1007/978-3-031-55558-9_10

Muthaluri, J. (2024). Optimizing supply chain management and marketing strategies: AI and ML integration for competitive advantage. Educational Administration: Theory and Practice, 8990–8997.

Muthu, S. E., & Kartheeban, K. (2023). Blockchain Enabled Secure Agri-Goods Traceability using RFID in Supply Chain Management. *Proceedings - 2023 3rd International Conference on Ubiquitous Computing and Intelligent Information Systems, ICUIS 2023*, 301–310. DOI: 10.1109/ICUIS60567.2023.00057

Muthukalyani, A. R. (2023). Optimizing Last-Mile Delivery in Retail Through AI-Powered Routing and Scheduling. [IJCET]. *International Journal of Computer Engineering and Technology, 14*(2).

Nandy, I., & Padhy, R. (2025). From traditional to consumer-centric: The evolution of themes in technology-focused last mile delivery. *Global Knowledge, Memory and Communication.* Advance online publication. DOI: 10.1108/GKMC-03-2024-0167

Narmadha, K., & Varalakshmi, P. (2022). Federated Learning in healthcare: A privacy preserving approach. *Studies in Health Technology and Informatics, 294*, 194–198. DOI: 10.3233/SHTI220436 PMID: 35612055

Nasrudin, M. F. (2024). Integrating Advance Technology and Logistics Customer Service for Optimal Logistics Performance: A Study at Shopee Express Pangalengan Branch. *Integrating Advance Technology and Logistics Customer Service for Optimal Logistics Performance: A Study at Shopee Express Pangalengan Branch.*

Negri, E., Fumagalli, L., & Macchi, M. (2017). A review of the roles of Digital Twin in CPS-based production systems. *Procedia Manufacturing, 11*, 939–948. DOI: 10.1016/j.promfg.2017.07.198

Nisha. (2025). Federated AI approaches in pandemic outbreak forecasting. South Asian Journal of Engineering and Technology, 15(2), 46–56.

Odumbo, O. R., & Nimma, S. Z. (2025). Leveraging Artificial Intelligence to Maximize Efficiency in Supply Chain Process Optimization. *Int J Res Publ Rev*, *6*(1), 3035–3050. DOI: 10.55248/gengpi.6.0125.0508

Oladele, O. K. (2025). AI in Retail: Personalized Shopping Experiences, Inventory Management, and Supply Chain Optimization.

Oyetoro, A. (2024). *The Application of Technology in Logistics.*

Pagallo, U. (2020). The Law and Ethics of AI and Robotics: A Literature Review. *Law, Innovation and Technology*, *12*(1), 115–137. DOI: 10.1080/17579961.2020.1724412

Pap, I. A., & Oniga, S. (2024). eHealth assistant AI chatbot using a large language model to provide personalized answers through secure decentralized communication. *Sensors (Basel)*, *24*(18), 6140. DOI: 10.3390/s24186140 PMID: 39338885

Park, K.-J., & Son, S.-Y. (2023). Residential load forecasting using modified federated learning algorithm. *IEEE Access : Practical Innovations, Open Solutions*, *11*, 40675–40691. DOI: 10.1109/ACCESS.2023.3268530

Patel, J. (2025). Leveraging digital twins for real-time supply chain visibility and decision-making. *International Journal on Science and Technology*, *16*(2).

Patil, D. (2024). Artificial Intelligence In Retail And E-Commerce: Enhancing Customer Experience Through Personalization, Predictive Analytics, And Real-Time Engagement. *Predictive Analytics, And Real-Time Engagement (November 26, 2024).*

Paul, R. K., & Sarkar, B. (2021). AI-powered forecasting algorithms to optimize last mile delivery. *Journal ID*, *2811*, 6201.

Pise, R., Patil, S., Patil, S., Shinde, S., & Gavkare, S. (2024). Decentralizing the Cosmetic Supply Chain with Hyperledger Fabric. *2024 IEEE International Conference on Blockchain and Distributed Systems Security, ICBDS 2024*. DOI: 10.1109/ICBDS61829.2024.10837300

Ponomarenko, I., & Ponomarenko, D. (2023). AI-Powered Logistics and Digital Marketing for Business Optimisation. *Economics & Education, 8*(4), 27–33. DOI: 10.30525/2500-946X/2023-4-4

Poornimathi, K., Kumar, A. D., & Srinithi, A. (2024, April). ROUTESENSE–An AI powered solution to Car pooling systems. In *2024 10th International Conference on Communication and Signal Processing (ICCSP)* (pp. 1168-1174). IEEE. DOI: 10.1109/ICCSP60870.2024.10543353

Prastyorini, J., Mudayat, M., & Ramadhan, C. A. (2023). Enhancing customer satisfaction in logistics services: The impact of service quality and trust. *Indonesian Journal of Law and Economics Review, 18*(3). Advance online publication. DOI: 10.21070/ijler.v18i3.930

Preskill, J. (2018). Quantum Computing in the NISQ era and beyond. *Quantum : the Open Journal for Quantum Science, 2*, 79. DOI: 10.22331/q-2018-08-06-79

Prosper, J. (2021). Scalable AI Architectures for E-Commerce and Retail.

Pugacheva, O. (2024). Basic directions for the use of artificial intelligence technologies in the transportation and logistics sector. In *Competitivitatea şi inovarea în economia cunoaşterii* (pp. 89-98).

Qamhieh, M., Sammaneh, H., & Demaidi, M. N. (2020). PCRS: Personalized Career-Path Recommender System for Engineering Students. *IEEE Access : Practical Innovations, Open Solutions, 8*, 214039–214049. DOI: 10.1109/ACCESS.2020.3040338

Queiroz, M. M., Wamba, S. F., & Joshi, A. W. (2022). Blockchain adoption for supply chain resilience: Integrating behavioral and technical factors. *Industrial Marketing Management, 105*, 55–68.

Quinn, P. (2004). Bar code: Stronger than ever. *Supply Chain Systems Magazine, 24*(10), 16–20. https://www.scopus.com/inward/record.uri?eid=2-s2.0-10444290713&partnerID=40&md5=6ee80358db84297bf590eab9ef5fb3a8

Ramasamy, I., Natarajan, S., & Sathyamoorthy, V. K. P. (2024). Does disruptive technology and AI (Artificial Intelligence) influence logistics management? *Multidisciplinary Science Journal*, *6*(12), 2024259–2024259. DOI: 10.31893/multiscience.2024259

Rane, N., Choudhary, S., & Rane, J. (2024). Artificial intelligence and machine learning for resilient and sustainable logistics and supply chain management. Available at *SSRN* 4847087.

Rao, J., & Prasad, R. (2018). Impact of 5G technologies on smart cities: Technical challenges, security concerns and future prospects. *Journal of Urban Technology*, *25*(4), 3–28. DOI: 10.1080/10630732.2018.1455113

Rashed, M. S., Fakhry, S., Satour, R., Abdelkarim, E. A., Sobhy, M., & Pathania, S. (2025). IoT and Digital Twins for Ssmart Food Supply Chains. In *Sustainable Development Goals Series: Vol. Part F102* (pp. 249–273). DOI: 10.1007/978-3-031-76758-6_16

Reddy, G. (2023). Study of faults in transportation management as a reason for delays in providing timely courier services to consumers. *Journal of Supply Chain Logistics & Management*, *13*(1), 57–65. https://www.mbajournals.in/index.php/JoSCLM/article/view/234

Reeyazati, A., & Samizadeh, R. (2025). Targeted and Personalized Online Advertising in the Age of Artificial Intelligence (AI): A Literature Review and Research Agenda. *International Journal of Supply and Operations Management*, *12*(1), 105–122.

Rezki, N., & Mansouri, M. (2024). MACHINE LEARNING FOR PROACTIVE SUPPLY CHAIN RISK MANAGEMENT: PREDICTING DELAYS AND ENHANCING OPERATIONAL EFFICIENCY. *Management Systems in Production Engineering*, *32*(3), 345–356. DOI: 10.2478/mspe-2024-0033

Rui, G., & Li, M. (2024). Utilizing Internet Big Data and Machine Learning for Product Demand Forecasting and Analysis of Its Economic Benefits. *Tehnicki Vjesnik (Strojarski Fakultet)*, *31*(4), 1385–1394. DOI: 10.17559/TV-20240318001408

Ruiz-Morales, B., Miranda-Ackerman, M. A., & Espitia-Moreno, I. C. (2021). Logistic strategies to minimize losses and waste in food supply chains. In *Research Anthology on Food Waste Reduction and Alternative Diets for Food and Nutrition Security* (pp. 302–314). IGI Global. DOI: 10.4018/978-1-7998-5354-1.ch015

Samuels, A. (2025). Examining the integration of artificial intelligence in supply chain management from Industry 4.0 to 6.0: A systematic literature review. *Frontiers in Artificial Intelligence*, *7*, 1477044. DOI: 10.3389/frai.2024.1477044 PMID: 39902380

Sani, S., Schaefer, D., & Milisavljevic-Syed, J. (2022). Utilising digital twins for increasing military supply chain visibility. In *Advances in Transdisciplinary Engineering*. IOS Press.

Santhiyagu, A. C., Vengadesh, S., & Chinna, P. R. (2025). The implications of digitalization in logistics after COVID-19. *International Research Journal of Multidisciplinary Scope*, *06*(01), 509–527. DOI: 10.47857/irjms.2025.v06i01.02336

Sarma, W., Nagavalli, S. P., & Sresth, V. (2020). Leveraging AI-Driven Algorithms to Address Real-World Challenges in E-Commerce: Enhancing User Experience, Fraud Detection, and Operational Efficiency. *International Journal of Research and Analytical Reviews*, *7*, 2348–1269.

Schrauf, S., & Berttram, P. (2016). *Industry 4.0: How digitization makes the supply chain more efficient, agile, and customer-focused.* PwC Strategy&. https://www.strategyand.pwc.com

Selvakumar, P., Shanthi, M., Pitchiah, R., Sharma, M., Dahake, P. S., & TC, M. (2025). The Role of Artificial Intelligence in Business Model Innovation: Overview of AI Technologies. *AI-Driven Business Model Innovation*, 219-246.

Shaikh, Z. P. (2025). Supply Chain Processes Through Artificial Intelligence and Machine Learning: Application of Demand Planning, Reinforcement Learning, and Product Clustering. In *Supply Chain Transformation Through Generative AI and Machine Learning* (pp. 379-408). IGI Global Scientific Publishing.

Shakeel, P. M., & Baskar, S. (2024). IoT in courier services: Impact on customer satisfaction and supply chain sustainability. *International Journal of Sustainable Development and Planning*, *19*(2), 547–554. DOI: 10.18280/ijsdp.190224

Shao, G., & Kibira, D. (2018). Digital manufacturing: Requirements and challenges for implementing digital twin. *Proceedings of the ASME 2018 13th International Manufacturing Science and Engineering Conference*, 1–10. DOI: 10.1115/MSEC2018-6485

Sharma, D., & Tripathi, K. (2024). Navigating the digital age: smart manufacturing and logistics. In *Recent Trends in Artificial Intelligence Towards a Smart World: Applications in Industries and Sectors* (pp. 99–144). Springer Nature Singapore. DOI: 10.1007/978-981-97-6790-8_4

Sharma, V., & Sharma, R. (2019). Assessment of lean supply chain practices in Indian automotive industry. *Global Business Review*, *21*(1), 65–81. DOI: 10.1177/0972150919890234

Shen, B., Dong, C., & Chan, H. L. (2025). Operational Research Models for E-Commerce Platforms: New Technology Innovation. *Asia-Pacific Journal of Operational Research*, •••, 2502001. DOI: 10.1142/S0217595925020014

Shiddiqie, S. R. A. (2024). Artificial Intelligence-driven Supply Chain Management: Exploring Adoption and Implications in the Turkish Context. *İKTİSAT VE İŞLETME*, 111.

Shinde, R., & Bansode, M. (2022). Managing the logistics distribution performance using digitalization in the FMCG sector. *Vision: The Journal of Business Perspective*, *27*(2), 178–186. DOI: 10.1177/09722629221143261

Shi, W., Cao, J., Zhang, Q., Li, Y., & Xu, L. (2016). Edge computing: Vision and challenges. *IEEE Internet of Things Journal, 3*(5), 637–646. DOI: 10.1109/JIOT.2016.2579198

Shobhana, N. (2024). AI-powered supply chains towards greater efficiency. In *Complex AI Dynamics and Interactions in Management* (pp. 229–249). IGI Global. DOI: 10.4018/979-8-3693-0712-0.ch011

Shuaibu, A. S., Mahmoud, A. S., & Sheltami, T. R. (2025). A Review of Last-Mile Delivery Optimization: Strategies, Technologies, Drone Integration, and Future Trends. *Drones (Basel), 9*(3), 158. DOI: 10.3390/drones9030158

Singh, B. (2025). Revolutionizing Supply Chains for Optimized Demand Planning, Inventory Management, and Logistics: An In-Depth Analysis of AI and ML Solutions in the Modern Era. In *Supply Chain Transformation Through Generative AI and Machine Learning* (pp. 103-128). IGI Global Scientific Publishing.

Singh, S., & Kaur, H. (2023, September). Analyzing the Impact of UPI on Supply Chain Performance: A Natural Language Processing Approach with Generative Pre-trained Transformers. In *International Conference on Entrepreneurship, Innovation, and Leadership* (pp. 107-122). Singapore: Springer Nature Singapore.

Siswipraptini, P. C., Warnars, H. L. H. S., Ramadhan, A., & Budiharto, W. (2024). Personalized Career-Path Recommendation Model for Information Technology Students in Indonesia. *IEEE Access : Practical Innovations, Open Solutions, 12*, 49092–49105. DOI: 10.1109/ACCESS.2024.3381032

Sohrabi, M. (2023). Artificial Intelligence in Logistic Industry. *Implementation of disruptive technologies in supply chain management, 73*.

Soni, M., & Shukla, S. (2023). A study on the impact of logistics management on customer satisfaction. *International Journal of Advanced Research in Engineering Science and Management*, 9(3), 34–39. https://www.ijaresm.com/a-study-on-the-impact-of-logistics-management-on-customer-satisfaction

Sorooshian, S., Khademi Sharifabad, S., Parsaee, M., & Afshari, A. R. (2022). Toward a modern last-mile delivery: Consequences and obstacles of intelligent technology. *Applied System Innovation*, *5*(4), 82. DOI: 10.3390/asi5040082

Sreerakhi, V., Balagopal, N., & Mohan, A. (2022). Transforming supply chain network and logistics using blockchain – a survey. *International Journal of Business Information Systems*, *39*(2), 193–218. DOI: 10.1504/IJBIS.2022.121430

Srinivasan, K., Chauhan, G. S., Jadon, R., Budda, R., Gollapalli, V. S. T., & Garikipati, V. (2024). AI-DRIVEN OPTIMIZATION MODELS FOR E-COMMERCE SUPPLY CHAINS: INTEGRATING HMO, MAXENT RL, TS, AND MDVRP FOR ENHANCED DEMAND FORECASTING, INVENTORY MANAGEMENT, AND DELIVERY EFFICIENCY.

Stephen, R. K., & Archana, T. (2025). IoT and AI integration for real-time supply chain monitoring. In *Ecological and Human Dimensions of AI-Based Supply Chain* (pp. 339–372). DOI: 10.4018/979-8-3693-7478-8.ch015

Strubell, E., Ganesh, A., & McCallum, A. (2019). *Energy and policy considerations for deep learning in NLP*. *Proceedings of the 57th Annual Meeting of the Association for Computational Linguistics*, 3645–3650. DOI: 10.18653/v1/P19-1355

Sumrit, D., & Sowijit, K. (2023). Winning customer satisfaction toward omnichannel logistics service quality based on an integrated importance-performance analysis and three-factor theory: Insight from Thailand. *Asia Pacific Management Review*, *28*(4), 531–543. Advance online publication. DOI: 10.1016/j.apmrv.2023.03.003

Sungheetha, A., Bharathi, B., Ganesan, D., Karthikeyan, T., & Madhavi, N. B., & KR, C. L. (2023, November). E-Commerce Business Model Analysis and Success in Urban Areas Using AI-Distributed Machine Learning. In *2023 International Conference on Research Methodologies in Knowledge Management, Artificial Intelligence and Telecommunication Engineering (RMKMATE)* (pp. 1-6). IEEE. DOI: 10.1109/RMKMATE59243.2023.10369718

Suraj, P., Shetty, P. P., Suhas, B. E., & Pranav, H. M. (2024, November). Predictive Analytics and AI in Logistics: Driving Operational Excellence and Cost Reduction. In *2024 8th International Conference on Computational System and Information Technology for Sustainable Solutions (CSITSS)* (pp. 1-6). IEEE.

Świtała, M., Cichosz, M., & Trzęsiok, J. (2019). How to achieve customer satisfaction? Perspective of logistics outsourcing performance. *Logforum, 15*(1), 105–116. DOI: 10.17270/J.LOG.2019.316

Tabasum, H., & Raghunandan, G. (2024). FUTURE TRENDS AND INNOVATIONS IN AI COMMERCE. *Applications of Artificial Intelligence in Commerce and Mathematics*, 98.

Taik, A., & Cherkaoui, S. (2020, June). Electrical load forecasting using edge computing and federated learning. ICC 2020 - 2020 IEEE International Conference on Communications (ICC). DOI: 10.1109/ICC40277.2020.9148937

Takawale, P. S., Omkar, K., Maitery, K., & Kale, A. (2024). DeliveRite AI Hub: A Review of Innovations in AI-Powered Logistics and Delivery Systems. *ITSI Transactions on Electrical and Electronics Engineering, 13*(2), 41–46.

Tamayo, P. A., Herrero, A., Martín, J., Navarro, C., & Tránchez, J. M. (2020). Design of a chatbot as a distance learning assistant. Open Praxis. Universidad Nacional de Educación a Distancia (UNED), Spain. Retrieved from https://search.informit.org/doi/10.3316/informit.219384622220499

Tamm, K., Leht, R., Vaher, M., Rebane, K., Poder, A., Batan, A., & Kask, L. (2020). Transformative Impacts of Artificial Intelligence on E-Commerce Supply Chain Management: Enhancing Transparency, Mitigating Risks, and Advancing Adaptive Logistics Strategies.

Tao, F., Zhang, H., Liu, A., & Nee, A. Y. C. (2018). Digital twin in industry: State-of-the-art. *IEEE Transactions on Industrial Informatics, 15*(4), 2405–2415. DOI: 10.1109/TII.2018.2873186

Terrada, L., El Khaili, M., & Ouajji, H. (2022). Demand Forecasting Model using Deep Learning Methods for Supply Chain Management 4.0. *International Journal of Advanced Computer Science and Applications*, *13*(5), 704–711. DOI: 10.14569/IJACSA.2022.0130581

Thaker, B., & Parilkar, S. (2024). UNDERSTANDING CUSTOMER PERCEPTION: EXPLORING THE ROLE OF ARTIFICIAL INTELLIGENCE IN PERSONALIZED SERVICE FOR Q-COMMERCE BUSINESS MODEL.

Thakur, S., Sandhu, S., & Yehuwalashet, F. (2024). E-Commerce and Trade: The Role of Artificial Intelligence. In *Handbook of Artificial Intelligence Applications for Industrial Sustainability* (pp. 232-248). CRC Press.

Tian, Z., Zhong, R. Y., Vatankhah Barenji, A., Wang, Y. T., Li, Z., & Rong, Y. (2021). A blockchain-based evaluation approach for customer delivery satisfaction in sustainable urban logistics. *International Journal of Production Research*, *59*(7), 2079–2098. DOI: 10.1080/00207543.2020.1809733

Tijan, E., Aksentijević, S., Ivanić, K., & Jardas, M. (2019). Blockchain technology implementation in logistics. *Sustainability (Basel)*, *11*(4), 1185. DOI: 10.3390/su11041185

Tošić, A., Vičič, J., Burnard, M., & Mrissa, M. (2023). A Blockchain Protocol for Real-Time Application Migration on the Edge. *Sensors (Basel)*, *23*(9), 4448. Advance online publication. DOI: 10.3390/s23094448 PMID: 37177653

Treiblmaier, H. (2018). The impact of blockchain on the supply chain: A theory-based research framework and a call for action. *Supply Chain Management*, *23*(6), 545–559. DOI: 10.1108/SCM-01-2018-0029

Tudisco, V., Perotti, S., Ekren, B. Y., & Aktas, E. (2025). Sustainable e-grocery home delivery: An optimization model considering on-demand vehicles. *Computers & Industrial Engineering*, *201*, 110874. DOI: 10.1016/j.cie.2025.110874

Ugrinov, S., Ćoćkalo, D., Terek Stojanović, E., Stanisavljev, S., Bakator, M., & Gluvakov, V. (2024). Enhancing Efficiency in Food and Beverage Supply Chains †. *Engineering Proceedings*, *79*(1), 2. Advance online publication. DOI: 10.3390/engproc2024079002

Umair, A. S., Zhang, W., Han, Z., & Haq, S. H. U. (2019). Impact of logistics management on customer satisfaction: A case of retail stores of Islamabad and Rawalpindi. *American Journal of Industrial and Business Management*, *9*(8), 1701–1718. DOI: 10.4236/ajibm.2019.98113

United Nations. (2015). *Transforming our world: The 2030 Agenda for Sustainable Development*. https://sdgs.un.org/2030agenda

Uvet, H. (2020). Importance of logistics service quality in customer satisfaction: An empirical study. *Operations and Supply Chain Management*, *13*(1), 1–10. DOI: 10.31387/oscm0400248

Vaka, D. K. (2024). From Complexity to Simplicity: AI's Route Optimization in Supply Chain Management. *Journal of Artificial Intelligence. Machine Learning and Data Science*, *2*(1), 386–389.

Vaswani, A., Shazeer, N., Parmar, N., Uszkoreit, J., Jones, L., Gomez, A. A., Kaiser, Ł., & Polosukhin, I. (2017). Attention is all you need. In *Advances in neural information processing systems* (Vol. 30). Curran Associates, Inc. Top of Form Bottom of Form

Venkateswaran, P. S., Sriramkumar, M., Vaddy, R. K., Kotagiri, A., Rajest, S. S., & Regin, R. (2024). Applications of Artificial Intelligence and Robots in Service Industries. In *Advancing Intelligent Networks Through Distributed Optimization* (pp. 61–80). IGI Global. DOI: 10.4018/979-8-3693-3739-4.ch004

Viellechner, A., & Spinler, S. (2020). Novel data analytics meets conventional container shipping: Predicting delays by comparing various machine learning algorithms. *Proceedings of the Annual Hawaii International Conference on System Sciences, 2020-Janua*, 1278–1287. DOI: 10.24251/HICSS.2020.158

Voigt, P., & Von dem Bussche, A. (2017). *The EU General Data Protection Regulation (GDPR): A practical guide*. Springer. DOI: 10.1007/978-3-319-57959-7

Vora, D. K., Patel, J. H., Shah, D., & Mehta, P. (2022). Application of Blockchain in Different Segments of Supply Chain Management. *Lecture Notes in Electrical Engineering*, *840*, 537–548. DOI: 10.1007/978-981-16-9012-9_43

Wamba, S. F., & Queiroz, M. M. (2022). Industry 4.0 and the supply chain digitalization: A systematic review and a research agenda. *Annals of Operations Research*, *308*(1), 1–38. DOI: 10.1007/s10479-020-03620-0

Wang, H. (2024). Linking AI supply chain strength to sustainable development and innovation: A country-level analysis. *Expert Systems: International Journal of Knowledge Engineering and Neural Networks*, *41*(5), e12973. DOI: 10.1111/exsy.12973

Wang, L., Deng, T., Shen, Z.-J. M., Hu, H., & Qi, Y. (2022). Digital twin-driven smart supply chain. *Frontiers of Engineering Management*, *9*(1), 56–70. DOI: 10.1007/s42524-021-0186-9

Wareewanich, T., Sukpasjaroen, K., Chankoson, T., Ruaengmaneeya, N., & Raviyan, N. (2019). Customer relationship management (CRM) and logistic customer satisfaction. *International Journal of Supply Chain Management*, *8*(2), 365–371.

Waseem-Ul-Hameed, N., Nadeem, S., Azeem, M., Aljumah, A. I., & Adeyemi, R. A. (2018). Determinants of e-logistic customer satisfaction: A mediating role of information and communication technology (ICT). *International Journal of Supply Chain Management*, *7*(1), 105–111.

Wasilewski, A., Chawla, Y., & Pralat, E. (2025). Enhanced E-commerce Personalization Through AI-Powered Content Generation Tools. *IEEE Access : Practical Innovations, Open Solutions*, *13*, 48083–48095. DOI: 10.1109/ACCESS.2025.3550956

Wei, H.-L., & Wang, E. T. G. (2007). Creating strategic value from supply chain visibility- The dynamic capabilities view. *Proceedings of the Annual Hawaii International Conference on System Sciences*. DOI: 10.1109/HICSS.2007.157

Wei, H.-L., & Wang, E. T. G. (2010). The strategic value of supply chain visibility: Increasing the ability to reconfigure. *European Journal of Information Systems*, *19*(2), 238–249. DOI: 10.1057/ejis.2010.10

Wirtz, B. W., Weyerer, J. C., & Geyer, C. (2019). Artificial Intelligence and the Public Sector—Applications and Challenges. *International Journal of Public Administration*, *42*(7), 596–615. DOI: 10.1080/01900692.2018.1498103

Xu, S., Zhang, X., Kim, R., & Su, M. (2024). Anthropomorphic last-mile robots and consumer intention: An empirical test under a theoretical framework. *Journal of Retailing and Consumer Services*, *81*, 104028. DOI: 10.1016/j.jretconser.2024.104028

Xu, Y., Bu, J., Cai, D., He, X., & Liu, W. (2018). Job recommendation with content-based and collaborative filtering. In *Proceedings of the 27th International Conference on Information and Knowledge Management (CIKM)* (pp. 2061–2064). ACM. DOI: 10.1145/3269206.3269289

Yaiprasert, C., & Hidayanto, A. N. (2024). AI-powered in the digital age: Ensemble innovation personalizes the food recommendations. *Journal of Open Innovation*, *10*(2), 100261. DOI: 10.1016/j.joitmc.2024.100261

Yerra, S. IMPROVING CUSTOMER SATISFACTION WITH PREDICTIVE ANALYTICS IN LOGISTICS AND DELIVERY SYSTEMS.

Yu, R., Pardos, Z., Chau, H., & Brusilovsky, P. ''Orienting students to course recommendations using three types of explanation,'' in Adjunct Proc. *29th ACM Conf. User Modeling, Adaptation Personalization*, Jun. 2021, pp. 238–245, DOI: 10.1145/3450614.3464483

Zemanek Jr, J. E., & Kros, J. F. (2024). Risk-Mitigation Strategies for Autonomous Delivery Vehicles in the Last Mile: A Comprehensive Overview of the Current State and Future Potential of Autonomous Delivery Technologies in the Supply Chain. *Journal of Comprehensive Business Administration Research.*

Zhang, F., & Hu, J. (2024). Research on logistics supply chain optimization strategy based on machine learning. In M. Mikusova (Ed.), International Conference on Smart Transportation and City Engineering (STCE 2023). SPIE. DOI: 10.1117/12.3024778

Zhang, C., Zhang, J., Sangaiah, A. K., Li, D., & Li, W. (2024). Evaluating edge artificial intelligence-driven supply chain management platforms using collaborative large-scale fuzzy information fusion. *Applied Soft Computing*, *159*, 111686. Advance online publication. DOI: 10.1016/j.asoc.2024.111686

Zhang, P., Chen, G., Sun, L., & Wang, S. (2024). A framework for demand response load forecasting based on federated learning. *Journal of Physics: Conference Series*, *2914*(1), 12008. DOI: 10.1088/1742-6596/2914/1/012008

Zhang, Y., Tao, F., Nee, A. Y. C., & Luo, Y. (2021). Digital twin-enabled smart manufacturing: Technologies and applications. *Journal of Manufacturing Systems*, *58*, 176–186. DOI: 10.1016/j.jmsy.2020.06.006

Zuboff, S. (2019). *The Age of Surveillance Capitalism: The Fight for a Human Future at the New Frontier of Power*. PublicAffairs.

About the Contributors

Omar Ali is an Associate Professor in Management Information Systems (MIS) at Abdullah Al Salem University (AASU), Kuwait. He is also acting head of Digital Marketing, Entrepreneurship and Innovation Department. In addition, he is the assistant of Vice President for Development and Intuitional Excellence at AASU. He received his PhD in MIS from the University of Southern Queensland (USQ), Australia. Also, he holds two master's degrees, the first one in Information and Communication Technology, and the second one in Information Systems and Technology by research, both from the University of Wollongong, Australia. His research interests include RFID; cloud computing; blockchain; artificial intelligence; security; and system analysis and design. He is the reviewer of many leading journals such as International Journal of Information Management, Government Information Quarterly, Information Systems Management, Technological Forecasting and Social Change, and Behavior and Information Technology. Also, he has published in top international leading journals such as International Journal of Information Management, Technological Forecasting and Social Change, Journal of Innovation and Knowledge, Government Information Quarterly, Information Technology and People, and Behavior and Information Technology.

***

Prathik CM is a researcher at DSCE. He is interested in Operations, Supply Chain and Analytics.

Venkatesh Ganapathy is a seasoned academician with over two decades experience in the corporate world. Mentored thousands of students pursuing MBA in soft skills and pre-placement. Teaching courses in marketing, strategy and supply chain management.

Ganesha K S is an Assistant Professor in the Department of Management Studies, at Dayananda Sagar College of Engineering, Bangalore, India. He has 15 years of experience in Corporate, Teaching and Research. He is a Member of the International Safety Quality Environment Management Association (ISQEM), UK. His primary research interests are tourist behavior, social media, sentiment analysis, human resource management, and labor studies. He has presented at multiple conferences and published articles in Scopus and other International Indexed journals. He has conducted FDP, workshops, and training in the areas of Digital Marketing, Statistical Analysis using SPSS, Project Management, Research Methodology, Entrepreneurship etc.

Ananya Pandey is a Research Scholar in School of Law at Christ University, Bangalore. She has her research interests in the field of Constitutional Law, Environment Law, Human Rights, Food Security, Intellectual Property Law and Jurisprudence.

Ramya R. completed her B.E and M.E degree in Computer science and engineering. She had 14 years of teaching experience in various Engineering colleges. She did PhD in computer science and engineering and published many articles and book chapters in her domain. She specialises in edge computing, cloud computing, Machine learning, artificial intelligence, Quality of services and resource management.

Venkateshkumar R. is a logistics professional based in Chennai, Tamil Nadu, India over 17 years of experience in automobile industry. He currently works in Outbound Logistics at Ashok Leyland, a leading commercial vehicle manufacturer. In addition to his professional role, he is a research scholar, indicating his engagement in academic pursuits. With a background in logistics and a commitment to research, Venkateshkumar combines practical industry experience with academic inquiry. His role at Ashok Leyland involves managing outbound logistics operations, ensuring efficient distribution of vehicles to various markets. As a research scholar, he is likely involved in studies related to logistics, supply chain management, or related fields, contributing to the advancement of knowledge in these areas. Venkateshkumar R dual engagement in industry and academia positions him uniquely to bridge practical logistics operations with theoretical research, fostering innovations that can enhance efficiency and effectiveness in the logistics sector.

Ravikumar R. Natarajan is an experienced academician with over 12+ years of teaching and research expertise across institutions in India, the UAE, and the Maldives. He currently serves as an Assistant Professor at Marwadi University, Rajkot, specializing in Machine Learning, Recommender Systems, and AI-driven applications in healthcare and security. He holds a Ph.D. in Machine Learning and Recommender Systems from Amity University, Jaipur, a Master of Engineering in CSE from VMRF University, Salem, and a Bachelor of Engineering in CSE from Anna University. He also has a MiniMBA from the Swiss eLearning Institute. Dr. Ravikumar has authored more than 8+ multiple SCIE/ Scopus-indexed journal articles, 25+ IEEE/Springer conference papers, and co-authored a book on Artificial Intelligence. He has also published 9 patents and contributed 10+ book chapters in emerging domains such as Federated Learning, Blockchain, and Digital Twins for IGI Global, Wiley and Springer publisher. He actively mentors students through initiatives like the Research Activities Club (RAC) and Student Research Internship Training (SRIT), promoting innovation and research culture.

Aarthi S is a dedicated Assistant Professor in Computer Science with over six years of teaching experience. She is currently pursuing her Ph.D. at Marwadi University, Gujarat, and holds an M.Phil. and MCA from Bharathiar University, Tamil Nadu. Throughout her academic career, Aarthi has specialized in programming languages such as C++, Java, and C, and contributed to research in recommender systems and AI-related data privacy. She has published journal articles, contributed to book chapters, and actively participated in technical workshops. Known for her student mentorship and engagement in academic events, Aarthi remains committed to fostering innovation and excellence in computer science education.

Denis Amirtharaj, Ph.D., is a distinguished academic and industry professional specializing in hospitality and management studies. He currently serves as the Associate Professor and Head of the BBA program at the School of Management, Hindustan Institute of Technology and Science (HITS), Chennai. Dr. Amirtharaj's academic journey encompasses a B.Sc. in Hospitality, M.T.M., M.Phil., M.B.A., and a Ph.D. in Management. His doctoral research focused on the "Impact of Training & Development on Employees' Performance, with Reference to the Hotel Industry in Chennai." With over a decade of experience in academia, Dr. Amirtharaj has also contributed significantly to the hospitality industry as a training manager at Savera Group of Hotels, Chennai. His research interests include employee training and development, service quality in hospitality, and consumer behaviour in the retail sector. Dr. Amirtharaj is an active member of the academic community, with profiles on platforms like ResearchGate and Academia.edu, where he shares his research work and collaborates with peers. He also engages with the broader community through interviews and discussions on career planning and industry trends. His dedication to education and industry collaboration continues to inspire students and professionals in the field of hospitality and management.

Index

A

B

C

D

E

F

H

I

www.ingramcontent.com/pod-product-compliance
Lightning Source LLC
LaVergne TN
LVHW080857300926
849162LV00003B/449
* 9 7 9 8 3 3 7 3 2 8 3 3 1 *